From
WALL STREET
to the
GREAT WALL

ALSO BY BURTON G. MALKIEL

A Random Walk Down Wall Street
The Random Walk Guide to Investing

5.19.23

From

WALL STREET

to the

GREAT WALL

How Investors Can Profit from

China's Booming Economy

BURTON G. MALKIEL

and **PATRICIA A. TAYLOR**

with **JIANPING MEI** *and* **RUI YANG**

W. W. NORTON & COMPANY

New York · London

For information about permission to reproduce selections from this book, write to Permissions, W. W. Norton & Company, Inc., 500 Fifth Avenue, New York, NY 10110

For information about special discounts for bulk purchases, please contact W. W. Norton Special Sales at specialsales@wwnorton.com or 800-233-4830

Manufacturing by RR Donnelley, Harrisonburg, VA
Book design by Charlotte Staub
Production manager: Anna Oler

Library of Congress Cataloging-in-Publication Data

Malkiel, Burton Gordon.
    From Wall Street to the Great Wall : how investors can profit from China's booming economy / Burton G. Malkiel and Patricia A. Taylor, with Jianping Mei and Rui Yang.—1st ed.
        p. cm.
    Includes bibliographical references and index.
    ISBN 978-0-393-06478-0 (hardcover)
    1. Investments—China. 2. China—Economic conditions—21st century. I. Taylor, Patricia A., 1938– II. Title.
    HG5782.M35 2008
    332.67'30951—dc22   2007036232

W. W. Norton & Company, Inc.
500 Fifth Avenue, New York, NY 10110
www.wwnorton.com

W. W. Norton & Company Ltd.
Castle House, 75/76 Wells Street, London W1T 3QT

2 3 4 5 6 7 8 9 0

To the
CHINESE MEN AND WOMEN

> *who we met in the course of our research in their country and who have taken part in China's amazing economic transformation over the past three decades.*

CONTENTS

PREFACE

FROM WALL STREET TO THE GREAT WALL—all four of us have literally made this journey. Burton G. Malkiel, the Chemical Bank Chairman's Professor of Economics at Princeton University, has spent close to half a century studying securities markets and actively participating in portfolio management. Patricia A. Taylor has worked for the Bank of America as an editorial officer and with Professor Malkiel for thirty-five years on all nine editions of *A Random Walk Down Wall Street*. Jianping Mei, a native of China, earned his Ph.D. in economics from Princeton University, has served as associate professor of finance and international business at New York University, and currently teaches at the Cheung Kong Graduate School of Business in Beijing. Rui Yang contributes the perspective of a mutual fund manager at Bosera Asset Management, one of mainland China's largest mutual fund companies.

We four thus view China from both inside and outside. Informed by this unique double vantage point, our book provides a practical guide for investors seeking to tap into China's riches. The biggest risk to any investor's portfolio today is not to have at least some exposure to China, and our book tells investors how best to accomplish that exposure.

Two hundred years ago, China was the world's greatest power in terms of both economic muscle and geographical territory. Although China's geographical boundaries have changed relatively little in the past two centuries, its economy suffered greatly under colonial exploitation and Mao's extreme economic policies. And yet, there is no question that China will shortly surpass the United States and once again become the world's mightiest economic power.

The first section of the book reviews China's past and present so that readers will have a background understanding of the unique hybrid economy that China has constructed. This unusual construct has its dangers, which we discuss in the context of perceived risks in the last chapter in this section. In the second section of the book, we review the investment opportunities available to investors living in and outside of China. We introduce readers to the uniqueness of the Chinese stock market, and examine whether market prices are efficient reflectors of shareholder values. We show that Chinese common stocks traded in international markets are attractive investments despite their substantial rise in value in 2006 and through the first half of 2007. In the last chapter in this section, we review investment opportunities in other assets such as real estate, art, and bonds.

In the third section of the book, we present strategies for profiting from the economic boom in China. These range from directly buying individual stocks to purchasing funds containing the equity securities of companies that are domiciled in China. We also discuss an indirect strategy of buying the securities of non-Chinese companies that benefit from substantial sales to China, or from China's abundant labor force, or the effect of China's growth on the prices of raw materials. In the concluding chapter, we present what we regard as the Optimal Strategy and give specific recommendations for implementing it.

Burton G. Malkiel
Patricia A. Taylor
Jianping Mei
Rui Yang

—*May 2007*

Section I

THE
SETTING

This book describes both the enormous profit opportunities and the substantial risks that China's growth provides investors. We believe it important to understand the setting in which these opportunities and risks exist, and so, in this first section, we review China's history, culture, achievements, and probable future directions. Armed with this knowledge, readers will be in an excellent position to develop sensible strategies to profit from the extraordinary economic growth that we anticipate China will achieve over the coming decades. In effect, this section provides the springboard to China's riches.

CHAPTER 1

The Past:
An Historical Perspective

Study the past if you would define the future.
— CONFUCIUS

FOR MOST OF THE PAST 2,500 YEARS China has been a huge, self-sufficient economic entity, set off from much of the world by the Great Wall to the north, towering mountains and sere deserts to the west, and the Pacific Ocean on its eastern coast. "Inscrutable" is a word frequently applied to the country and its people by outsiders.

It is not surprising that prospective investors often find China difficult to comprehend. Just think about it: Today, China is the world's fourth largest economy (second largest in terms of purchasing power), and yet just half a century ago it had abolished private ownership of assets and had the most anti-business policies in the world. Now it has one of the most pro-business governments to be found. In recent years, it has received the largest amount of foreign direct investment of any nation, making it a magnet for venture capitalists and others seeking to capitalize on the country's booming economy.

It is natural for investors to ask: What is it about China that has led to such a remarkable transformation? What can be learned from the ups and downs of China's past? What were the main drivers of China's development cycle, and how likely is it that its current business-friendly policy is going to continue? This chapter provides a brief cultural and economic review of China's long history so that investors can better comprehend the great attractiveness and the unique risks of a strategy designed to capitalize on the country's future growth.

As with all major nations, the China of today can be said to be the sum of its history. For simplicity's sake, we have divided this history into four major periods: Confucianism, Colonialism, Communism, and now Capitalism.

CONFUCIANISM: STATIC GREATNESS

In the millennium before Christ, the country known today as China was divided into dozens of viciously warring feudal states. From this turmoil arose the man who is arguably the most influential philosopher in Chinese history: Confucius (551–479 BC).

The philosopher proposes

Though conceived out of wedlock and raised in poverty, Confucius managed to become an accountant in the state of Lu and eventually was named its justice minister. Disgusted with the brutality and greed surrounding him, he resigned from his post and began a long journey around China, lobbying—unsuccessfully at the time—many different rulers for political reform. After twelve years, he returned home and spent the last years of his life teaching a large number of students, and writing and editing a set of Chinese classics.

Confucius's social philosophy emphasized the concept of *ren*, "compassion" or "loving others." For Confucius, such compassion is demonstrated through the practice of benevolence: "Since you yourself desire standing, then help others achieve it, since you yourself desire success, then help others attain it." He argued that it is a moral responsibility to better society and that one should use government to address social ills. Such intervention was generally not to take the form of coercion but rather to be achieved through the moral leadership exemplified by rulers and high-level officials.

Confucius also introduced the concept of *li*—proper social behavior or respect of social order. He emphasized respect for both ancestors and those in authority, as well as the importance of education. Indeed, Confucius was foremost an educator, one who believed in teaching all people, no matter their social standing. His teachings on morality, proper speech, government, and the refined arts, preserved in the *Analects*, form the foundation of much of subsequent Chinese education and culture. They have been so influential that generations of Chinese parents believe their children can only achieve social status and become ideal persons through tireless lifelong learning.

The emperor disposes

Though Confucius created the philosophical tone that was to be so pervasive throughout Chinese history, his ideas did not ameliorate the chaotic politics of the Warring States period that consumed the country after his death. That particular problem was decisively settled by Qin Shi Huang (259–210 BC). His solution was brutally simple: as king of the Chinese state of Qin, he set out to conquer all the other states. In the process he established a single country under his rule, the largest in the world. He did that in just twenty-seven years, becoming the first emperor of a unified China in 221 BC.

Qin Shi Huang next launched a series of major reforms to

consolidate his power. He standardized the Chinese script and units of measurements such as weights and currency. To avoid the anarchy of the Warring States period, he divided the empire into thirty-six units or commands, with each reporting to the central government. To avoid concentration of local power, he also separately appointed civilian and military governors in various localities.

Boosted by his military success, Qin undertook colossal construction projects, most notably a major extension of the Great Wall and a gigantic mausoleum, both of which are today considered wonders of the world. While the Great Wall—at over 3,900 miles the world's longest man-made structure—has been known for centuries, the mausoleum, located in Xian, was only discovered in 1974. Excavations at the site have currently unearthed a terra-cotta army of 8,000 life-sized men and horses. Now on display in this world-famous attraction, every soldier and horse is unique, with its own style of dress, rank designation, and weaponry. The seemingly indefatigable Qin also developed an extensive network of roads and canals connecting the provinces to accelerate trade and military movement.

Many scholars believe Qin Shi Huang also inadvertently created a lasting legacy with his forceful relocation and exile to southern China of former officials from conquered states, dissident scholars, convicted criminals, and merchants. Since the capital was located in the north, central government control tended to be less strict; as the popular saying goes, "The heaven is high and the emperor far away." Because of less government control and interference, business and trade started to flourish in the south. In addition, the exiled officials and refugees who populated the south tended to have a high risk tolerance since many had gone through terrible persecution and political turmoil. This risk tolerance, coupled with business and trade opportunities, made the south a traditional breeding ground for entrepreneurs in Chinese history.

The legacy is mixed

These two men—Confucius and Qin Shi Huang—set much of the tone for China's subsequent history. The natural creativity and ingenuity of the Chinese people flourished, with the result that they developed porcelain, gunpowder, the wheelbarrow, the compass, the stirrup, the rigid horse collar (to prevent choking), the spinning wheel, and paper.

And yet, China never seemed to capitalize on these discoveries, despite the fact that it is reputed to have had the highest gross national product in the world by the seventeenth century. At a time when Great Britain was laying the groundwork for the European industrial revolution, there was, as the economic historian David Landes has argued, an "ineffable stillness of immobility" within China. This immobility was epitomized by the idealized dictum of a fourteenth-century Ming dynasty emperor: The people "will be content with where they live and happy in their customs. Though the adjoining states be within sight of one another and cocks crowing and dogs barking in one be heard in the next, yet the people will grow old and die without having had any dealings with those of another."

Part of China's seeming placidness can be placed at the feet of the two men who were crucial in laying the footprint for its greatness. The peace and serenity of Confucius's teachings became entrenched over the centuries to the great detriment of the overall advancement of Chinese society. Businessmen, for example, were often seen as interested only in profits rather than the public good. And while China had perfected a rigorous civil service examination system in which anyone could participate, no matter how humble his social background, education became viewed as a tool for advancement in civil service rather than as an instrument for encouraging free inquiry and the consequent development of science and technology. The best and the brightest were selected into government service rather than into commerce. In Europe, commerce and mercantilism opened a unique path to riches, where creativity and daring were the sine qua non of success. In China, the road to social status and material well-being led to government employment, where the term "kowtowing" was coined.

On the other hand, Qin's unification of China—again according to Landes—created a monolithic entity that dampened competition and scientific advancement. While Europe around the time of the Renaissance consisted of dozens of competing states, thus encouraging small-state rulers to adopt new technology in order to stay ahead of the game, China lacked such a competitive atmosphere. A unified and centralized China that was rooted in Confucianism was ultimately a society that only changed slowly.

Admiral Zheng goes sailing

Given this state of affairs, consider the story of Admiral Zheng. A eunuch in the fifteenth-century Ming court, he sailed to the Indian Ocean seven times, reaching as far as Africa. The size of his fleet—300 ships and 28,000 sailors— was not exceeded until World War I. (Columbus's fleet some eighty years after Zheng's travels had only three ships and ninety sailors.) The purpose of this massive undertaking has never been discovered.

What is known is that Zheng's patron died and a power struggle between court eunuchs and Confucian officials broke out. The winning Confucians put an end to his expeditions. Worse still, the Ming court issued a formal ban on ocean sailing in 1500 and destroyed the many shipyards that built those large seagoing ships. The peaceable Celestial Kingdom had no need to seek out foreign trade; it needed only to wait for others to come to it. By the eighteenth century, thanks to such traders, China had become central to a global trade in which its unmatched teas, silks, and porcelains were eagerly sought throughout Asia and Europe.

The British come knocking—at first

Despite its complacency, China was the largest economy in the world at the beginning of the nineteenth century. Its GDP, as shown in Exhibit 1.1, was roughly a third of world output. Indeed, China's output exceeded that of Western Europe, Japan, America, and Russia combined. Because of its self-sustaining wealth, strong government, and insularity, the country—particularly the ruling classes—became imbued with a feeling of superiority and a conviction that there was no need to pay attention to what was going on elsewhere.

Thus, China was totally ignorant of the seismic change

EXHIBIT 1.1   *Selected GDPs: 1600–2001*

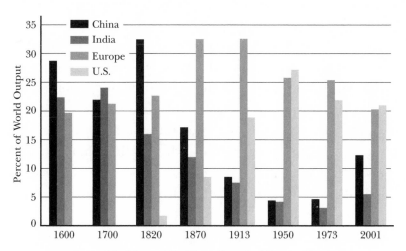

SOURCE: Angus Maddison, *The World Economy Historical Statistics.*

occurring in Europe as a result of the industrial revolution. Europe was embracing technology and new production methods; China was remaining still. Great Britain, in particular, with its rapid increase in production efficiency, needed to expand into overseas markets. Its rising living standards also created an insatiable demand for Chinese tea, silk, and porcelain. The result: In 1792, Britain sent its envoy, George Macartney, to see Emperor Qianlong to improve the terms of trade with China and to open up more trading posts in coastal cities. The rapidly rising British Empire's proposed cultural and trade exchange met with little interest from the insular Qing Empire.

Landes (2006) reports that Emperor Qianlong wrote the following lines to commemorate the occasion:

Now England is paying homage.
My Ancestor's merit and virtue must have reached their distant shores.
Though their tribute is commonplace, my heart approves sincerely.
Curios and the boasted ingenuity of their devices I prize not.

The emperor disparaged not only the gifts but also their bearer. The Qing court insisted that Lord Macartney kowtow to the emperor, an act that would require him to bow low enough to have his head touch the floor. The British rejected the demand, insisting Macartney would bend only one knee and bow to the emperor as he would do for the British monarch. In consequence, no agreement was reached. Rather, the court prepared an edict stating that vast and resourceful China had no need for any goods and services that the British could provide, and thus no interest in trading with them.

Lord Macartney was quickly dismissed and told to leave China immediately. In his journal, Macartney compared

China to an "old, crazy, first rate man of war . . . which may not sink outright; she may drift some time as a wreck, and will then be dashed to pieces on the shore." The Chinese court further gave strict orders to all local governors not to allow the British to carry out any trade or business in China, aside from the sole approved trading post for Europeans in the southern city of Guangzhou (called Canton in English).

COLONIALISM: A CENTURY OF HUMILIATION

Trade, though limited, was still carried on between the two countries, and the exchange was highly profitable to those involved. China exported tea, an expensive commodity unavailable at the time from anywhere else in the world, and received silver—much in demand at the Imperial Court—in return. As the price of silver soared, however, the British looked for another commodity to trade that was cheaper to produce. Opium filled the bill to perfection. The drug was grown on plantations in India under a British-sanctioned monopoly stipulating that it could only be sold in China.

The British scheme was extraordinarily profitable—for the British. For the Chinese, the result was calamitous, with thousands upon thousands of Chinese civilians becoming enslaved to the drug. Opium demand and opium addiction soared in deadly locksteps—with sales quintupling from 500,000 to 2.5 million pounds from 1820 to 1832. The Qing government, dismayed at the havoc created by widespread opium dependency and the outflow of goods and money used to purchase the drug, desperately tried to curtail the trade.

The British ignored the government's attempts because the money involved was just too good to give up. Desperate to arrest the trade that was devastating local life and the economy, the Qing court finally ordered a complete ban on opium in 1838 and confiscated over 2 million pounds of the drug. It then held a large ceremony in which the confiscated opium was dumped into specially constructed trenches filled with lime and seawater, and thus irretrievably destroyed. This act is sometimes referred to by the Chinese as their equivalent of the Boston Tea Party.

There is no question that opium addiction was detrimental to Chinese society. And there is little doubt that British traders were addicted to profit. The traders were not at all pleased with the heavy financial loss incurred by the confiscation and destruction of the opium. They lobbied their government for retaliation, and their government responded.

The British return, this time blasting

In 1839, the First Opium War broke out. The British navy and marines invaded China's southern coast under the pretense of free trade and the protection of British expatriates. Though its economy was several times larger than Great Britain's, China's military technology was outdated and powerless against British guns. In 1842, China was forced to sign the Treaty of Nanking in which it agreed to open five villages, which became known as treaty ports, to British consuls, businessmen, and missionaries, and to accept the secession of Hong Kong. Not even this resounding defeat could dim the feeling of innate Chinese superiority. The government saw little reason to change and innovation was not encouraged.

In the turbulent years that followed—capped by widespread unrest known as the Taiping Rebellion—the Qing court continued its precipitous decline. Taking advantage of this situation, the British initiated the Second Opium War in 1856, which the French soon joined. In 1860, the two European armies marched into Peking (now Beijing) and burned down the old Summer Palace, which is reputed to have rivaled Buckingham Palace in its grandeur and artistic collections. The French writer Victor Hugo called this action one of the greatest tragedies of history.

Literally under the gun, China signed another unequal treaty that gave the two foreign countries additional privileges. Numerous other treaties soon followed that allowed other countries, including Germany and Japan, to establish foreign concessions and military bases on Chinese soil.

Xenophobia hardens and yet teaches

At the close of the nineteenth century, the Chinese had finally taken to heart their repeated defeats by the Europeans. Although the disdain—in many cases burning hatred—of foreigners increased, so too did the recognition of the need to understand Western doctrines and beliefs. Both the disdain and the need were the direct result of their experiences with the two totally different kinds of foreigners who had successfully entered China.

The first were the missionaries, who began to arrive in the sixteenth century to spread the word of Jesus Christ. In order to demonstrate the rightfulness of their beliefs, these preachers—particularly the Jesuits—sought to prove the superiority of their culture by introducing new forms of education and technology.

Jesuits such as Matteo Ricci and Johann Adam Schall von Bell learned the Chinese language and translated the Western science of cartography and the astronomy of Galileo. To the delight of the court, Jesuits introduced and built clocks and other mechanical devices. Other Jesuits directed the Imperial Bureau of Astronomy and supervised foundries producing both astronomical instruments and heavy artillery.

The second influx of foreigners, those who arrived in the eighteenth and nineteenth centuries, primarily came to make money. For the most part, these people looked down on the Chinese, did not learn the language, and clustered geographically in enclaves where their governments had obtained extraterritorial rights. To this day, Shanghai tour guides point out where the British posted a sign saying: NO DOGS AND NO CHINESE. (Although the historical authenticity of such a sign has been questioned, martial arts hero Bruce Lee elicited cheers from moviegoers when he kicked one to pieces in his classic *Fist of Fury*.)

But while the Chinese resented both the petty and the major humiliations imposed by the latest influx of foreigners, they were also impressed by their accomplishments and wealth. Shanghai, for example, was little more than a fishing village when the British took it as a treaty port. Within five decades it was the largest commercial city in the Far East and trailed only New York and London as a financial center. Foreigners built handsome homes and commercial buildings in the Bund—an area on the banks of the winding Huangpu River. This area, in turn, was part of a larger entity known as the International Settlement, where European rules and customs held sway.

The heady mix of opium and money attracted people from all over the world. Popular culture, vice, intellectual discourse, and political intrigue flourished. In 1912, the Qing dynasty was toppled by Sun Yatsen and his Kuomintang political party (KMT). If anything, the intrigue became even thicker over the years. In 1921, the Chinese Communist Party was founded in the city (Mao Zedong was one of the twelve founders); four years later, Chiang Kai-shek took over leadership of the KMT. In 1929, the Cathay Hotel (now known as the Peace Hotel) was built as the most luxurious establishment of its kind in the Far East. Lalique glass panels decorated its doors; Charlie Chaplin and Bernard Shaw came to stay; Noël Coward completed his play *Private Lives* in one of its rooms; and Chiang Kai-shek held his engagement party in one of the ballrooms.

Amidst the gaiety of this international high society in this one city, however, the rest of the country was sliding into chaos as warlords fought one another and income disparities increased. At its core, China fundamentally remained a semi-colonial country, dominated and insulted by foreign powers. The result of these humiliations was the development of xenophobia even among the enlightened elite, including the descendants of those whom the Jesuits had first touched centuries ago. The true intentions of the West became suspect; political ideals such as democracy, equality, and justice came to be seen as slogans used to put China down and to justify barbaric colonial acts. Woodrow Wilson was a particular disappointment. Despite the fact that China was on the winning side of World War I, the German concession in Northeast China (officially a 99-year lease similar to that for Hong Kong) was not returned in the end, but was given to the Japanese to win their support at the Versailles Conference in 1919.

The Japanese, newly modernized themselves and anxious to have their own empire, wanted more. In 1931, they invaded Manchuria; in 1932, they sent troops into Shanghai and obtained further concessions in the city; in 1937, they set out to conquer the whole country. In December of that year, they occupied the capital of China at the time—Nanjing—and committed one of the most appalling atrocities of World War II: the massacre of 300,000 civilians, and the rape and mutilation of hundreds of thousands more. The objective of the atrocities was to completely crush the Chinese will to fight. That objective was not met.

Mao makes his move

Indeed, with the Japanese launch of a full-scale invasion, the Communists and the KMT, which had been engaged in a civil war throughout the country, joined forces—temporarily. The Communists were under the leadership of Mao Zedong (1893–1976), son of a wealthy peasant family. Unlike many of his comrades such as Deng Xiaoping, Mao never traveled to the West or received any Western education. He went to traditional Chinese schools and was heavily influenced by the Chinese tradition of using government to address social inequality and injustice. As a patriot, he hated foreign occupation and special privileges. But he did not hate foreign ideas. He was attracted to Karl Marx's analysis of class warfare and used that as his basis for establishing a socialist society, free of foreign domination and appalling inequality.

A brilliant strategist, Mao seized upon the astonishingly uneven distribution of income between landless peasants and landlords and formed an innovative strategy for a peasant uprising. He quickly assembled a large peasant army attracted to his proclaimed objective of redistributing land and urged them on with anti-Japanese slogans. Sensing a deepening dissatisfaction with China's weakness and disunity among the elite, Mao convinced a large group of intellectuals to join him in his revolution.

With the official defeat of the Japanese in September 1945, Mao quickly took advantage of the postwar chaos and the widespread resentment against what had become the corrupt and incompetent rule of Chiang Kai-shek's KMT government. Despite (or because of) American backing of the KMT in the resumption of civil war, Mao successfully defeated Chiang Kai-shek and established the People's Republic of China in 1949. Foreigners fled to their home countries and 2 million KMT followers crossed the waters to Taiwan. With that, what Mao called China's "Century of Humiliation," the century of foreign domination, ended.

Communism: A Great Leap Forward — and Backward

It is ironic that in its rejection of foreign domination and its rampant xenophobia, China next embraced a radical European philosophy. And then it invited Soviet Russia to help implement that philosophy, probably the first time foreigners were ever asked by the Chinese to help enrich their country.

Under Mao's leadership, China adopted a Soviet-style planned economy with rigid government control and asked Soviet experts to participate in China's development. Although there was a centuries-old tradition of strong government in China, nothing could compare with the Communist creation of the largest proactive government in the nation's history. Backed by a growing bureaucracy, Mao set out to pursue his ideal of a strong and prosperous China. He wanted to build a modern, industrialized nation and to relieve the wrenching poverty of the peasant population.

The country was such a wreck after decades of civil war and years of Japanese occupation that it had no place to go but up. Between 1949 and 1952, considerable economic progress was made with the initiation of infrastructure repairs, the distribution of farm holdings from landlords to peasants, and the centralization of the monetary system.*

Having brought stability and the beginnings of prosperity

*In December 1948, even before they had taken complete control, the Communists introduced the renminbi, a currency based on the traditional, centuries-old yuan. In 1955, in a complete revamp to put to rest once and for all the rampant hyperinflation, the government declared that one renminbi yuan was henceforth equivalent to 10,000 old yuan. The two terms— "renminbi" and "yuan"—remain in use today and, while essentially interchangeable, can be confusing to those outside mainland China. We have followed *The Wall Street Journal* style in this book and use the term "yuan" to denote the mainland China currency.

to the Chinese people, the Communists—true to their Soviet Marxist role model—next began a series of Five-Year Plans (the strategy continues to this day, although the implementation and content of these plans have changed drastically). The first, 1953–57, emphasized industrial growth over agricultural output and planned for the state to control everything. All privately owned establishments were swallowed up by the government. By 1958, over 97 percent of China's economy was under the direct control of the government, primarily through state-owned enterprises (SOEs). Agriculture activities were conducted under a commune system, in which over 90 percent of farmers were forced to participate.

The Communist control of the country was extensive and involved not only economic matters but social aspects as well. A rather puritanical atmosphere prevailed. Shanghai's Peace Hotel, closed during the war years, reopened in 1956—minus the glamour and decadence of the 1920s. As the business consultant Tim Clissold relates in his book *Mr. China,* a prominent sign in the lobby told foreign guests that they were not "allowed to up anyone in their room for the night." Drug use and prostitution were banned; violators were executed or thrown into prison. The status of women was enhanced with regulations eliminating foot-binding and child marriage, and the introduction of laws allowing them to initiate divorce. In 1956, an internal passport system was introduced that effectively forbade all nonauthorized internal travel. All were to work for the good of the country, and previous titles and status counted for little.

Mao creates a new system with a Great Leap Forward

It was not enough. Mao deemed that a Great Leap Forward was necessary, and this was implemented in the Second Five-Year Plan (1958–62). In order to leapfrog economic development, Mao ordered the implementation of a variety of unproven and unrealistic techniques to boost agricultural and industrial production. Karl Marx's motto of "From each according to his ability, to each according to his needs" appeared to rule. Unfortunately, the Maoists had not perfected a professional measure of ability; millions of unskilled city residents and farmers were mobilized to produce steel in backyard furnaces, which resulted in poor product quality and a huge waste of resources. The diversion of unskilled labor to industrial and infrastructure projects, the lack of personal incentives (somehow, "to each according to his needs" was not widely accepted), and the appearance of regional droughts and floods led to a sharp drop in grain production. It is estimated that 20 to 30 million people died in the resulting famine, probably the largest such tragedy in Chinese history.

In 1960, in the midst of so much personal and economic devastation, a great split opened up between the Soviets and the Chinese. Tensions over boundaries and nuclear capabilities had simmered quietly for years; they erupted in June 1960 when Nikita Khrushchev publicly called Mao "a nationalist, an adventurist, and a deviationist." The Chinese responded by branding Khrushchev "a revisionist." The name-calling stung; a month later, the Russians summarily withdrew 1,390 experts—among them engineers, technicians, and agronomists—and unilaterally stopped all shipment of vital parts to factories that it had been jointly producing. The withdrawal left hundreds of large projects in limbo, and China had to further tighten its belt. This withdrawal also strengthened China's distrust of foreigners.

After "Three Bitter Years," as the period is sometimes called, the Great Leap Forward was brought to a screeching halt. In its wake, Mao's reputation was severely tattered and his huge political aura damaged. Following a Politburo meeting in 1961 that effectively ended his disastrous policies, he was forced to take a more backseat role. And with that reduced visibility, the government concentrated on improving food production and neglected preparing a third Five-Year Plan.

Mao wipes the slate clean with a Cultural Revolution

Though agriculture did revive, Mao was not happy taking a backseat; true believers in the purity of the revolution shared this view. In 1966, with their backing, Mao brought about a third Five-Year Plan (1966–70) and started the infamous Cultural Revolution, in the process precipitating ten years of utter chaos—years in which the Chinese world was turned upside down. Whereas in the Great Leap Forward farmers and peasants were told to make steel, in the Cultural Revolution skilled workers and educated youth were uprooted from their families and sent to work in the fields. Politicians were uprooted, too; among them Deng Xiaoping, who was sent to a tractor factory in rural Jiangxi Province.

Mao's stated objective was to get rid of those pragmatists whom he labeled "capitalist running dogs," but on whom the party had come to depend, and to establish a socialist paradise. The revolution led to a purge of pragmatic officials at all levels. The prosecution caused hundreds of thousands of deaths and millions of personal injuries. Mao encouraged young students to mobilize as "Red Guards" to propagate his theory. They closed universities, shut down factories, and disabled national transportation. The economy almost completely collapsed. They burned books and destroyed countless historical sites, objects, and buildings. Wealthy families voluntarily destroyed antiques and family heirlooms to demonstrate their loyalty to the revolution. Perhaps because the destruction is so recent, many Chinese view this revolution as the most damaging to their culture throughout their history.

The Cultural Revolution left China profoundly isolated. It was half-surrounded by hostile American military bases (in South Korea, Japan, Taiwan, and Southeast Asia), and as its quarrel with the Soviet Union escalated, it also confronted a serious Soviet threat from the north and west. Relations between the two had so deteriorated that the hot line between Moscow and Beijing was abandoned. As the *New York Times* correspondent Patrick Tyler recounts in *A Great Wall* (1999), Soviet premier Alexei Kosygin tried to reopen the line in April 1969. The Chinese operator wouldn't let the call go through, telling Kosygin, "You are a revisionist and therefore I will not connect you." Since he was refused contact with Mao, Kosygin asked to speak to Premier Zhou. Again calling Kosygin a revisionist, the operator hung up. Shortly afterwards, China and the USSR fought a nasty border war.

At the beginning of the 1970s, China's economy was a wreck. Most villages were without electricity; the automotive industry was based on 1930s technology; and perhaps worst of all, the Taiwan economy was thriving. Drastic measures were needed to address the internal crisis and the external threats. At this historic moment, Mao demonstrated his capacity for extraordinary statesmanship. Despite the fact that he had lost his son during the Korean War to American cluster bombs, he initiated the establishment of a working relationship with the United States to counterbalance the Soviet threat. On April 6, 1971, in what *Time* magazine called "the ping heard round the world," the American Ping-Pong team participating in a tournament in Japan received an invitation from the Chinese players for an all-expense-paid trip to mainland China. The trip received worldwide press coverage. What was not recorded was Henry Kissinger's clandestine visit to China that summer, a trip that laid the groundwork for President Richard Nixon's historic visit to China in February 1972. That in turn laid the foundation for China's eventual opening up to the world.

Today, most Chinese have mixed feelings about Mao. While they are grateful to Mao for his patriotism and his unification of China after decades of civil war and a century of foreign domination, they are also angry about the millions of lives lost or destroyed as a result of the Great Leap Forward and the Cultural Revolution, and the wrong path China took for economic development. And it is truly ironic that the face of the man who had no regard for money now appears on the currency used by the largest country in the world.

CAPITALISM: A UNIQUE VERSION

Soon after Mao's death in 1976, Deng Xiaoping became the paramount leader in China. Born in 1904 to a small landlord family in Sichuan Province, he went to France at the age of sixteen as a work-study student. Among the young and idealistic student revolutionaries in France, he stood out as a pragmatist and a bon vivant—one who enjoyed croissants and other French delicacies. He was assigned to deal with such mundane issues as finance and printing.

Deng is universally credited with reintroducing capitalism into modern China's economy. He called it "socialism with Chinese characteristics," and, probably harking back to the Cultural Revolution, defined it as a philosophy that did not mean shared poverty. As he declared on June 30, 1984, "Pauperism is not socialism, still less communism." A popular joke in Beijing vividly summarizes Deng's strategy for China's reform: On the superhighway to the future, Clinton, Yeltsin, and Deng meet at a crossroads. Clinton makes a right turn.

Yeltsin tells his driver to follow Clinton. Deng tells his driver to give a left-turn signal and make a right turn.

Deng's long political life was filled with all the vicissitudes associated with power. A veteran of the Long March of the 1930s, he was prosecuted as the number two "capitalist running dog" during the Cultural Revolution in the 1960s. It was during this period that one of his sons was paralyzed for life after being pushed from a tall building by Red Guards. Deng was called back from disgrace by Mao in 1974 to restore order, but he came under attack a year later when Mao's politically powerful wife and her cronies, known as the Gang of Four, charged him with starting to change some of Mao's more radical policies. After the disgrace and imprisonment of the Gang of Four in 1981, Deng was free once more to put his pragmatic reforms into effect.

The reforms are implemented

Deng, as opposed to Mao, is notable for not letting ideology shape policy. Rather, he saw what worked or looked promising and encouraged it. Indeed, his period of leadership is known as the era of reforms or simply the reforms without any grand title attached to them. At the same time, he began to roll back some of the more extreme Maoist arrangements.

In agriculture, for example, Deng became aware of what was happening in one small Feng Yang County village, Xiao Gang, in Anhui Province. During the Mao years, twenty farming families had been herded together to form a production unit within a huge agricultural commune. Constantly hungry, they wanted to divide the land among themselves. In 1978, they held a secret midnight meeting and put seventeen fingerprints and three seals on a land division contract. Under this contract, with each family essentially working for themselves, food production increased dramatically.

Despite surging production and the absence of hunger among the farmers, the experiment initially met with disapproval and resistance from the local Communist government. Deng became aware of the situation and advised high-level officials that it was the production arrangement developing better living standards that mattered most, not ideological purity. He agreed with the farmers that the biggest problem with the planned economy was its deadening effect on people's productivity. In December 1978, he oversaw a new government policy that relaxed various government controls.

Under Deng's influence, agricultural communes throughout the country were dismantled and farmers were told that they could do whatever they liked with the surplus they generated above a set quota. The results were dramatic. Feng Yang County became one of the food baskets of China, with great improvements in both output and living standards. The World Bank has reported that in the 1980s alone, 250 million Chinese were lifted out of absolute poverty, which is one of the greatest improvements in human history.

Hunger is not forgotten

In one sense, the Cultural Revolution laid the basis for the success of Deng's post-Mao reforms. The radicals had gone to such extremes and things had gotten so bad that everyone wanted change. To this day, memories of hunger still haunt the generation that was born and grew up under Mao's later years. One high-ranking government official reminisced to us about his days as a youngster in a village where fish was served only once a year. Today, fish is available daily. He uses this story to remind hardline Communists, of which many still remain, of the difference between now and the harsh, puritanical Mao years.

Another high-level financier, born in 1963, told us that when he thinks of his youth, the specter of hunger is a constant. When he entered university, he weighed about half of what he now does (he did add that his wife thinks he should lose some pounds today). What an extraordinary transformation for this person in a little over four decades: from a constantly hungry, rail-thin youngster to a senior official in a large Chinese financial firm hosting an extraordinary meal of Yunnan delicacies.

A new atmosphere prevails

Under Deng, massive class struggle campaigns disappeared. Intellectuals and technicians who had been banished to the countryside were welcomed back and encouraged to once more participate in economic activities. Universities were reopened and Chinese capitalists—those who had formerly owned businesses—were allowed to join the Communist Party.

Deng also promoted an open door economic policy, saying that "The experience of the last thirty some years has taught us: we cannot adopt a closed door policy to develop our economy." Foreign trade was encouraged, and special economic zones, where foreign investment flourished, were established in major cities such as Shanghai, Guangzhou, and Shenzhen. Large numbers of students traveled overseas to learn modern technology and business techniques. Deng joined theses students in overseas treks, becoming in 1970 the first Chinese leader to visit the United States since the Communists assumed power in 1949.

Deng, as Patrick Tyler wrote, "trusted what Mao had never trusted in his own people—their unstoppable industry. Mao had sought to control it, to channel it for revolution; Deng's simple genius was to turn it loose."

A reaction sets in

With entrepreneurship set free in China, many of the old vices returned. Drug use and prostitution reappeared, and corruption flourished. Millions were losing their jobs as inefficient state-owned enterprises were forced to adapt or sink in the new competitive atmosphere. Students started to speak, and then shout, in ever larger gatherings. The last famously culminated in a series of demonstrations in Tiananmen Square, Beijing, in the summer of 1989, just when the Soviet Russian leader Mikhail Gorbachev was visiting China. During his years in power, Gorbachev had initiated a series of economic *and* political reforms. While he endorsed economic reform, Deng believed that the political reforms advocated by Gorbachev would be disastrous for China. Thus, Deng forcefully put down the student demonstrations in Tiananmen Square (a year later, the Union of Soviet Socialist Republics collapsed and splintered into many different national entities).

The hard-liners felt that Deng had waited too long for this crackdown. In a period of fierce political infighting, they fostered internal repression and economic retrenchment. Foreign investors fled and economic activity was sharply curtailed. Inflation also slowed, and for the hard-liners, the resulting downturn meant that the good old days of pure communism were coming back.

Deng heads south

After Caesar crossed the Rubicon, Rome was never the same. Deng took a similarly momentous journey at the age of eighty-seven. Leaving the hard-liners in Beijing, the old man headed south in 1992 to remind the country that the old days were not good and that conditions should be much better. With this dramatic trip, Deng restarted China on its remarkable transformation from a Maoist dead end to one of the largest economies in the world today. "To get rich is glorious!" he told the people, and they listened with all their hearts and responded with enthusiasm. The hard-liners in Beijing could not ignore the message.

Deng stressed the importance of economic development and criticized those who were wavering on reforms and on opening up to the outside world. The timing of his famous "Southern China Tour" could not have been better. It coincided with an historic low in world interest rates. Attracted by the newly unleashed high growth opportunities, foreign capital poured in. Many investors found that China was less risky than originally thought and investment returns were higher than expected because of these high growth rates. In 2005, this so-called "Communist" country overtook the giant U.S. "Capitalist" country as the largest recipient of foreign direct investment. Investors clearly are driven not by labels but by expected returns.

The next chapter discusses the full impact of Deng's reforms; suffice it to say here, that foreign direct investment in China today differs significantly from that undertaken earlier. China's "open door" policy exemplifies the harsh lesson learned from its dealings with the West during Colonialism and Communism: there is much to incorporate from the outside world, but that incorporation should be done only under Chinese terms and conditions. China is determined to maintain the country's economic and diplomatic independence.

In his last years, the remarkable Deng made an important contribution to China's political stability. In comparison to most Communist leaders who died on the job, he was the first leader who retired voluntarily from his post. He started a process of orderly succession and some form of term limits. When he died at the age of ninety-two in February 1997, the only title Deng held was that of Honorary Chairman of the Chinese Bridge Association.

A Summing Up

In this brief review of China's history, it appears to us that many elements of its past are incorporated in its outlook and strategies today.

Confucianism. Throughout China's history and to this day, education and respect for ancestors have been an integral aspect of its society. Although many cultures emphasize family ties and veneration of ancestors, China stands out as one that also emphasizes education. Today, that reverence for education has broadened from interests in the arts and governance to commerce, science, and technology. For centuries, China was the world's most powerful country, and that memory imbues the government and the people today with a longing to once more demonstrate their nation's superiority.

Colonialism. The end of the "Century of Humiliation" left a China determined to recover its past position of power and respect. It also brought home forcibly the realization that the country must learn from the outside world, particularly Western science and institutions. The age of globalization has further reinforced both these aspects: China will remain open to new ideas and new technology, but it does not want to have foreigners dominate or control any aspect of its society ever again.

Communism. Class distinctions, while perhaps not erased, were dealt a heavy blow during the Mao years. There was little differentiation as to whom to debase and crush: peasants and intellectuals, landlords and workers—all suffered horribly. In a sense, the social slate was wiped clean, and there is a feeling today that upward mobility is possible on a scale never known before under the Confucian and Colonial systems. Finally, the Mao years left an indelible mark in that the Chinese never want to be hungry and destitute again; the Confucian concept that profit is bad—practiced so brutally under Mao—is no longer viable in China.

Capitalism. Building on the commercialized economy of the past, the country's form of socialism with Chinese characteristics—capitalism by any other name—has brought tremendous wealth and opportunity to its people. Rising international prestige has made clear that the economic reform started by Deng works and should not be abandoned. Nevertheless, the reform and its further refinement is a unique experiment, one in which China will define its own way with the goal of returning to its rightful glory and power.

As we shall see in subsequent chapters, all these factors must be taken into account when devising a strategy for investing in China.

CHAPTER 2

The Present:
China's Stunning Accomplishments

*What makes China's success so striking is the
contrast to the economic failures of the European
countries that abandoned communism.*

—HARVARD SOCIOLOGIST EZRA F. VOGEL

"WE HAVE SEEN THE FUTURE, AND IT IS CHINA." After our
2006 visit to the country, we couldn't help paraphrasing Lincoln Steffens's famous quote.

We saw Shanghai, which in less than twenty years has transformed itself into a megalopolis of a city where the number of
stunning skyscrapers and upscale apartment complexes
dwarfs those punctuating the Manhattan skyline.

We felt the palpable excitement of Chinese citizens
throughout the coastal areas, millions of people who always
seem to be in an optimistic hurry as they dash about the
streets talking on cell phones, carrying their attaché cases and
Coach bags, and wearing their Prada shoes, Piaget watches,
and Gucci suits.

We were impressed by the savvy and practicality of the government officials we met, some of whom had left lucrative
financial jobs in Western countries to come back to China to
partake in its great renaissance.

We could see for ourselves that an average annual growth rate of 9 percent is not an exaggeration. Our anecdotal evidence was confirmed by Peking University's Professor of Economics Guoqing Song when he told us at a private dinner in Beijing that China should continue to grow at an astounding 9 to 10 percent annually, even though our own projections were more moderate. We did not accept his statement on simple faith: Professor Song is consistently singled out by Chinese institutional investors for the accuracy of his gross domestic product predictions; he has also won admirers in the United States during his times as a visiting scholar at Princeton University and at the University of Chicago, where he conducted research on the Chinese economy.

China, we felt, is no longer an emerging country. It has emerged, spectacularly so. As Federal Reserve chairman Ben S. Bernanke noted, there is no historical antecedent for this development. "Columbus's voyage to the New World," he said in a 2006 address at the Fed's annual retreat, "ultimately led to enormous economic change . . . but the full integration of the New and Old Worlds took centuries. In contrast, the economic opening of China, which began in earnest less than three decades ago, is proceeding rapidly and, if anything, seems to be accelerating."

In this chapter, we briefly review the past thirty years and describe the steps China has taken to reach its current status.

The statistics are impressive

To set the mood for what follows, consider the following widely accepted statistics:

- China is the world's third largest trading nation.
- With its official foreign exchange reserves now exceeding $1 trillion, it is a major international investor.

- Depending on the measurement used (and economists love to create new kinds of calculations so that they can argue about the results in major publications), China is either the world's fourth or second largest economy.

- China now has 170 cities with more than 1 million people (the United States has 10 such cities). And these cities contain some of the most modern and striking architecture in the world. Given the huge building boom, it is not surprising that recent statistics show China annually consuming over 45 percent of the cement and more than 30 percent of the steel, iron ore, and coal produced in the world.

- There are over 400 million Chinese subscribers to wireless phone services, 100 million more than the entire U.S. population. And by 2011, Chinese subscribers are expected to number well over 600 million.

- China's citizens now account for more than 12 percent of the world's luxury goods sales, spending their country into the world's third biggest high-end buyer, trailing only the United States and Japan. Goldman Sachs & Co. analyst Jacques-Franck Dossin believes that within ten years China will become the world's top luxury market.

- Bentley boasts the world's most expensive car—the $1.2 million 728 stretch limo—and it has sold more of these in its Beijing dealership than in any other dealership in the world.

The economic transformation is unprecedented

These statistics are even more compelling when you look at China's recent history and realize the speed at which the country has accomplished such an astounding economic transformation. Consider the following examples from different areas of the economy.

At the beginning of the 1970s, China's automotive industry was based on 1930s technology. In 2005, China became a net exporter of cars and trucks for the first time in its history. In 2006, China's Geely Automobile Co. exhibited at the Detroit Auto Show; and at the 2007 show, Changfeng's innovative W-CT3 concept car stole headlines from GM and Ford. China is now aiming to increase its vehicle and autoparts exports to $120 billion by 2116, the equivalent of 10 percent of the world's total vehicle trading volume, according to Wei Jianguo, vice minister of commerce.

During the Cultural Revolution, universities and schools throughout China were closed. Chairman Mao's works alone were officially available, libraries were shut, novels and poems out of reach. "Educated youths," those with at least some high school education, were denied further learning and sent into the countryside to work alongside peasants. In 2005, according to the World Intellectual Property Organization, a UN agency, China's patent applications rose 44 percent from the previous year, pushing the country into tenth from thirteenth place in the number filed. The surge continues. In 2006, the agency reported that China's application increased by 56 percent, boosting it to eighth place in the number filed.

Forty years ago, China's rail network was less developed than that of the United States during the American Civil War. The Chinese government put a positive spin on this with a creative slogan that appeared on a huge sign in the Beijing railroad station: BETTER A SOCIALIST TRAIN THAT IS LATE THAN A CAPITALIST TRAIN ON TIME. Today, segments of China's rail system are far superior to those in the United States. For example, China boasts the world's only commercially operated Maglev train, which speeds along at up to 260 miles per hour using magnets to elevate it above the track. And in July 2006, China inaugurated a luxury train to coddle

passengers on a 48-hour trip to Tibet. As the five-star train—
billed as the world's most environmentally friendly—sweeps
through the snow-clad mountains that have been described as
"the roof of the world," passengers will view the scenery from
specially pressured carriages. No pressure-induced clogged
ears on this trip!

At the height of the Cultural Revolution, Tsinghua University—the MIT of China—literally became a battlefield as student factions used machine guns, rifles, and Molotov cocktails
against each other and burned buildings in their war to determine the right way to educate people. The disgraced revision-
ists felt that the purpose of education—particularly at this
science-based institution—was to have experts train students
through regular study in various specialties. Maoists felt that
education should enhance the socialist consciousness of workers and that this could best be brought about through less in-
class time and more practical time working in fields and
factories. This university—home to Nobelists in physics—actually witnessed senior faculty confessing to the error of their
ways and vowing not to teach the principles of science. Just over
three decades later, Chinese universities now graduate 200,000
engineers a year, compared with 60,000 in the United States.

China is consuming more, creating more, graduating
more, and—with its increasingly economic clout—buying
more, particularly prestigious international brands at bargain
prices. Since the beginning of the new millennium, Chinese
companies have bought Benelli, the oldest motorcycle manufacturer in Italy; the 140-year-old German toolmaker Schiess;
a French cannery selling tomato sauce in Provence; and
IBM's personal computer business. Perhaps the splashiest
purchase, in terms of brand name, is Nanjing Automobile's
acquisition of the legendary British MG. At the company's
heyday in the swinging, anything-goes twenties, MG stood for

EXHIBIT 2.1 *What a Difference Thirty Years Makes: China in 1977 and 2007*

	1977	2007
Political indoctrination:	Several times a week	Almost none; people are too busy making money
Private ownership:	Not allowed	Encouraged
Status clothing:	Blue or green Mao jacket	Armani suits
Cosmetics:	How dare you wear them!	Avon; Revlon; Lancôme Paris
Power lunch:	Lo mein	Starbucks sandwich
Blockbuster movie:	*Shining Red Star*	Harry Potter series
Favorite music:	*The East Is Red*	Heavy metal
Status drink:	Mao Tai	Bordeaux wine
Entertainment:	Card playing	Golf

"Morris Garages"; today, the initials for the new Chinese sports car (built with machinery from the British factory shipped to China) stand for "Modern Gentleman." "It's just like cooking," Nanjing chairman Wang Hongbiao said. "You have to keep the original flavor."

Scholars cite five factors of success

The outline above provides but a peek at the scope of China's unprecedented economic growth over the past three decades. In *China: The Balance Sheet* (2006), the think tank economist and former U.S. Treasury official C. Fred Bergsten and his colleagues argue that five factors are key to China's stunning transformation: "the embrace of market forces, the opening of the economy to trade and inward direct investment, high levels of savings and investments, the structural transformation of the labor force, and investments in primary school education."

Embrace of market forces. Throughout the Mao years, consumer goods were rationed and few consumer staples were available. University students were assigned jobs upon graduation; the idea of interviewing for a job one might like was unknown. Wages were set by the state, and internal migration was severely limited. The government planned citizens' lives from cradle to grave. In the past thirty years, market forces have slowly but inevitably replaced many of these government-mandated arrangements. Companies have increased both productivity and profitability, and thousands of inefficient state-owned enterprises have been disbanded or gone bankrupt. Rationing has disappeared and consumer goods now flood the markets.

Openness to the global economy. China today has one of the most open economies in the world. The level of effective tariff protection granted to its domestic firms is among the lowest of any developing country. In true free market fashion, this openness has led to increased efficiency and competitiveness among domestic firms, making China the most cost-effective manufacturing center in the world. This, in turn, has led to greater profitability and a subsequent increase in capital resources.

High savings level. China's savings rates are among the highest in the world and have actually increased under the reforms. Before 1978, the gross annual national saving rate was estimated to be at 27 percent of GDP; today, it is hovering around 50 percent. (In contrast, the U.S. rate is essentially zero.) The capital from savings has been used for modernizing production, which in turn has increased profitability and its attendant creation of more capital. With its high pools of money, China has easily been able to invest in infrastructure improvements.

Transformation of the labor force. Because of China's extreme shortage of arable land, agricultural productivity is very low. As economic reform led to labor mobility, hundreds of millions of laborers, totaling more than the size of the U.S. labor force, have left agriculture for the more profitable business and manufacturing sector.

Investment in education. China is unique among major world powers in that it has valued education throughout its history. Indeed, China's pre-university public education system is now the largest in the world. Mass literacy was a proclaimed goal as early as the 1950s; by 1977, China's adult literacy rate was 66 percent; in 2003, it was reported to be 89 percent. In 1986, a Compulsory Education Law was instituted that mandated nine years of education for all children. In a debt to the Mao years, females were included in defining the goal of mass literacy. Bergsten and his co-authors believe that this has been particularly important in attracting foreign investment in manufacturing: "the work force is disproportionately female" and "basic literacy has been a crucial prerequisite to the creation of a relatively productive work force in these foreign manufacturing establishments."

Tiananmen Square's economic shadow disappears

The Chinese economy was severely set back following the Tiananmen Square crackdown and the subsequent exit of foreign investment. After Deng headed south, the Chinese embraced his message with so much enthusiasm that just seven years after Tiananmen, Barton Biggs, at the time a renowned Morgan Stanley investment guru, proclaimed: "After six days in China, I'm tuned in, overfed, and maximum bullish."

While it is easy for gurus to make bold proclamations and

EXHIBIT 2.2 *Tiananmen Aftermath: Selected Statistics, 1989 and 2006*

	1989	2006
GDP *(billions of $)*	451	2,687
Consumption *(billions of $)*	226	1,019
GDP per capita *($)*	403	2,043
FDI* *(billions of $)*	3.39	63
Total number of private cars	730,000	23,000,000

*Foreign Direct Investment.

SOURCE: Bosera Asset Management Co.

for venture capitalists to invest in Chinese companies, many individual investors fear that they could lose everything if another Tiananmen should occur. As the table above shows, China has come so far and the middle class has grown so much since 1989 that the possibility of another such economic downturn is considerably lessened. There is simply too much to lose and too many people for the government to alienate at this stage of China's emergence.

China joins the WTO

The major reason for China's openness to the global economy is its participation in the World Trade Organization (WTO). Once Deng had succeeded in getting his message across, and the economy was again taking off, China began lobbying to join the WTO in order to obtain greater market access for its manufactured goods. Officially chartered in 1994, the organization demanded a quid pro quo in the form of foreign direct investment in China. Chinese officials—especially the old-line Maoists—bristled at this requirement. The negotiations, with the United States playing a leading role, were intense. This intensity was aggravated by the powerful Taiwan lobby, which had hoped to torpedo the arrangement.

While the negotiations dragged on, economists, politicians,

and many others debated the implications of China's joining the organization. In a prescient paper, two Australian economists, Kym Anderson and Anna Strutt, argued that China's WTO accession would cause the rate of GDP growth to accelerate from an annual 7.8 percent to 9.2 percent. The two also argued that accession would raise China's trade volume by more than one quarter. Such arguments were not unknown within China, and the economic reformers used them forcefully to convince the hard-liners to accept a wide range of demands to open the economy.

In December 2001, China officially joined the WTO. The results have been dramatic for both China and the United States. In its 2007 Background Note on China, the U.S. Department of State's Bureau of East Asian and Pacific Affairs reported that "China is now one of the most important markets for U.S. exports: in 2005, U.S. exports to China totaled $41.8 billion, more than double the $19 billion when China joined the WTO in 2001 and up 20% over 2004. U.S. agricultural exports have increased dramatically, making China our fourth-largest agricultural export market (after Canada, Japan, and Mexico). Over the same period (2001–2005), U.S. imports from China have risen from $102 billion to $243.5 billion."

And China's exports and imports are not confined solely to the United States. China is now the third largest trading nation in the world. As Bergsten and his colleagues noted in their book, "China's WTO commitments are further enhancing the role of the market, particularly in financial, distribution, and other services—domains where the introduction of market forces had lagged compared to the goods and labor markets. China's WTO commitments have locked in and even added, at the margin, to the openness that had already existed prior to accession in 2001."

EXHIBIT 2.3 *Increase in China's Real Gross Domestic Product, 2002–06*

YEAR	INCREASE (%)
2002	9.1
2003	10.0
2004	10.1
2005	10.2
2006	10.7

SOURCE: China National Bureau of Statistics.

The table above shows that the predictions by Anderson and Strutt were on the conservative side.

China's entrepreneurs seize the possibilities

The statistics cited above do not do full justice to the creative energy and the entrepreneurship that have been unleashed since the era of Deng's reforms. Today, savvy industries and individuals are keeping close watch on the evolution of their economy, and are adapting, changing, or creating entirely new kinds of businesses in order to remain competitive.

Adaptation: An uplift for bras. Under agreements with the European Union (EU) and the United States, China has to limit its flood of textiles into both areas. This has had a major impact on the "bra towns"—centers of manufacturing which had until recently been inundating the world with cheap bras. Several of China's top bra manufacturers have responded by investing heavily in designing and marketing premium, high-margin bra products (all Victoria's Secret bras are made in China). These high-margin items not only increase profits but also get preferential treatment from the government in determining the volume of allowable exports.

One manufacturer, the ACE Style Intimate Apparel Ltd., has gone so far as to fund a two-year course, leading to a BA in

Intimate Apparel, at the Hong Kong Polytechnic University. Dr. Joanne Yip, a faculty member of the university's Institute of Textiles & Clothing, gave us a guided tour of this program. It was unlike any other college tour we had been on.

We walked into a room filled with mannequins decked out in colorful lace and satin bras and thongs designed by first-year students. These mannequins, created from a 3D scanning of a model, are unique in that they are the first "to simulate a live woman for the fitting assessment of bras and panties." The mannequins are, in other words, soft in key places, and can be stroked and squeezed to accommodate various fits and design goals. An application has been made with the U.S. Patent Office.

The mannequins are lauded in printed literature for prospective students:

• Feel the softness

• Feel the smoothness; close-fitting fabric skin as soft and resilient as a lady

• Flexible cup size; detachable and exchangeable artificial breasts

These mannequins are particularly useful for male students; female students have private dressing rooms in which they can personally test out various bra concepts and fabrics. Even so, much as artists call on nude models, students in the program often use live models for fitting sessions.

With one exception, all the mannequins in the program are constructed for size 34B bras. That works for the hordes of slim Chinese women that we saw throughout our trip, but, as we mentioned to Dr. Yip, it just would not do in the United States. She did point out one new mannequin constructed for size 36C bras. The program, then, must rely on live subjects for larger-size bras, and for these, foreigners are always called in. "The problem," she said, "is that it's extremely difficult to find people here who need a 40D bra."

Believe it or not, this is all serious stuff. As a professor who teaches bra studies in England declared, "It is clear that China's bra makers are no longer relying on cost advantage; they are at the top of seamless construction—we couldn't duplicate it."

There were 150 applicants for the program's first year; 33 were accepted. Whereas half of China's new liberal arts graduates spend considerable time finding jobs, this is not the case in bra studies. Dr. Yip said that some companies were trying to hire students even before they completed the program.

Change: A metamorphosis for Christmas trees. The Kao family story aptly illustrates the entrepreneurship and willingness to accept change so prevalent in China today. The senior Kao, Michael, was six years old when his family left Shanghai to escape the Communist takeover. They went to Hong Kong, where Michael grew up to discover a new way of making fake pine needles and with that knowledge went on to create a billion-dollar artificial Christmas tree business. When labor costs started increasing in Hong Kong, he moved his factories to lower-cost mainland China. He also acquired a racehorse named Super Treasure and took singing lessons to improve his karaoke skills in performing Chinese ballads and love songs. Michael, in other words, was a very hip Chinese businessman. And, like so many of his status at the time, he sent his two children to college in the United States.

His daughter, Vivian, joined the business when she graduated in 1994. She continued the company's record of annually shipping millions of fake trees to such major U.S. retailers as Wal-Mart, Target, and Kmart, but took it a step further with the introduction of high technology. She oversaw the building of a fifty-person research team devoted to Christmas tree technology, a team that brought the world trees that glow in psychedelic colors and others that are embedded with microchips that act as traditional lights. (The team also developed a tree that sang "Let It Snow"; that got buried in a blizzard of bad press.)

When Francis, Vivian's brother, returned to China with his college degree in 1998, he felt that neither his sister nor his father were hip enough. He looked at the company's books and believed that the future was not one of exponential growth—even with those sparkling trees in shades of pink and lime. Michael convinced his father to sell the bulk of the business to an American group (Vivian stayed with the tree business as chief executive officer) and to back him with the proceeds in starting up a computer animation company. That firm, Imagi, is now one of Asia's biggest digital animation studios. Its 350 plus animators, working in Hong Kong for wages far less than those earned by their counterparts in Hollywood, recently completed the latest *Teenage Mutant Ninja Turtle* movie.

From green plastic Christmas trees to green animated turtles in less than twenty-five years—now that's a story of how Chinese entrepreneurs are willing to change to keep ahead of the economic game.

Creativity: A new business concept. Several years ago, Jason Jiang, a thirtysomething Shanghai advertising executive, found his mind drifting as he waited for an elevator to reach its destination. (Unlike most Western countries, where elevator rides are often measured in seconds, the journey from lobby to top floor in China's skyscrapers can take up to ten minutes.) Though the lone poster in the enclosed space was boring, Jiang's mind kept coming back to it. How could the poster be made more interesting? How could it help while away the time? And just like that, Focus Media was born.

True to its name, this company captures consumer attention with ads on LCD screens placed strategically in elevators, office reception areas, and apartment lobbies. There are now many, many thousands of those screens in over seventy-five cities throughout China, catapulting Focus Media into China's largest publicly traded advertising firm and Jiang into the ranks of multimillionaires.

Among the companies tuning in to have their ads featured on the flickering screens, which air only TV commercials twenty-four hours a day, are Samsung, Nokia, HSBC, Unilever, and McDonald's. Investors have also been tuning in to get a piece of Focus Media action. Prominent among these is Goldman Sachs, which was one of the firm's original backers. When Focus Media made its debut on the NASDAQ exchange in July 2005, buyers snapped up shares—so much so that the stock price tripled in less than a year.

The flash memory cards that hold the ads in each LCD must be changed manually, which circumvents the need to get a TV license from the government. Among the thousands of bike riders to be seen on streets throughout China are Focus Media employees, pedaling from location to location to ensure that a twenty-first-century concept will continue to be profitable. In many senses, then, Focus Media is truly a China story. And then, too, "Chinese culture is different," as Jiang has said. "We like TV and we don't mind noise. We also seek out information about new products, so many Chinese actually like advertisements."

China is too often presented to the world as a static economy—one that survives solely as a low-cost source of manufacturing activity. As the examples above illustrate, this is not an accurate picture of the China of today. Rather, it is a dynamic entrepreneurial economy, one that is evolving and growing and ultimately destined to become a world leader.

The government also proves to be shrewd in business

Borrowing from Yogi Berra's classic comment that "The future ain't what it used to be," it is clear that China's state-owned enterprises (SOEs) also ain't what they used to be. Back in 1958, when they accounted for 97 percent of China's gross domestic product, they were hopelessly inefficient messes. And although these huge behemoths still dominate the economy (recent data indicate that they account for the majority of the assets of the 500 largest companies), they do so with a twist: they are now open to private investors.

Consider China Mobile, one of the country's most profitable companies and, with a subscriber base of over 300 million, the world's biggest mobile phone operator. Most people simply cannot conceive of using the terms "profitable" and "major world player" in discussing a mainland China company, and yet there you are. And it has all come about through careful government guidance.

The government first let private equity into its telecommunications industry during the 1990s, when it became obvious that more money was needed to put it on a firmer footing. About 30 percent of China Mobile's shares were released to the public; technically, the company remained (and still is) an SOE, but the public now participates as a minority owner. Shortly after private money infused its operations, the company established a mobile network that covered the whole country. Unsung government officials, who could recall the disasters of monopoly-controlled SOEs from the Mao years, took steps to protect the public by backing another SOE, China Unicom, to create a competitive situation. To further strengthen the free market concept, the government next formed China Telecom and China Netcom.

China Mobile has thrived in this atmosphere, constantly

innovating and continually expanding. It is a leader in the concept of a mobile phone serving as a one-stop shop of digital services. As its chief executive officer Wang Jianzhou has proclaimed, "We want to make the mobile phone a Swiss Army knife that can do anything for you." Few companies throughout history have grown so fast and so profitably in such a short period. Furthermore, China Mobile is publicly committed to increasing its dividend payments to shareholders. Think about it: the world's largest mobile phone operator is a company that is less than twenty years old. And it arose from the ashes of a country in which over 20 million citizens died of hunger a half century ago. In the case of China Mobile, at least, socialism with Chinese characteristics has been a stunning success.

Shanghai transforms itself

Perhaps the best illustration of China's tremendous accomplishments is the story of Pudong, a swampy area on the other side of the Huangpu River, the body of water that bisects Shanghai. Until the 1990s, the only way to reach this area from downtown Shanghai was by ferryboat. In 1990, however, Shanghai officials drew up a $10 billion plan not only to develop the area but also to connect it directly with the city through a series of bridges, tunnels, and subways. Backed by this development plan and Deng's blessing, the city won national government approval in May 1992 to create tax exemptions for foreign joint ventures and a zone for the importation of duty-free materials in the Pudong area. That year alone, Pudong attracted $3.3 billion in foreign investment; the figure more than doubled the next year.

Within a decade, the barren wastes were transformed into a platform exhibiting some of the most exciting architecture in the world. The stunning Oriental Pearl Tower, with its three spheres said to be based on a Tang dynasty poem, was completed in 1994. Four years later, the soaring Jin Mao Tower, with the Grand Hyatt Hotel nestled within its fifty-third to eighty-seventh floors, made its debut. The Bank of China Tower with its lentoid glass shaft appeared in 2000. The Shanghai Oriental Art Center, an elegant building suggesting a butterfly and illuminated at night in rainbow colors, opened in 2004. As the noted American architect Ben Wood commented, "here was someplace where I could do more in 15 years than most architects could do in their entire career."

The transformation is far from complete. Shanghai's World Financial Center, touted to be the world's second tallest building, is scheduled to open in 2008. It features a rectangular opening at the top—a wonderful yet practical design element in that it reduces the stress of wind forces. This construction boom, and the myriad financial, trade, and arts institutions behind it, has attracted millions of construction workers from the hinterland and thousands more smartly dressed Chinese to staff the new offices.

As a result of Pudong's metamorphosis, construction and modernization have spread throughout the city. One of the most ambitious projects—the largest new city development in a century—is in a new Shanghai city district known as the Luchao Harbor City project. Scheduled to be completed in 2020, it will house 800,000 residents in buildings surrounding a large circular man-made lake, complete with promenades and a bathing beach.

With all this exciting and striking new development, the Bund area—that formerly glamorous section where colonial vice and elegance ruled—began to look a wee bit shabby. More prestigious architects were called in, among them the American Michael Graves. His firm restored the historic facades of three of the buildings and created spaces inside for high-end shops, including an elegant Jean-Georges restaurant with its *haute cuisine*. Crowning it all and situated in the

Cupola, in the rooftop of one building, is the world's most romantic restaurant: it seats only two.

The construction boom went beyond renovating older buildings in Shanghai. Swaths of derelict buildings—particularly those housing the poorer workers—were cleared to make way for new hotels, such as an elegant Four Seasons in the heart of old Shanghai. There was no question, however, about protecting one particular building: the old schoolhouse where Mao attended the first meeting of the Communist Party has been carefully preserved.

Even with its renovation, the Bund today—or so, at least, we think—somehow looks not quite as glamorous as it was said to be a century ago. Rather, as one stands on the newly reconstructed pedestrian promenade in front of the Bund and gazes through the ever present pollution across the Huangpu River, it is Pudong—the epitome of today's resurgent China—that seems ever so much more interesting and exciting. Pudong soars above China's imperial past, is infinitely more splendid than its bitter colonial heritage, and is certainly more vibrant than what existed during its Mao years. Pudong is the China of today—a robust, exciting entrant into the global economy.

Perhaps this pride in the China of today—yet with it a respect for an ancient cultural heritage—is best exemplified in the Shanghai Stock Exchange. When the exchange first opened in 1991 as a Chinese entity, the municipal government had dictated that it be located in the Bund area, the location where foreigners had forbidden Chinese to participate in the first stock exchange. Today, the Shanghai Stock Exchange's gleaming new quarters are located in Pudong. And here, it carries an echo from China's far distant past—the past when China was the world's most magnificent country. In this most modern and technologically advanced of all stock exchanges, there are exactly 1,608 seats. Such an odd number, a Westerner might think. But to a Chinese person, steeped in the ethos of a many-thousand-year-old culture, the number "8" is associated with prosperity and is revered as being very special. The number had to be included for good luck.

China wins bids to host the Olympics and the World Expo

China is rightly proud of its real-this-time great leap forward. Not only that, it wants to brag and show the entire world that its past greatness was not a fluke. Hosting the Olympic Games is one of the surest methods of focusing world attention on a country's glories. Starting in the 1990s, China began lobbying extensively to serve as a host. U.S. congressional opposition, fueled by the Taiwan lobby, resulted in China losing out to Sydney, Australia, for the 2000 Olympics. By 2001, however, it was clear that China could no longer be denied—not only did it join the WTO at the end of that year; it was named host of the 2008 Olympics.

Beijing was chosen as the primary host city within China. The opening ceremony is scheduled to begin at 8 p.m. on August 8, 2008 (observant readers of the Shanghai Stock Exchange story will already understand the full import of this; those who are not so observant should now note that the time can be transcribed as 08-08-08-08, a truly auspicious and prosperous combination).

Current plans call for the government to renovate or construct thirty-six gymnasiums and stadiums and fifty-nine training centers. This has led to a multi-billion-dollar construction boom rivaling that taking place in the Pudong area. Architects throughout the world vied in competitions for the right to be represented. Probably the most prestigious assignment went to the Swiss firm of Herzog & de Meuron, collaborating with the Shanghai-based China Architecture Design & Research Group, to design and build the Beijing National Stadium. The stadium features a radical, eye-catching design: a latticelike concrete skeleton, which is supposed to invoke a bird's nest made of interwoven twigs. Radicalism does have its price, however, and in 2004—after only eight months of construction work—the design was modified because of ballooning costs; the retractable roof was abandoned.

It is expected that 7 million tickets will be sold to the 302 events featuring 28 different sports. To handle the influx of visitors, ultra-modern new subways and gleaming new hotels and housing complexes have been created. Furthermore, in April 2006, the Beijing municipal authority announced that all those without resident permits and without tickets would not be allowed in the city during the games. To reduce air pollution, some factories were physically moved to other locations hundreds of miles outside the city, and the sale of gasoline will be restricted during the events so that residents will not be able to drive their cars. The Beijing Olympics, in short, will be a thing of splendor, and the Beijing government is leaving nothing to chance.

Not to be outdone by its northern rival, Shanghai learned in December 2002 that it had won its bid to host the 2010 World Expo. This event, to take place from May 1 through October 31, will be first ever held in a developing country. The Shanghai government has committed over $10 billion for infrastructure improvements to its harbor, airports, transportation, and cultural facilities. Current plans call for over 200 national exhibitions and business pavilions. Over 70 million visitors are expected to attend.

A Summing Up

In the past thirty years, China has transformed itself from an economically and technologically backward nation into one of the world's most dynamic economies. It has opened its doors to new ideas and techniques, introduced competition to all aspects of production, strengthened its commitment to widespread literacy and education, and taken advantage of the opportunities offered by its WTO membership. Its people, on their own, continue to have one of the highest savings rates in the world—a feat especially noteworthy when one considers that the savings rate in the United States is essentially zero. China is now getting ready to strut on the world stage and is making every effort to ensure that its appearance will be an impressive one.

History majors (and we trust that history majors pay at least some attention to finance and economics) and perhaps others may have seized on the fact that our opening reference to Lincoln Steffens's quote was a paraphrase of his reaction to his 1921 visit to Russia. Specifically, he said, "I have seen the future, and it works." What a ghastly future he envisioned! Under Communism, Russia killed millions of its own citizens, created the term *gulag*, and saw its economy wrecked to almost total destitution.

Some readers might have read our paraphrase to mean that China's future is similarly bleak. Could we be wrong? Could China's future be as devastating as Russia's was in 1921? Again, history majors and, let us be honest about this, economics majors as well know that this is a totally rhetorical question. We wouldn't have asked it if we believed the answer to be yes. But many do feel that the future is not so bright in China, that China is doomed to trip over numerous roadblocks and obstacles. In the next chapter we show why we believe such feeling is, for the most part, ill informed.

CHAPTER 3

The Future: Perceived Risks

Let China sleep, for when she awakes she will shake the world.

—ATTRIBUTED TO NAPOLEON

NOT EVERYONE IS CONVINCED THAT CHINA will continue on its rapid growth path. As many China experts and not-so-experts have proclaimed, China has a plethora of serious problems. These problems, they feel, will ultimately sink the nation. Or as the publication *Strategic Forecasting* put it in their forecast to 2015: "China will suffer a meltdown." In this chapter, we examine the risks to China's economy and whether these widely perceived impediments are based on fact or fiction.

Risk #1. A huge aging population will drag down the economy

Flat-out fiction. Aging populations are a common headache throughout much of the developed world. In the United States, doomsters point to the tidal wave of Americans who will soon be tapping into the underfunded Social Security and Medicare systems, systems that a smaller number of younger, taxpaying workers are supposed to support. Europe's problems are even worse because the promised old-age benefits are even larger than those in the United States and the proportion of retirees to workers is even greater. With the world's largest population, China has the greatest number of older people. This has created a field day for people who love to grab media attention. Consider, for example, these words of so-called wisdom from a fall 2005 *Wall Street Journal* article: "Of all the impending Third World aging tsunamis, the most massive is set to strike China." Dramatic, yes; misleading, terribly.

Indeed, in the short term, China's aging population, as a percentage of total population, is more favorable than that of the United States. Furthermore, according to predictions prepared by the UN Population Division, China will not even rank among the top twenty-five countries with the largest percentage of those over age sixty in 2050. And while the

EXHIBIT 3.1 *Population Aged 60 Years or Above, as Percentage of Total Population*

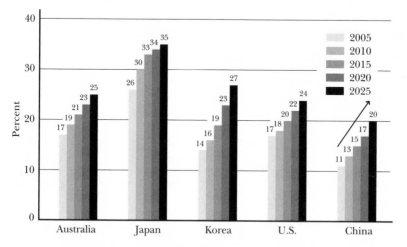

From Merrill Lynch Research "China in 2007–2010: Key Trends and Risks," November 22, 2006.

SOURCE: United Nations and Merrill Lynch Research.

increase in the aging population is of some concern, it will not be a major detriment to economic growth in either country over the next ten to twenty years. China in particular is in a more favorable position than the United States with regard to funding health and pension obligations. Though the Chinese government's pension fund faces as much as a $100 billion shortfall over the next decade, more than enough reserves exist to cover this obligation.

It should be noted that all the hue and cry about graying populations presupposes that people overnight become mentally challenged and physically infirm when they reach their sixtieth birthday, an assumption that some of us find highly insulting. The "gray hairs" or "bald heads" are classified in statistics as dependents, being unable either to earn income or to have the mental capacity to care for themselves and handle their affairs. Research by neuroscientists over the past fifteen years has been attacking this thesis with a vengeance. It has been found, for example, that while an adult brain is less "plastic" than that of a child, it nevertheless turns out to be more supple and open to new learning than was previously believed. The University of California–San Francisco neuroscientist Michael Mezerich predicts that these findings are creating a "new brain fitness culture." In visiting China's city parks, we were impressed with the number of older Chinese people dancing, practicing Tai Chi, playing musical instruments, and creating sidewalk calligraphy with the use of large brushes dipped in water. On a strictly anecdotal basis, we believe that China's older population is already engaging in a culture of brain fitness. Furthermore, with the country's Confucian tradition of honoring parents and the lack of spacious quarters, it is extremely rare for older people to be left alone to become inactive and depressed.

Graying-of-population doomsayers also totally ignore the

relative position of those over sixty compared to the rest of the population. At this point, it is helpful to have a brief lesson in demography, the study of population growth and change. In one sense, demography can be said to be the most exact of all the social sciences. This is because the number of people born in any given year will never increase after the year ends. Thus, if 1 million children are born in, say, 1946, the cohort size—the term used to describe the number of births in a given time period—will never be larger than 1 million. Although the birth cohort size can be decreased by deaths due to wars, disease, and accidents, it will never increase. Knowing the size of a birth cohort is a powerful economic prediction tool.

Recall the baby boom in the United States. In the period from 1946 through 1964, an average of 4 million babies were born per year, a record at the time. These babies, dubbed the boomers, led to one of the biggest hiring bonanzas in education, to a burst of housing construction, and now to a plethora of financial planners. Savvy entrepreneurs profited handsomely as the boomers went through the various stages of the aging process. The boomers were followed by the Birth Dearth generation. These fortunate people entered schools overflowing with teachers desperate to keep their jobs and went into a workforce eager to hire them. For those born in 1973, there were no easier years than 1991 and 1992 to get into an Ivy League school; there was simply less competition.

Demographers take this certainty about cohort size and then look at the numbers over all age groups. And here is where China, according to Yale professor Deborah Davis, has an unprecedented demographic advantage among developing economies. How can this be so when China is supposedly going to be swamped by a tsunami of useless oldsters? Simple. China is not inundated by even larger masses of diaper-wearing babies and angst-ridden, uneducated youths. While much of China's low birth rate is the result of the government's one-child policy, this policy is no longer widely enforced through the draconian measures occasionally used when it was first introduced. Indeed, China's current birth rate is higher than that in Italy.

Demographers like to combine the proportion of those under fifteen and the proportion of those aged sixty-five and older and compare that number with those of working ages. The result is called the "dependency ratio," and China today has one of the most favorable in the world. China does not have to train thousands of new teachers to educate its youth. It does not have to build new schools to house them. It does not have to set aside massive sums for education in its state budgets. Because the number of youngsters has actually declined in the past fifteen years, classes are smaller. And unlike many developing nations—particularly India—there are fewer entrants to absorb into the workforce every year. Thus, China has both a low youth and, as shown in Exhibit 3.2, a low elderly dependency ratio. Even forty years from now, the differences between China and the United States will be minor.

As Professor Davis wrote in the *Yale Global Online*, "Even if the growing number of elderly places greater demands on

EXHIBIT 3.2 *Dependency Ratios: U.S. and China*

	% AGE 65 AND OVER		ELDERLY DEPENDENCY RATIO*	
	2000	2050	2000	2050
United States	12.3	20.0	19	32
China	6.8	22.9	10	37

*The ratio of those 65 and over to those of working ages 15–64.

SOURCE: UN Population Division, 2003, *World Population Prospects: The 2002 Revision Population Database*.

medical services, the falling percentage of young children suggests that both local governments and families will maintain or even increase their investment in primary and secondary education. Given the excellent core curriculum across the entire country, China is therefore well positioned to continue to upgrade its 'human capital' over the next decade."

Risk #2. Bad bank loans will sink the economy

Fiction. The savings rate of Chinese people—probably the highest in the world—and the lack of opportunities for investment both at home and abroad have led to a banking system awash in cash. By some estimates as much as $1.7 trillion, which translates to 65 percent of the country's GDP, are stuffed into Chinese bank accounts. The Chinese, in other words, save more than they spend. In the United States, the situation is the exact opposite: Americans consume more than they save. And with the constant push to do something with all that Chinese money, the banking system has made a huge number of loans, without any level-headed thinking as to how viable those loans ultimately would be. Often the banks had no choice, as the government frequently dictated that the loans be made to hopelessly inefficient state-owned enterprises.

As a result, it is widely accepted that the nonperforming loans are a cancer in the financial system. For many investors, the situation brings back memories of the heavy debt loads that were associated with the late 1990s economic collapse of the four "Asian Tigers" economies, and the downward fiscal spiral that plagued several Latin American countries as well. China really is different, however. The difference in this case is that the China bank loans are actually the government's responsibility since financial institutions are owned and controlled by the government. And while an inordinate number of loans were made to inefficient state enterprises, these loans did contribute to social stability by helping to keep unemployment down. Nevertheless, there are those who argue that the loans constitute a staggering amount of bad debt and that they will eventually lead to a meltdown of the entire Chinese economy. This is certainly a dramatic conclusion but, as with the supposed tsunami of oldsters, it is definitely a faulty one.

It is our contention that China's nonperforming loans should be considered as government debt. The influential financial economist Franklin Allen of the University of Pennsylvania comes to a similar conclusion. Indeed, 2006 data compiled by the Bosera Asset Management Company indicate that China's total government debt (which includes nonperforming loans) is 25 percent of its GDP and 60 percent of its cash reserves. In contrast, U.S. government debt constitutes 29 percent of GDP and a truly astounding 5,400 percent of reserves. Japan's financial statistics also pale in comparison with China's: debt is 165 percent of GDP and 886 percent of reserves. Seen in this light, it is Japan on which financial doomsayers should be concentrating. Indeed, as Federal Reserve Chairman Ben Bernanke wrote in late 2006 to Senator Richard Shelby, head of the U.S. Senate Banking Committee, "Although the [Chinese] banking sector is burdened with an enormous and probably growing stock of problematic loans, the government possesses sizable resources and is unlikely to allow the banking system to fail."

The China "meltdown scenario" also ignores the shrewdness of Chinese government financial experts. They are attacking problem loans primarily through three different strategies: shoring up the banks with government money; allowing foreign institutions to participate in the cleanup through private investments; and letting the banks raise new money through initial public offerings (IPOs).

Government funding. Of all the government-owned banks, Bank of China is probably one of the worst with its colorful history of bad loans and corruption. So blatant was this corruption that the government actually cracked down on the chairman and president, Wang Xuebing, who received a twelve-year prison term in 2003 for taking bribes (and this in a country where bribes are almost a daily part of doing business). The government then followed through with an injection of $22.5 billion to clean up bad loans. According to Fitch Ratings, a global credit-rating agency, this infusion reduced the bank's nonperforming loan ratio from an extraordinary 33.4 percent in 2003 to a more acceptable 4.4 percent in mid-2005.

The Bank of China has not been alone in receiving "cleanup" money from the national government. The China Construction Bank received a $22.5 billion infusion. And the central bank transferred $15 billion of the country's foreign exchange reserves to the Industrial & Commercial Bank of China.

Private investments. Much as the Rockefeller family trusts boosted their fortunes when they sold Rockefeller Center to the Japanese in the 1980s, the Chinese government has allowed foreign institutions to buy into state-owned banks. For example, a Citigroup-led consortium beat out ABN Amro and Société Générale for the right to pump $3.2 billion into China's Guangdong Development Bank, a medium-sized Chinese lender. At the same time, Citigroup announced it was increasing its stake in the Shanghai Pudong Development Bank, with which it had been jointly offering a credit card since 2004. (Recall that China has 1.3 billion consumers, many of whom see both their appetite for retail goods and their incomes rising.)

The Chinese government is not only shrewd in allowing the injection of foreign capital into its banking system but also practical. Such investments are part of the obligation the government incurred when it joined the World Trade Organization. If China wants—and it does—to remain a member of the WTO, it has to allow foreign institutions to participate in China's undeveloped consumer finance market.

And let it be noted that the mainland China banks of today want more than money from foreigners. They also want their management expertise. The China Construction Bank (CCB), for example, which received a $3 billion investment from Bank of America (BofA) in 2005, also obtained a seven-year agreement in which BofA is providing advice and assistance in improving call centers and retail branches, and in establishing procedures for database management and information technology planning. Approximately fifty BofA executives are working closely with CCB personnel on over twenty partnership projects to transform CCB into a modern, competitive bank.

Issuing IPOs. The Chinese government also recognized that its citizens would want to participate in the newer, cleaner banking system. This was all music to many, many ears dreaming of new wealth. The newly somewhat squeaky clean Bank of China responded with an IPO in 2006. In the early days of planning for this, the bank easily got the Royal Bank of Scotland Group, Merrill Lynch, and Temasek Holdings (the Singapore government's investment arm) to take investment stakes before the IPO was launched.

And then the frenzy started. Thousands of Chinese packed the bank's Hong Kong branches to obtain the necessary forms for the June 1 listing on Hong Kong's stock market. Some were driven by the fact that they had missed out on a small

IPO for Tianjin Port Development, which operates China's fifth largest port. It was the most heavily subscribed IPO in southern China, with offers for nearly 1,700 times the number of shares scheduled to be sold. Other would-be buyers were aware that shares of China Construction Bank had climbed over 40 percent since its IPO six months before.

On May 24, 2006, when stock markets around the world were sinking, the Bank of China raised $9.7 billion—at the time the largest offering ever in Hong Kong, and the world's biggest since AT&T Wireless floated an offering in 2000. The portion of shares allocated to retail investors was oversubscribed by a factor of 80 and those to institutional investors by 20. On June 1, the day the shares made their debut on the Hong Kong Stock Exchange, the price rose 15 percent.

That one-day gain was eclipsed in September, when shares for the China Merchants Bank jumped 25 percent on the first day of trading. As with the Bank of China IPO, the offering was heavily oversubscribed. Even though the bank is only the country's sixth largest, it raised $2.4 billion in its Hong Kong Stock Exchange debut. And then all else paled in October 2006 when the giant Industrial & Commercial Bank of China raised $19 billion in the world's biggest IPO. It was not only the world's largest IPO, it was also the first to list in both Hong Kong and Shanghai. More than 1 million people tried to participate in the Hong Kong offering, placing orders worth almost $54 billion. Institutional orders for the offering were more than thirty times oversubscribed, attracting $325 billion in orders from investors. Goldman Sachs was one of the favored ones, and rumor has it that the company made a $1 billion paper profit at the end of the opening day.

With the government committed to cleaning up its banking system through cash infusions, and with both its citizens and international investors eager to shell out money to own shares in that system, it appears highly unlikely that bad bank loans could sink China's economy today.

Risk #3. Tensions with Taiwan and Japan could disrupt the economy

Fact—but. There is no doubt that enmity between China, Taiwan, and Japan is thick. In a distant echo of General MacArthur's famous "I shall return" declaration, Chang Kai-shek vowed he would ultimately return to the mainland when he and 2 million refugees withdrew to Taiwan in 1949. The Chinese promptly pooh-poohed this and simply reaffirmed their historical stance that Taiwan is part of their country, and further, that the island would eventually be folded into China's governing structure. The United States, with the backing of a powerful Taiwan lobby, then muddied the waters separating the two Chinese entities when it passed the Taiwan Relations Act in 1979. This states that if Taiwan is attacked by an outside source, the United States must come to its defense. China, under this act, is considered an outside source. Reacting to this "in your face" provocation, China has proceeded to place hundreds of missiles across the strait separating Taiwan from the mainland and every one of them is aimed directly at the island.

As for Japan, the Rape of Nanjing—the 1937 Japanese massacre of hundreds of thousands of Chinese in and around Nanjing—still resonates among the Chinese public. The decades-old bitterness is fueled by several of today's conservative Japanese politicians who not only refuse to accept the actuality of the massacre but also honor the graves of generals who participated in it.

Despite the heavy and real presence of such tensions, the three economies are becoming ever more mutually entangled. Both Japan and Taiwan have outsourced a substantial share of their manufacturing to China; in turn, China both imports from and exports to the other two entities. Indeed, China is the biggest export destination for Taiwan and accounts for a large portion of exports from Japan. Toyota alone, for example, has poured over $2 billion into its China operations since 1998. This is a profitable situation for all involved. In the early 1970s, Mao said that while Taiwan would eventually be an integral part of the Chinese state, it could take a hundred years for this to come about. There's still another sixty plus years left.

Politicians, however, often tend to ignore the economic aspects of a situation. Vested interests—especially military and military manufacturers—can also profit from increased tensions. In 2005, a top Pentagon official declared that China may be preparing to deal with its dispute over Taiwan through other than political means as it increases its offensive military power. The statement was widely viewed as part of a Pentagon strategy to obtain funds for new long-range weapons and a greater U.S. Navy presence in the Pacific.

The bottom line is that any military outbreak would be detrimental to economies worldwide—this is not solely a risk to the Chinese economy. And, sadly, no one can predict to what length demagogic politicians will go to stir up popular resentment to further their own agenda. Given that a military conflict could just about destroy all three economies and perhaps countries, we feel it unlikely that war will break out— although periodic saber rattling will no doubt continue.

Risk #4. Widespread environmental degradation will impede growth

Not necessarily. There is no doubt that rampant pollution has ravaged China's environment during the past quarter century of breakneck industrialization. Among the frightening statistics that are bandied about are: sixteen of the world's most polluted cities are on the China mainland; more than 70 percent of China's lakes and rivers are polluted; 25 percent of its population are without clean drinking water; and less than 20 percent of solid wastes are treated. And that says nothing about the air, which is downright life-threatening throughout the country.

Indeed, the situation has become so bad that the government has been forced to respond. In fact, their winning bid for the 2008 Olympics obligated them to ensure air clean enough for athletes to engage in strenuous activities. In 2006, the government enshrined its commitment to environmental protection in its eleventh Five-Year Program. It has publicly stated that environmental quality in key areas and cities must be "improved" by 2010 and "markedly improved" by 2020. The State Environmental Protection Administration now daily publishes on its Web site the air quality index for eighty-four major cities, with the goal of such publicity forcing local officials to adhere to cleaner air guidelines. (Nothing, however, is being done to impede the growth of private car ownership, which is contributing mightily to air pollution in major cities.)

As part of its latest program, the country aims to have its use of environmentally friendly energy sources such as wind, hydro, and solar power increase to 15 percent of its energy needs by 2020; to build thirty nuclear power plants by that date; and to invest heavily in new technologies.

When we met with Yang Guoxiong, deputy Director of China's National Research Center, he explained in greater depth some of the steps the government is taking to halt and even repair environmental degradation.

• The government is insisting that old buildings be renovated to conform to new efficient energy standards; for example, between 2006 and 2011, 20 percent of all old buildings in Beijing will be updated. In addition, there are stringent energy-efficient standards for all new construction. Factories that do not reach environmental standards within five years must close.

- Unlike many areas of the China economy, there are no restrictions on foreign companies introducing green technologies. Not only can these companies fully own their operations, they also receive tax benefits if they introduce certified new environmental technology.

- The Chinese car emission standard is much higher than that in the United States (This has not gone unnoticed in the United States, where Fred Krupp, president of the advocacy group Environmental Defense, has commented that "If the United States would adopt energy-efficiency standards like China, that would be a big advance for us.")

- Between 2001 and 2006, the percentage of clean air days in Beijing rose from 60 to 65 percent. Given the enormous amount of construction (it appears that a new building is going up every day) as well as the burgeoning number of cars, this is an impressive accomplishment.

- The government has made a huge commitment to wind power. Western China is home to the world's largest wind power generation facility.

The 2008 Olympics will be a marvel of green technology, featuring solar power, green roofs, and waterless urinals. Say that last again? Yes, waterless urinals, and there are even plans to have a drawing of a bee prominently displayed on each urinal's interior to help users aim correctly. One year of correctly hitting that little bee equals a saving, per urinal, of almost 40,000 gallons of water that would have been flushed. Contrast this with water conservation efforts in the United States. When builders in Los Angeles and Philadelphia wanted to include waterless urinals in new construction, plumbers' unions vetoed the project, saying it would take work from them.

In addition to increased regulation, the Ministry of Science and Technology is pioneering new "green technology" that will not only benefit the Chinese people but will also enhance a new field of manufacturing and technological capabilities. As the *New York Times* columnist Thomas Friedman wrote in November 2005, "Within a decade . . . we'll have to import our green technology from Beijing."

It appears, however, that the Chinese aim to shorten that time prediction. In the April 2007 Shanghai Auto Show, for example, China's automakers demonstrated their environmental high-tech prowess by exhibiting experimental fuel-cell sedans and cars running on ethanol. In comparing his alternative energy vehicles with those of major foreign manufactures, Shanghai Automotive Industries president Chen Hong noted that "we're all starting from almost the same line." Backed by government grants and tax breaks, Chen believes that China will be a world leader in the development of clean energy and high-mileage vehicles.

Of course, in China as in many of the world's countries, there is often a big difference between what a government says and what it enforces. Given the horrendous, world-publicized 2005 chemical spill that disrupted drinking water supplies in the northern China city of Harbin, the dust storms in Beijing, the desertification brought about by deforestation, and the public outcry over what is happening, China's national government is getting very serious in this area. It has already put on hold road construction and other projects deemed to pose environmental hazards. What has not stopped, however, is the construction of highly polluting coal-fired plants to meet the country's growing demand for energy.

In one sense, the government has entered a race between its determination to halt and repair past environmental degradation and the urge of Chinese consumers to emulate the wasteful energy-spending habits of Western countries. There is a handicap in this race, however, and it is the local governments. Indeed, Zhou Shengxian, director of the State Environmental Protection Administration, has publicly blamed much of the continuing—and in some areas increasing—environmental problems on corruption and fraud by local officials.

In one notable example, two paper mills in Inner Mongolia were heavily fined and ordered to upgrade their pollution equipment after a serious Yellow River spill in 2004. The fines and publicity were widely praised as demonstrating the government's efforts to crack down on industrial pollution. And then nothing happened—even after local officials were ordered to close the factories if they continued polluting. In April 2006, after a violent storm, sludge from the factories spilled out of a temporary containment basin and literally sank a small village in a toxic, foul-smelling brown mess. The *New York Times* quoted one resident as saying, "The reason this accident happened is that the local government didn't follow the directives of the central government."

Environmental degradation, then, is closely entwined with rural unrest and corruption, risks that are discussed below. Suffice it to note here that the national government is aware of the problem, and that its efforts in this area are recognized by both domestic and international environmental groups. At the very least, environmental problems are not being ignored on the national level and much is being done to ameliorate them.

Risk #5. The remaining poverty is leading to disruptive and dangerous internal unrest

Fact—but. Since the late 1990s, reduction of poverty has slowed markedly, particularly in rural areas, in spite of the fact that China's economic growth has been the wonder of the world.

According to the Princeton University economist and China expert Gregory C. Chow, about 59 million rural residents still lived under the poverty line of 800 yuan per capita in 2003. He noted that more than 60 percent of rural households do not have access to flush toilets. Six percent of villages are still beyond the reach of highways; 2 percent have no electricity. Some 150 million rural households face problems in fuel supply. And only one fifth of rural residents are covered by the government's medical care insurance system; the remainder have no coverage whatsoever.

The United Nations Development Program reports that in 2006 the gap in China between wealthier urban dwellers and poorer rural residents was about 3.3 to 1. This is not only an extremely wide divergence but also a growing one—in 1985, the ratio was 1.85 to 1. It is worth noting, however, that this most recent degree of inequality is still low compared with that in Latin America. The gap in China has led to an increasingly audible grumbling among those left out of the current economic boom, as attested to by the frequent headlines about police cracking down on protestors in Chinese villages. Official statistics have even admitted that "mass incidents of unrest" have occurred well over 200 times in a single year, while annual public protests throughout the nation have exploded from 10,000 in 1994 to 74,000 in 2004.

The Chinese unrest, however, is on the whole very different from that expressed in Latin America. There, recently elected populist politicians argue against free market economies and the presence of foreign investment. The Chinese people, on the other hand, appear to fully back Deng's assertion that "To be rich is glorious!" with the result that civilian unrest often represents the flip side of the Chinese being more educated and wanting to work harder than those in other emerging market countries. Many are striving for a better life, and when they see extravagant displays of new wealth, they want their share. Others are scared. As many as 30 million workers have lost their jobs with the closing of tens of thousands of unprofitable factories over the past ten years. Though these people may not mourn the passing of Mao's Communist economy—albeit one that provided at least a minimum of a safety net—they bridle at seeing so many getting wealthy while they sink into abject poverty.

Millions of these literally displaced persons have flocked to urban areas, where they have become a drifting population with no permanent residence. Like illegal immigrants in the United States, this flotsam of ill-educated, ill-prepared workers takes on the most menial jobs to support themselves and their families. According to a 2006 report by the China Academy of Social Sciences, the combined incomes of the poorest fifth of the urban population is less than one twentieth of the combined incomes of the wealthiest one fifth.

We have seen some of the sullen faces of the underclass in the cities and we have witnessed, in brief forays into the country, the bleak conditions under which many of these people live. Even in the cities, we were told, there are families who are packed into one room and who must share kitchen facilities at the end of a hall and an outhouse in a courtyard. And these wretched accommodations are often only blocks from gleaming Grand Hyatt and Four Seasons hotels.

It is this potentially explosive situation that now confronts a government riding a wave of tremendous economic growth. The government answered that challenge in its eleventh Five-Year Program in 2006. Speaking before the national legislature's annual meeting, Prime Minister Wen Jiabao promised free education for every rural child, increased funding for

rural infrastructure and agricultural modernization, the abolition of an agricultural tax, an increased grain subsidy to
farmers, a higher budget for improving the rural hospital network, and a higher government contribution to individual
health insurance plans in rural areas.

This is a huge government program. According to Fan Jianping, director of economic forecasting at the State Information Center, spending on rural programs could well exceed
the approximately $15 billion in annual outlays during the
government's special urban development campaigns undertaken from 1998 to 2003. And while these measures will not
transform rural China overnight, they do ensure that the well-
being of residents in these areas—in terms of education, rising income, and health care—will be far above that in other
emerging countries.

Perhaps the most revolutionary of the acts announced by
the prime minister is the abolition of the agricultural tax, a
tax that had been collected for 2,600 years. Indeed, the prime
minister called it a "change of epoch-making significance." In
practical terms, as *The Economist* has reported, its impact is
almost purely psychological: the annual per capita saving is
only $19. Nevertheless, when we went into the countryside
after the prime minister's announcement, we found that this
one act alone has made an enormous attitudinal difference
among those farming the land—for the first time in their lives
they are free from the dreaded tax collector.

The measures embedded in the current Five-Year Program
are designed to build a "new socialist countryside" and are part
of an overall goal of creating a more harmonious society. They
are aimed at depressing the migration to cities by making rural
life more attractive and viable. In addition, officials hope that
domestic consumption will increase in these areas, stimulating
further growth. Such economic growth, the Harvard econo-

mist Benjamin Friedman argues in his book on *The Moral Consequences of Economic Growth* (2005), is essential to social progress. He believes that during times of increasing prosperity, societies tend to liberalize. By contrast, during eras of economic depression, they veer toward authoritarianism. With continuing economic growth, he writes, there is "greater opportunity, tolerance of diversity, social mobility, commitment to fairness, and dedication to democracy." China will be the great proving ground as to whether or not his thesis is correct.

Professor Guoqing Song of Peking University believes that the new government programs are definitely a step in the right direction and will do much to mitigate widespread unrest. In addition, he feels the floating populations of migrant laborers are too poorly organized to launch massive political actions; and then, too, many are entrepreneurs who have a strong desire to profit from rather than protest actively during their time in the cities. Those left behind in rural areas are now aware that the national government is working to alleviate their plight.

And don't forget China's demographic advantage. Unlike every other developing country, China is not faced with growing hordes of young people seeking jobs. With a stable age structure and increased economic incentives, we believe there is a guarded hope that much of the unrest will be quieted and that China's path to economic abundance will continue unimpeded. In any event, continued growth in the Chinese economy is part of the solution, especially as increased economic activity becomes more geographically widespread.

Risk #6. Rising factory wages and cheaper labor elsewhere will slow down the economy

Probably fiction. An interesting thing happened to China on its way to becoming a world economic power. Wages in the manufacturing sector started rising, exerting pressure on profit margins. According to the well-known global economist Steven Roach, there has been a manufacturing wage inflation of about 12 percent every year since 1999. As a *BusinessWeek* online article put it, these rising wages are changing the game in China. A study by China's Institute of Contemporary Observation, a labor research organization, indicated that employee turnover in low-tech jobs is approaching 50 percent. High-tech industries are also facing shortages of skilled workers. Emerson Climate Technologies in northeastern Suzhou, for example, competes with nearby Samsung, Siemens, and Nokia for workers. "It has gotten to the point," David Warth, Emerson's general manager, has said, "that we are just swapping folks and raising salaries." There is even talk of some companies moving their low-tech operations to lower-wage countries such as Vietnam and Indonesia.

In the long run, the rise in wages will bolster China's future because it helps to create a more consumer-oriented economy, one that is not so heavily dependent on exports. Indeed, McKinsey & Company predicts that China's middle class will number 520 million by 2025, with an anticipated purchasing power in excess of $2.5 trillion. The rise in wages is also spurring greater manufacturing development in the country's interior, where the level of poverty is such that wages are lower.

But what about the short run? The Chinese, it should be noted, are not idly twiddling their thumbs while these economic changes are occurring. Many, as we saw in the previous chapter, are already making the necessary adjustments for their businesses to not only survive but thrive. Furthermore, the national government has recognized the danger to the country as a whole and addressed it in the latest Five-Year Program, which encourages a "harmonious society" through measures designed to help smooth the economic transition.

Without question, there will be disruptions and tragedies on an individual level as China moves from a low-wage, export-oriented economy to one that is wealthier and more consumer-oriented. This is true of past economies that have made such a transition and no doubt will be true in China. But China is different. Given the adaptability, receptiveness to change, and creativity so prevalent throughout its society today, the change should not be as traumatic as it has been in other countries, and there will be, with the government's awareness and direction, greater positive benefits throughout its society.

Risk #7. China's growth is unbalanced and unsustainable

Fact—but. Thus far, the growth of China has rested on two sectors of the economy: private and public capital investment, and exports. Neither can continue to grow at their recent rates. It is a well-established fact that countries enjoying years of investment-led growth inevitably succumb to the economic laws of gravity. This is because overinvestment in the corporate sector can lead to diminishing returns and to a decline in the return on invested capital.

In China's case, however, the huge investment in infrastructure has been an unambiguously positive development that is widely credited with allowing China to grow more rapidly than India. As the western regions of China are developed, continued large infrastructure investments will be required.

On the other hand, China's reliance on exports has severe international implications, particularly with regard to relations with the United States. Consider, for example, the view expressed by Commissioner Patrick A. Mulloy in the November 2006 *Report to Congress of the U.S.-China Economic and Security Review Commission*: "America's policymakers must understand that the interest of the multinational corporations and the policies they advocate toward China are not necessarily serving the larger interests of our citizens and our nation." The report as a whole urges the U.S. Congress to acknowledge "the harm that Chinese practices do to workers, consumers and investors."

There is little interest, particularly among politicians, in heeding reports from the U.S. Bureau of East Asian and Pacific Affairs because such reports contradict what the politicians are saying. In 2006, the Bureau pointed out that though the U.S. deficit with China has grown, its overall deficit with Asia has remained roughly the same for the past decade. The Bureau concludes that the U.S.-China "bilateral" trade deficit is more accurately a trade deficit with East Asia because East Asian economies that once shipped directly to the United States now do substantial processing and final assembly in China.

The bottom line, however, is that according to bookkeeping standards today, the United States is running a huge— and ever-growing—trade deficit with China. This situation is not politically sustainable. Rising protectionist sentiment in the United States might well lead to legislation that would sharply curtail the growth of Chinese exports and thus the growth of China's GDP.

There is no doubt that China must engineer a shift in the composition of its GDP as it cannot rely on net exports and capital investment to the same degree that it has in the past. But we believe a shift in the mix of GDP is both feasible and likely in the future as incomes rise. Consumer spending in China accounts for less than 50 percent of GDP today versus 70 percent in the United States. Even while maintaining extremely high savings rates, China can still increase its share of consumption substantially. Anecdotal evidence indicates that the younger generation—hip twentysomethings—have bought into the consumption mode in a big way. They presage a shift that will both make the growth path more sustainable and help China achieve its harmonious society.

Risk #8. Corruption

Fact. The noted China scholar Gregory Chow has written that "The major factor that will hinder further economic reform in China, in my opinion, is the bureaucratic behavior and corruption of government officials." We not only concur with his considered judgment but would also expand it further: Private individuals are not immune to this vice. A 2006 poll by Nanjing University found that 94 percent of the respondents agreed that bribery is widespread in China. In its *2006 Annual Report*, the Congressional-Executive Commission on China noted: "The International Monetary Fund has estimated that money laundering in China may total as much as US$24 billion annually, while the Asian Development Bank estimated that more than 2 percent of China's gross domestic product is laundered in mainland China each year." As one China watcher commented, in the old days corruption used to be concentrated at the top, but now, with liberalization, it has become more democratic and is spread throughout many levels of government and society.

As a start, there is the inefficiency in Chinese government, which is at its most bloated in history. China has five levels of government (township, county, regional, provincial, and national) and five major government bodies at each level (the party, administrative, legislative, political consultative, and the court). It is not surprising that the large number of government agencies has bred bureaucracy and corruption.

The current government has made administrative reform a top priority. Local elections—as opposed to government appointments—are being introduced to encourage accountability. And both elections and appointments now feature term limits to increase official turnover and transparency. Despite these efforts, China has a long way to go toward an effective, service-oriented government. Citing misappropriation of city pension funds, underreporting of nonperforming loans, bribery, and embezzlement, *Forbes* columnist James Grant has written that scandal chases scandal in the People's Republic. "Out of a population of 1.3 billion," he has commented, "there must be one honest Chinese citizen." Herb Greenberg, a senior columnist for the Web site MarketWatch, put it slightly more delicately: "Investing in China demands being very, very careful."

It should be noted that not everyone is corrupt; far from it. As Professor Chow has pointed out, many Chinese still uphold the old cultural standards of honesty and integrity. The story of Liu Shuwei, a scholar at the Central University of Finance and Economics in Beijing, typifies a side of China that rarely gets publicized in the Western press.

Liu's field is financial accounting. At the turn of this century she became intrigued by all the hype surrounding Ju Zhaomin, a savvy entrepreneur who in four years had transformed Lantian, a humble fish and lotus roots business, into the first publicly listed Chinese ecological agricultural company. The year was 1996, a heady time of stock manipulation on the Shanghai Stock Exchange. Lantian's annual net profits increased nearly tenfold during the next three years and its market cap more than quadrupled. In 2000, the company reported $222 million in sales. Chinese banks appeared to think this justified their competing to lend the company another $225 million. Many of these bankers didn't need to examine the company's books to make the loans; they were quietly padding their own books with the bribes that Ju and other Lantian executives were extending to ensure the company's apparent prosperity.

Liu, however, did examine the books and financial reports —they were her area of interest and not a source of funds for her savings account. What she found was disturbing: though the company had reported $222 million in sales, there was only $1 million in accounts receivable, an impossible gap for a legitimate company. In October 2001, she published a research paper questioning the company's financial viability and sent warnings to state bank officials about the company's financial affairs.

The banks' cash spigots to Lantian dried up almost overnight. The company retaliated by suing Liu for defamation. Despite receiving an anonymous death threat, Liu did not budge from her conclusion. Rather, she sent copies of her research report to news media throughout China. That did it. Her findings were juicy enough to make major headlines. In 2002, Ju and several other top Lantian officials were arrested on charges of accounting fraud and trading of the company's stock was suspended. And the bankers? Five were ultimately charged with illegally pocketing approximately $500,000.

The Lantian scandal and Liu's part in exposing it has several interesting aspects. Among them is the fact that many academics as well as government officials are solidly against corruption. Indeed, stories abound of old Communist cadres becoming increasingly upset at the turn the country is taking from its theoretically pure Communist activities to such practices as those embedded in the Lantian affair. And then there is the honor received by Liu. For her work in exposing the Lantian scam, she was named the Economic Person of the Year in 2002, the first woman to be so honored. Among the write-ups hailing her achievement, however, there was one asserting that her success was a result of Chairman Mao's philosophy. Because of Chairman Mao, the article said, women in China are now free to unbind their feet and pursue

careers. Thus, the rampantly capitalistic China cloaks its economic progress—and pacifies Communist ideologues—by
declaring that it is following Chairman Mao's dictates.

Still, there are not enough citizens like Liu who actively
seek to rein in the corruption so prevalent in China's society,
corruption that has internal and external effects. As Steve
Hanke pointed out in a *Forbes* column, of the 155 countries
ranked according to level of corruptness by the World Bank's
Investment Climate Department, China at 100 ranks below
the bottom third. Hanke went on to show how easy it is for
insiders to loot Chinese companies.

Investors need to be particularly wary when investing in Chinese stocks because of the level of corruption. Those of us who
hail from the country that gave the world Enron and World-
Com realize that we could sound sanctimonious when we
inveigh against corruption elsewhere. We do also acknowledge
the hard work the Shanghai Stock Exchange has done to
increase transparency and monitor violations, as well as the
government's recent introduction of political reform measures
to curtail corruption at all levels. Nevertheless, much more
needs to be done in this area to make investors more comfortable about buying stocks listed on domestic exchanges. As
Shanghai mayor Han Zheng acknowledged in the aftermath of
a major city pension scandal in 2007, "Sunshine being the best
disinfectant, transparency itself is a form of supervision."

The overriding importance of culture

Despite the risks, perceived and actual, in China's economic landscape, we remain convinced that the country's
future is extraordinarily bright, and we base our feeling on
China's inherent culture. This is a culture that has evolved
over thousands of years, one that is still rooted in many ways
in the Confucian tenets of loyalty to the family and to the

state. This loyalty today expresses itself in a deep sense of pride in the country and its accomplishments.

Confucianism encourages a reverence for education and applauds hard work, values that appear to be embedded in Chinese communities throughout the world. In a *New York Times* article in May 2006, columnist Nicholas D. Kristof asked, "Why are Asian-Americans so good at school?" He noted that Chinese villages still contain monuments to those who had obtained the Ming dynasty equivalent of a perfect SAT score, and that those who migrated to the United States brought the values of honoring education and hard work with them. Not only that, they made sure that these values were transferred to their children. Kristof's conclusion: "the success of Asian-Americans is mostly about culture."

Sir W. Arthur Lewis, one of the outstanding economists of the twentieth century, also emphasized the importance of culture. He spent his life studying such economic development questions as: Why do some nations grow in prosperity while others stagnate? Does it depend on the system of government and the organization of the economy? Do planned economies have an advantage over those that are unplanned? These questions formed the core of his great work, *The Theory of Economic Growth*, which was published in 1955. In 1979, Professor Lewis was awarded the Nobel Prize in Economic Science for his "pioneering research into economic development research with particular consideration of the problems of developing countries."

After a lifetime of studying the fundamental forces determining the rate of economic growth, Sir Arthur became convinced that one factor was more important than any other. The primary determinant of the rate of economic growth is the creative energy of the population. It is the entrepreneurial drive and the ambition of the people that fuels economic growth. The best that government can do is to create the conditions under which the creative enthusiasm of the people can build an empire of bricks and steel. We think Sir Arthur would consider the recent success of China after the economic reforms to be a shining example of how, when unleashed, the culture, drive, ambition, and creativity of a people can produce economic miracles.

A SUMMING UP

China is determined to show the world its richness and sophistication, and this determination is backed by a culture that venerates its past greatness and is eager to participate in a future grandeur. Perhaps equally important, the country possesses a government that can generally carry out whatever it deems necessary to realize its goals.

The aging of the population and the financial stability of the country are not—on closer examination—major problems. Additionally, the government is actively taking steps to alleviate environmental degradation and income inequality. Rising wages, though detrimental to some in the short term, will encourage the transition from an economy dependent on an export-driven manufacturing base to one where internal consumer consumption plays a much larger role. And while no one can predict what political tensions might bring, China's desire to successfully sponsor the 2008 Olympics and the 2010 World Expo provides a great incentive on the part of the government not to fuel such discord. One can only hope, however, that greater steps will be taken to rein in corruption. It is the cancer that in many ways destroyed both the Mandarin dynasty and Chiang Kai-shek's Kuomintang, and it threatens to have equally devastating effects on the current government's prosperity.

Yes, there are problems. Yes, there are risks. But changes are occurring, and at the very least the direction of these changes is positive. Setbacks will arise and the growth path in the future is unlikely to be smooth. Nevertheless, we are convinced that with a practical government devoted to a market system, and with an ambitious, educated, and entrepreneurial population, China is likely to enjoy many more years of rapid growth.

Now, having covered the broad setting under which Chinese investment opportunities have emerged, it is time to review specific types of investments.

Section II

THE
INVESTMENTS

Having briefly reviewed China's history, culture, achievements, and probable future directions, we turn next to the kind of investments that one can make in order to profit from China's extraordinary economic growth. The major part of this section is devoted to equities, because these represent the most readily available instruments for investors to purchase. And just as China is now practicing socialism with Chinese characteristics, so too is the country's stock market a unique construct imbued with Chinese characteristics. We also devote a chapter to China's real estate, art, and bonds. This section provides the basic understanding needed to undertake the specific investment strategies that will be described in Section III.

CHAPTER 4

The Uniqueness of the Chinese Stock Market

It does not matter whether the cat is black or white, only that it catches mice.

— DENG XIAOPING

IT MAY SEEM SURPRISING, BUT ECONOMISTS do agree on at least one thing: systems for the allocation of resources fall within a spectrum bounded by two extremes. On the one end is the market economy, where prices and transactions are determined solely by individual consumers and producers, and on the other is the planned economy, where all prices and transactions are under government control. These two extremes are also known as capitalist and socialist economies. A well-functioning stock market is key to a successful market economy (indeed, Nobel laureate John Hicks suggests that the industrial revolution would not have occurred without the development of financial markets); planned economies do not make use of such institutions.

China today is attempting to straddle the middle of this economic spectrum and is the first country ever to do so on such a large and complicated scale. China's hybrid economy features a mixture of government-owned and privately owned

enterprises. Some companies, like the Internet search company Baidu.com, are privately owned. Others, like Petro-
China, the big Chinese oil company, are majority-owned by
the government. But even though the government owns the
bulk of the shares, PetroChina's stock trades in the open market. PetroChina is not an unusual example. Most major Chinese companies traded in New York and Hong Kong have
significant government ownership.

A well-functioning stock market is critically important for
three reasons. It gives signals to management regarding the
direction of future investment; it supplies the capital that
fuels future expansion; and it provides an outlet for individual savings. One can say then that China's future depends to a
large extent on its attempts to create a well-functioning financial market. Further, because of the unique features of the
Chinese economy, it will have to differ from all others in existence. It is useful, therefore, to understand the important
functions of any stock market before we describe the history
of the Chinese stock market and its unusual structure.

The Role of the Stock Market in a Market Economy

The allocation of capital resources plays a critical role in any
economy's ability to sustain real economic growth. If capital is
not made available to those enterprises and industries capa-
ble of increasing both productivity and production, the economic growth rate will suffer. The flexibility and speed of the
capital allocation process is essential to ensure the adaptability of the economy's productive process and thus its long-run
rate of growth.

In economies with capitalist features, stock markets offer
important signals to corporate management about the cost of

investment capital, which is vital to ensuring that an optimal amount of real investment in plant and equipment is undertaken. During China's Mao years from 1949 through 1977, there were no stock markets and the country was almost completely at the planned end of the economic spectrum. In 1958, for example, state-owned enterprises (SOEs) accounted for more than 97 percent of GDP. These enterprises were not disciplined by the profit motive and they invested in large numbers of nonproductive projects.

With the institution of the reforms under Deng Xiaoping, China came to recognize that a stock market could play an important role in the restructuring of its hopelessly inefficient SOEs. The country's new leaders understood the principle that the privatization of the SOEs through stock ownership would provide both the financial discipline and the hard constraints that force managers to act in the interest of shareholders rather than in the interest of the state or the managers themselves. In this way, a stock market can help to improve corporate governance. At its best, it can help to correct the poor management, lack of accountability, and widespread corruption associated with many of the SOEs. While recognizing the attractiveness of the principle, however, China has only partially implemented it, as will be discussed later in this chapter.

For the most part, stock markets also offer easy-to-understand evaluations of the financial conditions of individual companies as well as their future prospects. Finally, stock markets perform what the economist William J. Baumol has called "an act of magic" by permitting long-term investments to be financed by funds from individual savers who may tend to hold those investments for only limited periods of time. In the case of China, stock markets are particularly important since they offer investment outlets for the substantial amounts of individual savings as well as for Chinese institutional investors. This provision of liquidity tends to lower the cost of capital funds and facilitates the low-cost financing of long-term investments. As Baumol concludes in his book *The Stock Market and Economic Efficiency* (1965):

> For all these reasons . . . one has come to look upon the stock market as the allocator of capital resources par excellence, and aside from some uneasiness about the untoward effects of speculation, one is readily inclined toward the view that the stock market constitutes an allocative mechanism of remarkable efficiency.

How effectively the Chinese stock market fulfills these expectations of efficiency is the subject of chapter 5.

THE FIRST STOCK MARKETS IN CHINA

After the Second Opium War ended in the 1860s, Westerners brought the concept of the stock market to China. And, as they did with so many of their activities, they excluded the Chinese from participation. In June 1866, an informal foreign shares brokers' association opened in Shanghai to facilitate the exchange of shares; the Hong Kong and Shanghai Banking Corporation was among the original companies whose shares were traded. In 1881, the arrangements became more formal with the establishment of China's first equity exchange in Shanghai—one limited to foreign corporations.

That example of raising funds through the issuance of public shares spurred Chinese intellectuals to examine the role of joint stock companies. Previously (and as we will note later, to some extent even today), business relationships in China relied totally on personal relationships and not on the impersonal dealings of a stock exchange. In 1868, under the aegis of Chinese native Yung Wing, an 1854 Yale graduate, China's first joint stock corporation by and for natives was formed. This attracted the attention and the approval of the Qing mandarins.

Thus, two forms of stock exchanges sprang up in China in the late nineteenth century. The first, the entity that is widely regarded as the forerunner of today's Shanghai Stock Exchange, was run by and for foreigners. The second was a series of formal and informal stock-trading arrangements carried on by Chinese throughout the country.

By 1911, Shanghai traders in Chinese stocks had centered their activities at the Beneficent Fragrance Tea House. Three years later, the traders established the Shanghai Securities Dealers Association. In 1918, the first formal Chinese securities exchange was started in Peking (as it was then called). By the end of 1921, there were more than 140 securities exchanges in Shanghai and an additional 52 in cities across the country. According to Yale Finance Professor Zhiwu Chen, these early markets were largely vehicles for speculation; investors typically bought stock without any knowledge of the issuing company and its prospects. Moreover, these early Chinese stock markets were basically oriented toward agriculture and family operations and never played an important role in the economy.

The foreign-operated and -controlled Shanghai Stock Exchange was a different story. In addition to the financial acumen of the controlling colonial powers, the exchange benefited from the talents of an influx of wealthy refugees fleeing the turmoil of World War I and its aftermath. In 1932, for example, 40 percent of the seats on the exchange were held by Sephardic Jews.

All About Shanghai, a guide published in 1934, described this stock exchange:

Shanghai offers locals and foreigners opportunities for speculation in commodities and stocks, gold bars and silver. Prompt execution is given in all of the leading and most of the minor markets of the world. London, Paris and New York stocks are quoted as well as local issues, of which there are many . . . both bonds and shares. Closing quotations on the New York Stock Exchange are available in Shanghai early in the morning. . . . There is perhaps a wider range of foreign exchange in Shanghai than in any other place in the world.

With the onset of the Great Depression and the Japanese incursions into China, the local stock exchanges—never financially strong in the first place—began to disappear. The Shanghai Stock Exchange, however, continued to operate until December 8, 1941—the day the Japanese assumed complete control over the city.

THE SECOND ROUND OF STOCK MARKETS IN CHINA

And then came the great silence. When the Communists took power in 1949, they never even considered reestablishing a stock exchange. Such an entity was a capitalist institution that was inconsistent with the Marxist ideology of the Mao revolutionary government. To make matters worse, Chiang Kai-shek, chairman of the deposed Kuomintang Party, was himself a former Shanghai stockbroker. The issuance and trading of stock was forbidden. Neither private ownership, nor the receipt of earnings from capital rather than from labor, could be tolerated by the People's Republic of China. The markets remained closed for almost four decades.

A second revolution occurred in 1978 when Deng Xiaoping executed his plan to revitalize the ailing Chinese economy. This was to be accomplished by transforming the economy from one that was centrally planned to one that was market-oriented, where individual initiative would be encouraged and rewarded. The early success was remarkable: Deng's economic reforms transformed a stagnant economy into one that was rapidly growing. It soon became clear, however, that partial reforms could not sustain economic prosperity. Two problems in particular needed solutions. Economic growth requires capital investment, and mechanisms had to be established to ensure that the capital could be provided. Second, many of the companies operated by the state (the SOEs) proved to be very poorly managed and highly inefficient. To cope with these problems, the Chinese government then permitted the issuance of common stocks and bonds in an attempt to ameliorate capital inadequacy and to help improve the efficiency of SOEs. Stock markets can be a disciplinary tool that provides a direct measure of management's effectiveness. This permission was codified in the Constitution of 1982.

In China's hybrid economy, however, stock market shares did not appear overnight. Rather, there was a gradual process, which began with the issuance of sharelike securities during the 1980s. The process was initiated in the township and village enterprises (TVEs), which sprang up in response to the economic reforms of Deng Xiaoping. In order to raise capital for the TVEs, a co-operative shareholder structure was introduced to augment whatever capital could be raised by the village. The first such enterprise to issue share certificates was a Shenzhen TVE named Bao'an County Joint Investment Company. A year later, Beijing Tianqiao Department Store became the first SOE to be restructured as a share-issuing company.

A government decision to accelerate the economic system's reform gave impetus to an explosion of share issuance. From 1984 to 1989, shareholding companies with 3.8 billion yuan worth of shares were set up all over the country. In order to entice the public to purchase shares, the issuing companies had to promise dividends at rates that exceeded bank deposit rates. Some companies even promised to redeem shares from their owners at a fixed rate. Thus, initially, many shares resembled bonds more than stocks. But no formal secondary market for trading the shares existed. Not surprisingly, when holders of securities needed cash, informal arrangements sprang up to facilitate the buying and selling of shares. Not sanctioned by the government and thus considered an illegal "black market," the arrangements were far from satisfactory. Secondary purchasers demanded compensation for the risks involved and typically offered sellers very low and quite inadequate prices for their shares.

The Shanghai branch of the People's Bank of China (PBC) decided to allow public transfers of securities in order to eliminate black market trading. Still, this market was extremely restrictive. To complete a transfer of shares, both buyers and sellers were required to go to the bank (or to the original issuing company) in order to finalize the transaction. Moreover, the trading prices were fixed by the bank and were essentially independent of the forces of supply and demand. As a result, black market trading remained popular.

The next step in the development of a modern Chinese stock market occurred in September 1986, when the Shanghai branch of the PBC authorized the establishment of the first over-the-counter market in China. This kind of market relied on networks of securities dealers linked by phone banks rather than located on a centralized trading floor. Within a year, fifteen financial institutions had set up trading centers in Shanghai and Shenzhen. Although the trading that ensued did embody some elements of supply and demand, prices were far from efficient. Professional scalpers, who were usually very well informed about the value of the securities they traded, would hide or exaggerate relevant information about the securities in order to negotiate a price that was dramatically in their favor. Prices were artificially manipulated and a daily range of fluctuations of 20 percent was common. Moreover, residents in other provinces were expected to go to Shanghai or Shenzhen to complete their security trades.

CHINA'S STOCK MARKETS TODAY

Clearly, a national stock exchange was required to enable China to reap the benefits of well-functioning financial markets. The government recognized this and then instituted a unique system. The new Shanghai Stock Market (SSE), established in 1990, reflected many elements of China's past. When we met with Wu Yalun, SSE's executive vice president, we were told that Zhu Rongji, then mayor of Shanghai (and later premier of China), was determined that the city should regain its luster as a financial capital of Asia and lobbied extensively for a new exchange. Once the national government approved the establishment of a stock exchange in the city, the municipal government dictated its location on the Bund, the former financial center of the East and the site of the earlier "Westerner's" exchange, where Chinese were typically allowed only as menial laborers. Wu, who was in charge of siting the new institution, searched the area in the vicinity of the original stock exchange and found that the former ballroom for the Peacock Hall was available. This ballroom, with its still intact inlaid wooden dancing surface, became the trading floor for the reconstituted SSE. Amid loud applause, an opening gavel banged down on December 19, 1990, and brokers wearing red waistcoats sat down at their desks.

Mayor Zhu's financial coup was met with envy and some bitterness throughout other major cities in China. Shenzhen alone was bold enough to take action. On December 18, the day before the SSE was set to open amidst dignitary pomp and splendor, Shenzhen officials announced they had unobtrusively converted their existing over-the-counter market into an open exchange with a centralized trading floor. This was done without Beijing approval and amounted to a minor insurrection. Not wishing to engage in a public quarrel, Beijing quietly gave Shenzhen permission to have an exchange—but only if the opening was delayed until the following spring. The government further forbade any other open exchanges in the country. With the establishment of these two open stock markets, and the subsequent trading with competitive bids and offers and unified settlement procedures, all black market and over-the-counter trading ceased.

The trading system was electronic from its inception, the first in Asia to use this method. It remains more modern and technically more efficient than the trading systems in Hong Kong and Taiwan. All Chinese cities are electronically linked to the two exchanges. Wu Yalun noted that in Japan, Nomura had to train its traders in the use of hand signals used in non-electronic exchanges. In exchanges like Tokyo and the New York Stock Exchange, floor traders would often communicate with hand signals to transmit their orders. This was never the case in China; Wu said that while it is easy to say one inadvertently made a hand mistake, it is harder to deny actions that are entered on the computer. Today, the SSE can handle 30,000 transactions per second, the highest in the world. Its trade settlement times (T + 1 or one day after the trade is made) are the fastest in the world (in the United States, it is T + 3, or three days to settle after the trade). The Shanghai Stock Exchange—the world's youngest—is equipped to handle 30 million transactions per day, as opposed to 5 million on the Tokyo Stock Exchange and 10 million on the U.S. NASDAQ.

China's past also played a role in the unique way companies were initially chosen to be listed on the exchanges. The controlling hand of the government was prominent throughout the process; and private enterprises were not allowed to list. The country had long been divided into regional governments, and now these governments were each given a quota for determining which SOEs under their purview should be listed. There was a lot of internal money to be made with regard to those listings. Most of the shares went to company owners (i.e., the local governments were, in effect, granting shares to themselves) and a few to company employees. Regional governments that successfully listed companies were then given larger quotas. Given the unique circumstances under which they came into being, the two Chinese stock exchanges did not get off to a resounding start: during the initial year of operation, only a combined total of fourteen companies were listed on both exchanges and the total market capitalization of all the listings was a modest 6.72 billion yuan. The first block of listed companies in Shanghai were restructured former SOEs. The main characteristics of companies listed in Shenzhen were joint venture companies.

The quota system, however, did possess an element of competition in that it rewarded those local governments that found the most successful companies to be listed. In 2000, the government's role was significantly reduced when it gave security dealers the right to recommend enterprises to be listed. This effectively ended the ban on the listing of privately owned companies. The quota system and then the listing of privately owned companies successfully jump-started the markets so that within twelve years, the China stock market was the eighth largest in the world in official capitalization. No other stock market in history had grown so rapidly. By 2006, over 1,400 companies were listed on the exchanges, with a total market capitalization of 9 trillion yuan. Monthly trading volume was almost half a billion yuan.

This growth is particularly noteworthy when one realizes that institutional investors play a relatively minor role in the stock market of China today. In the United States, for example, institutions such as insurance and pension funds are major players in the stock market. On a typical day, they will account for as much as 90 percent of the trading activity. In China, the government limits the proportion of stocks in the portfolios of institutions such as life insurance companies and banks. Typically, a life insurance company can hold no more than 10 percent of its investments in equities. In addition, Chinese mutual funds hold only about 26 percent of all tradable shares. Many mutual funds consist primarily of bonds and money market instruments rather than equities. Furthermore, as opposed to the United States where mutual funds seem to spring up overnight, it has been very difficult until recently for mutual funds in China to receive government approval.

The growth and structure of the Chinese stock market reflects the very practical nature of the Chinese government and its willingness to experiment at each stage of its economic development. The approach has been one of trial and error, and the country's leaders have described the process in terms of "crossing a river by feeling the stones underneath." During his Southern China Tour in early 1992, Deng Xiaoping gave a speech that exemplified the experimental approach. He asked: "Are securities and the stock market good or bad? Are they peculiar to capitalism? Can socialism make use of them? We allow people to reserve . . . judgment, but we must try these things out." Deng went on to say that if the stock market proved to be useful, it could be expanded; otherwise, it could be terminated. The growth of the market attests to its usefulness as well as to the pragmatic policies of the Chinese government.

Nevertheless, as this book went to press, the Chinese stock market was still modest relative to markets in the Western world. The percentage of GDP represented by all the shares traded in Shanghai and Shenzhen was relatively small (at about 50 percent) compared with developed stock markets such as the United States (where the total capitalization of the stock market is about 150 percent of GDP). The figure is somewhat misleading, however, since well over half of the Chinese stock market shares are held by the state or by state-controlled agencies and are not actively traded.

The domestic stock market remains a very small source of financing for the growth of business enterprises. But regulatory changes are underway that promise to release many of the state-owned shares for general trading and to make the market more accessible to foreign and domestic investors. These changes should make the stock market a far more significant source of corporate financing. Moreover, it appears that the government has quietly stipulated that all new issues floated in either Hong Kong or other financial capitals must also be listed in China. We therefore expect very large increases in the total market value of the shares traded in the local Chinese stock markets. In the future the capital allocation in China may thus depend less on the state and much more on the economic signals provided by the market.

REGULATIONS OF THE SECURITIES EXCHANGES

When ownership shares were first established, few Chinese were aware that stock prices could fluctuate. That all changed during the late 1980s in a period generally described as "Share Fever." The stock of the Shenzhen Development Bank was initially floated in 1988 at a price of 20 yuan per share. In March 1989, the bank announced the payment of a dividend that represented over 100 percent of the value of the shares. As might be expected, the shares soared in price. By the end of 1989, the bank's shares traded at 90 yuan per share, representing an increase of 350 percent from the original issue price. This event presented Chinese investors with a mouth-watering example of the profit potential from owning equity shares.

That signature event is usually described as the genesis of a speculative equity culture in China. Indeed, as we shall see more clearly in the next chapter, several waves of rampant speculation and market manipulation were evident during the 1990s. Such events made it abundantly evident that the country needed a regulatory system within which the stock market could operate with some degree of efficiency and in a manner consistent with overall government policy.

Although extensive regulations were drafted in 1989, the market was still relatively unregulated during the early 1990s. But an event occurred on August 10, 1992—called the "8.10 Incident"—that made a more formal regulatory framework imperative. On that day, tens of thousands of Chinese citizens lined up to purchase an IPO to be traded on the Shenzhen Stock Exchange, only to be told that all the subscription forms had already been distributed. The unruly demonstrations of frustrated and angry investors that followed made it very clear to the government that the stock market needed to be properly regulated.

The China Securities Regulatory Commission (CSRC) is the chief regulating body that oversees the Chinese stock market. The CSRC is analogous to the Securities and Exchange Commission (SEC) in the United States. The CSRC plays a role in regulating trading, avoiding fraud, promulgating listing standards, setting rules for initial public offerings, and releasing state-owned and other illiquid shares for trading. In addition, the CSRC helps determine the quotas given to foreign investors that permit them to purchase limited amounts of local Chinese shares.

Especially surprising to those who view the Chinese government as a kind of monolithic entity, rulemaking authority for the Chinese financial markets is quite diffuse in actual practice. The Ministry of Finance, the State Planning Commission, the People's Bank of China, provincial authorities, and others all participate in certain decisions. Considerable differences of opinion exist regarding the pace at which the Chinese should convert to a true market economy. Moreover, the initial structure of ownership, with two thirds of all shares controlled by the government, has impeded the development of an independent private litigation system.

In our discussion with government officials, however, we were impressed that there were no disagreements regarding the direction of the changes. China appears committed to a path that will make the Chinese stock market an alternative financing vehicle for the state-owned enterprises and ultimately a mechanism for their reform and full privatization. Only when the SOEs are fully privatized will it be possible to achieve judicial and regulatory independence and to establish a well-functioning legal framework that will permit the stock markets to flourish.

THE PRIVATIZATION OF EQUITY SHARES

A distinctive feature of the Chinese stock market is the sometimes bewildering bifurcation of shares into tradable and non-tradable categories. With the founding of the new Shanghai Stock Exchange—the SSE—in 1990, listed equities in the modern Chinese stock market were consigned to two categories: shares held by private investors that could be sold or purchased in the stock market; and shares controlled by state and other "legal persons" that could not be traded in the market. A "legal person" is generally another state or local government agency that participates in ownership of the company. The Chinese stock market was and remains to this day the only stock market in the world in which a majority of the listed companies are state-owned enterprises. And a large portion of the listed shares cannot be traded. As the line from *The King and I* goes: "Is a puzzlement."

This structure was designed by the "founding fathers" of the new Chinese economy in order to ensure that the state retained control of the SOEs even after they were listed for trading, and that no pressures for a change in that status would occur in the future from subsequent trading activity. Approximately two thirds of the capitalization of Chinese stocks listed in Shanghai and Shenzhen were held until recently by government agencies or by other economic entities on behalf of the state. Until the end of 2006, state-owned shares were not allowed to be traded on the open market. "Legal person" shares have only limited marketability, as their trading is subject to cumbersome state approval.

The existence of state-owned shares has created a significant obstacle to the conversion of the Chinese economy to one that is fully market-oriented. They have also interfered with the growth and development of the Chinese stock market. Since 1999, many mainland financial analysts believe, the rise and fall of the Chinese stock market has been closely tied to the state's efforts to reduce its holdings in listed companies.

Two important problems have concerned investors. First, there are troublesome governance implications. Shareholders would like to believe that company management will be making decisions with the sole objective of benefiting the shareholders of the enterprise. When the government is the major shareholder, the minority owners have good reason to believe that the government is likely to have other objectives in mind. The government has little interest in the behavior of the share price. It neither benefits much from rising prices nor need it fear a hostile takeover if prices fall.

The behavior of the majority-state-owned banks exemplifies this conflict. Often the banks would find a manufacturing SOE that would need financing to keep afloat. While the SOE might be unprofitable, with little chance of repaying the loan, the enterprise might also be a major employer in the region, and a collapse of the business could create widespread unemployment. The government would want to ensure that the bank makes the loan and thus preserves jobs, despite the small likelihood of repayment. This general example illuminates the actual situation responsible for many of the "nonperforming" loans that have plagued the Chinese banking system.

A second problem arises if the state-owned shares are immediately made tradable and then quickly sold to the public. Dumping large numbers of previously locked-up shares could swamp the market and lead to devastating price declines. Investors call this phenomenon the "overhang" problem. In 2001, a state share reduction program was announced in which the sale of all state-owned shares would be completed over a five-year period. After the program started in mid-2001, prices in the Shenzhen and Shanghai markets plunged by about 40 percent and the program was suspended later that year. In the trial and error game, this was a big error. It became clear that a solution to the overhang problem required considerable care.

In 2005, Shang Fulin, chairman of the China Securities Regulatory Commission, achieved what many in China's financial community considered an impossible mission: he set up a method of compensation whereby public owners of a state-owned enterprise would receive a bonus when the nontradable shares were converted to tradable shares, thus alleviating the precipitous drops in value that usually resulted. In the summer of 2006, for example, Sinopec (SNP), Asia's largest oil refiner by capacity, announced that mainland holders of its stock would receive 2.8 shares for every 10 shares held as compensation for allowing the company's nontradable shares to become tradable. Shang's plan provided holders of exchange-traded shares with the reassurance that the release and trading of state-owned shares would be achieved gradually and according to a timetable. Many in China's financial community feel that this plan has contributed to the rise of the Chinese stock market during 2006 and 2007.

On September 4, 2005, the China Securities Regulatory Commission officially issued a regulation with the rousing title "Listed Company Stock Ownership Diversification Reform and Management Methods." Despite the bureaucratic name, it represents one of the world's largest privatization movements. Wu Yalun explained its basic ramifications during our interview with him at the Shanghai Stock Exchange. First, there is an internal lock on all converted shares for one year after conversion. Second, those who originally held over 15 percent of the nontradable shares can sell no more than 5 percent of their holdings within the year following the lockup period, and no more than 10 percent within two years following the lockup period.

With the conversion of nontradable shares into tradable equities, and the slow but steady release of these newly tradable shares into the market, both trading activity and market value have begun to climb dramatically. Still, with 70 percent of the shares nontradable at the start of the conversion effort, the practical but slow process of making all stock-trading activity truly market-oriented means that the overhang issue will be around for a number of years.

THE ALPHABET SOUP OF SHARE TYPES

As if the tradable/nontradable share story isn't confusing enough to those who just want to make some money investing in China, there is also the quagmire of a literal alphabet soup of share designations that indicate where the shares are traded and who can buy them. This is the second distinguishing feature of the Chinese stock market. In alphabetical order, these shares are described below.

A shares: Available to local investors. The predominant class of publicly held shares—comprising about 30 percent of the total—is called A shares. These shares are denominated in yuan and traded on the Shanghai and Shenzhen stock exchanges. Originally, only Chinese nationals were allowed to own A shares, but as we will see below, a limited number of foreign investors now have access to these shares as well. Ticker symbols for A shares are given in numbers, e.g., 600028.SH. The numerals identify the company and the two letters the exchange (here Shanghai).

Throughout much of China's stock market history, A shares tended to represent ownership in the smaller, less well managed companies. That began to change in 2006, when the A-share market started heading for the sky. Worried that a bubble was in the making, one that could burst just as the country was to demonstrate its modern economic power at the Beijing Olympics, the government started introducing new measures to increase the breadth of the market, thus reducing a situation in which a lot of money—much of it pouring out of savings accounts where the Chinese had traditionally put their assets—was chasing too few stocks and thus contributing to the rise in prices.

Whereas in the past the larger, better-managed companies

could not list locally and only appeared on foreign exchanges, in spring 2007 the government stepped up the transformation of the A-share market by unofficially requiring that any company wishing to list overseas had to also list locally. In addition, many of the larger companies, such as China Mobil and Aluminum Corporation of China, that had been listed only on overseas markets requested and received government permission to list locally. The hope is that the newly available A shares of these larger, better-managed companies will mop up some of the excess liquidity and reduce some of the speculative frenzy that appeared to be infecting the market.

Furthermore, A-shares buyers have tended to be individuals rather than institutions (in the United States, institutions account for over 70 percent of stock ownership). When we talked to senior staff of the CSRC, we were told that the development of an institutional shareholder base is one of their top objectives. At the time we had our discussions, banks and insurance companies were legally limited to holding only a minute percentage of their assets in stocks.

B shares: Available to foreign investors. These shares were created solely to allow foreign investors to participate in the domestic markets. The aim was to have outlets available for the investment capital of nonmainland Chinese investors so that Chinese companies had access to another source of capital. The B shares are traded in Hong Kong dollars on the Shenzhen exchange and in U.S. dollars on the Shanghai exchange. Since no arbitrage trades are possible between the two types of shares (mainland residents do not have ready access to B shares and foreigners have only limited access to A shares), the B and A shares of the same company typically trade at different prices. Moreover, the number of B shares is small and thus they are quite illiquid. The Chinese authorities currently are considering the termination of trading in the B-share market, so we have not considered B shares in developing our strategies.

H shares: Available to Hong Kong investors. The inability of the B shares to attract international capital led the government, in 1993, to allow the establishment of H shares. H shares represent mainland companies that are registered in Hong Kong and that trade on the Hong Kong Stock Exchange. They include SOEs that have gone through a major restructuring that satisfies the requirements for international issuance. Chinese government approval is required for an SOE to pursue an international listing, and in general the companies listing in Hong Kong have been strong ones selected in part to showcase Chinese companies on the international stage. H shares are traded in Hong Kong dollars. As with A shares, the ticker symbols are in numbers (e.g., 0386.HK). Since Chinese residents cannot freely convert yuan to Hong Kong dollars, they have effectively been denied the opportunity to buy stock in some of China's largest and most profitable companies. This situation started to change in 2006, and gained momentum in 2007, when the government gave permission to major companies such as Bank of China and China Life to list on the mainland, as well as on the international stock exchanges. As we shall see in the next chapter, however, during 2007 these companies tended to trade at higher prices in Shanghai than their equivalent prices in Hong Kong and New York.

In addition, so-called Red Chip shares trade in Hong Kong. The Red Chips are Hong Kong–registered companies that have a mainland Chinese corporate shareholder holding at least 35 percent of the shares. In many cases these listings are, in effect, "back door" listings. A nonlisted Chinese company purchases a relatively dormant Hong Kong–listed company and inserts mainland assets into the Hong Kong "parent." The Red Chip then becomes a kind of holding company with access to international financing that can be used as an acquisition vehicle for Chinese assets. All the shares traded in Hong Kong are available to international investors.

N shares: Chinese shares traded in the United States. Some of the strongest Chinese companies have been chosen by the Chinese government to register with the U.S. Securities and Exchange Commission and trade in the United States. These companies are widely regarded as being "the best of the best," strong and profitable enough to undergo the listing requirements of the U.S. exchanges. The trading typically takes place on the New York Stock Exchange or, particularly for high-tech companies, on the NASDAQ market—hence the designation "N shares." Ticker symbols for shares traded on U.S. stock exchanges are given in letters (e.g., SNP for Sinopec).

The shares are generally traded as American depository receipts (ADRs), which means that the trades take place in U.S. dollars; dividends are also credited in U.S. dollars. That would appear to make it easy for an American citizen wishing to invest in a foreign company. But, alas, things are not always what they seem in this case. ADRs are frequently bundled shares. Bundled shares! Where did that come from? When a foreign company lists on a U.S. exchange, it wants to look as enticing as possible. Because single shares of many foreign firms are so inexpensive, the feeling is that a single share listing would create the impression of a small, fly-by-night enterprise. Thus, foreign firms often will combine or bundle several shares and have these listed as one ADR share on a U.S. exchange. For example, one share of Sinopec

(SNP) traded in New York represents 100 shares traded in Hong Kong.

And all the rest: Shares listed on other international exchanges. Some of the Chinese companies that are permitted to list internationally have chosen to bypass New York and opted instead to list on the London Stock Exchange (L shares), the Tokyo Stock Exchange (T shares), or the Singapore Stock Exchange (S shares). While available to all international investors, they are traded respectively in British pounds, Japanese yen, and Singaporean dollars. Listing in places other than New York avoids the costs of complying with SEC and Sarbanes-Oxley requirements, which some companies find increasingly burdensome.

Slightly confused? Never strong on the alphabet? There's more. If you have been paying close attention, you now know that some Chinese companies are only listed as A shares, others are listed only as H shares, some are listed as A and H shares, about two dozen are listed as H and N shares, about a dozen are only listed as N shares, and a growing number are listed as A, H, and N shares. Yes, a puzzlement indeed. To make this incredibly complex situation even more confusing, the same company often trades at different prices in the local and international markets. This price differential reflects extremely limited foreign access to mainland shares and limited local access to shares listed internationally, as we shall see in the following chapter. Thus, should a foreigner hold a share of Sinopec, for example, and see that it is trading at a 25 percent premium in Shanghai, it does her no good—because she is not allowed to sell her shares short in Shanghai while buying them in Hong Kong or New York. Whenever arbitrage is restricted, prices can deviate from market to market.

Changes in Chinese Regulations
During the 2000s

Since joining the World Trade Organization in 2001, China has accelerated the pace of reform to bring the legal environment for its capital markets up to international standards. The WTO, for example, calls for allowing foreign investment in all industries, with the exception of sensitive companies associated with national security. This meant that China had to open its investment doors. It did so in a very Chinese way.

Cuefee and Quidee quotas. While they sound like new athletic challenges for Harry Potter, these are the pronunciations for two programs that China has initiated to further solidify its capital markets. The Qualified Foreign Investor Program (QFII—pronounced "Cuefee"), begun in November 2002, permits a limited number of qualified institutional investors, on an annual renewal basis, to participate directly in China's domestic stock markets. UBS, Europe's biggest bank, based in Zurich, was the first foreign bank to be issued a QFII quota. Since then a number of banks, insurance companies, brokers, universities, and other investors have acquired QFII quotas. Although the quotas have been expanded over time, they are still relatively small. Moreover, there are limits to the number of A shares that QFIIs may acquire in any single company, and the program does not permit the unrestricted repatriation of the funds. The regulatory authorities are worried that since the capitalization of the domestic market is relatively small, it would be overwhelmed if foreign investors were given full access. In addition, the size and renewal of a QFII quota is often determined by the areas in which the institutions have invested. As this book goes to press, the government does not encourage foreign investment in real estate and new construction; thus, any institution concentrating its QFII quota investments in these areas will probably find it difficult to obtain additional quota the following year.

The China Securities Regulatory Commission and the State Administration of Foreign Exchange administer the quotas. There are, we believe, many advantages to liberalizing these quotas substantially. China badly needs to develop an institutional investment culture, and the presence of foreign institutional investors can help foster a domestic professional investor culture as well. Institutional investors can perform an important monitoring function and thereby help improve corporate governance. They can also help smooth out some of the market anomalies created by the alphabet soup where companies trading in Shanghai, Hong Kong, and New York often sell at different prices in the domestic market.

The CSRC is well aware of these advantages and very much wants to establish an institutional investment climate in China. However, in our discussions with officials there, they also expressed a fear that moving too fast to liberalize the quotas could overwhelm the market. The total capitalization of all Chinese equities was less than 2 percent of the world market in July of 2007. The CSRC, therefore, has opted for gradualism in its policies over the liberalization of quotas and limitations on QFII's ownership of the shares of any single company. But there is no question about the likely direction of policy change in the future as state-owned shares become fully tradable. China is moving to a system of private ownership where corporations will be run for the benefit of shareholders rather than the government. And the release of the state-owned shares to the private sector will lead to increased market liquidity, greater protection for minority investors, and increased efficiency for the state-owned firms themselves.

In July 2006, the government introduced the Qualified

Domestic Institutional Investing (QDII, pronounced "Quidee") program. Similar to the QFII program, it allows local institutions to exchange yuan into foreign currencies in order to buy shares on international exchanges. The government believes that this program can, at least in part, reduce the mounting pressure on the yuan to appreciate because of the deluge of foreign exchange flooding into China.

Nontradable share conversion. The nontradable share conversion is probably the biggest and most far-reaching reform underway in the Chinese market. At the start of 2007, all companies on the Chinese market had either announced or already completed a program to make restricted shares tradable.

The full-flotation reform instituted in 2005 also included an additional QFII-like system. Foreign investors who do not have an unused QFII quota will be able to purchase some state-owned shares through a private transaction. Five government agencies issued a joint decision in 2006 that allows non-QFII foreign investors to purchase strategic interests in the state-owned shares. Such private purchases would comprise a minimum of 10 percent of the listed company's shares and a three-year holding period would be required.

New accounting standards. Until recently, the Chinese stock market has been without universally accepted accounting standards. It is widely believed that Chinese firms traditionally carried four sets of books—one for the government; one for official company records; one for foreigners; and one (obviously not widely available) for what was actually going on. Thus, when reviewing a financial statement, what one saw was not necessarily what one was paying for. In its inexorable effort to create a functioning world-class market, the government has acted to correct this situation.

As of January 1, 2007, China's Ministry of Finance now requires all companies listed on the Shanghai and Shenzhen stock exchanges to report their annual performance in terms of International Financial Reporting Standards (IFRS). This is an enormously ambitious project, particularly given the overlapping interests of many Chinese companies that consist of numerous subsidiaries, as well as the woeful lack of qualified accountants to process and clarify the raw numbers (the Chinese accounting profession is still recovering from having been sent lock, stock, and barrel to the countryside to be reeducated during the Mao years). To give some idea of the task facing the listed companies, it has typically taken three years for expectant Chinese corporations to meet the listing requirements enunciated by the IFRS and mandated by the Hong Kong Stock Exchange. Though listed companies were supposed to have complied with the Ministry of Finance's directive by 2007, there is widespread feeling that many have yet to fully adhere to IFRS requirements. While progress has been slow, the new requirement is clearly a step in the right direction. As Martin Fahy, director of development for the Asia-Pacific region of the Chartered Institute of Management Accountants, has said, "You can't have a functioning financial market and economy without objective and independent accounting."

Futures and other modern techniques. The Chinese government continues to work to make its capital markets more rational. For example, in September 2006, the Chinese Financial Futures Exchange inaugurated a new exchange focusing on financial derivatives trades. This will allow institutions to hedge against market risk by investing in the Shanghai and Shenzhen 300 Index futures.

Furthermore, we anticipate that the government will soon be introducing two additional trading techniques: These are margin trades and short selling. Margin trades allow equity investors to borrow money to buy stocks. Short selling allows investors to sell stock they don't own—perfectly legally—in the hopes of buying it back at a lower price. Without short selling, investors can only make money if their stock goes up. Since money can be made in both directions—and you do have to pick the directions correctly—short selling leads to more balanced trading patterns.

A Summing Up

As this chapter has made clear, China has gone a long way toward reforming its financial markets and embracing a market-oriented economic system. In so doing, however, it has created what can only be termed a Chinese Puzzle. There's an alphabet soup of different kinds of shares, the national government's controlling hand in the release of shares, and the constant tinkering in devising new programs. Somehow, this hybrid conglomeration works—and recently has worked surprisingly well. But China is far from a full market system. State-owned enterprises still control a large portion of the nation's economic output, and the privatization of state-owned shares, we feel, could be moving at a faster pace. Certainly, much more needs to be done. China's markets are far from problem-free, and there is still far too much reliance on the state.

China, then, is in an unprecedented position with regard to the development of its domestic stock market. It continues to restrict outside access, is trying to dampen domestic speculative enthusiasm for share ownership, is introducing new accounting standards and requirements for transparency, and is also trying to rein in corruption. It is an extremely delicate balancing act, one that will affect the future not only of China but of the entire world economy. Having met with officials at many levels and in many government agencies, we are impressed with the creativity and the dedication devoted to this task.

CHAPTER 5

The Efficiency of the Chinese Stock Market

"Stir frying"
—CHINESE SLANG FOR SPECULATING IN SHARES

FINANCIAL ECONOMISTS, DULLARDS THAT THEY ARE, use the term "efficiency" to communicate whether or not a market is free of corruption or manipulation, or, as they like to put it, whether or not the stocks in a market properly reflect all the information that is known about their conditions and prospects. Financial economists would never accuse an institution of being lax in morals or wanting in the tools to control roguery; rather, they simply say that the market is "inefficient." The efficiency, or lack thereof, of the Chinese stock market is the subject of this chapter. Though there is definitely some eye-closing prose here, the information is important because the investment strategies that we recommend depend upon the extent to which the Chinese market conforms to the ideal of efficiency.

In a further challenge to staying awake, we examine both the local A-share market, which is open to Chinese citizens and is for all practical purposes closed to foreign investors, and the markets for H, N, and other shares that are available to all international investors (but are restricted for local Chinese investors because they cannot freely move large sums of money out of the country). Readers who have absolute faith in our judgment can easily skip this chapter; those in the financial industry or who like to manage their money themselves would do well to pay attention because the information here is essential to profiting from China's economic boom. Or, as a financial economist would put it, the extent to which Chinese stocks are efficiently priced is crucial to the development of optimal investment strategies that are most likely to allow investors to benefit from the continued enormous growth that we foresee for the Chinese economy.

EFFICIENCY IN A STOCK MARKET

Financial economists took all the fun and excitement out of investing when they developed the concept of an efficient market. This kind of market is exceedingly bland. All relevant news is absorbed into stock prices completely and without delay. There is no outguessing other traders, no hunches, no emotion. When news does arrive, whether it be good or bad, investors and traders respond instantly; in turn, stock prices adjust immediately. Thus—so the theory goes—at any point in time, the price of every stock fully reflects the prospects for the company involved. In such a market, all stocks are perfectly priced. An investor could select a portfolio by throwing darts at the stock pages and do just as well as any other investor since one stock is just as good a buy as another. The better analogy is to have the investor throw a blanket over the stock pages and simply buy and hold all the stocks available in the market. This is what an all-market index fund does, although the people who construct the index may not actually throw a blanket over the stock pages. Rather, they select and then bundle together a representative group of securities, which they feel will provide an investor with a portfolio whose performance closely represents that of the market as a whole.

Not only do financial economists disdain the glamour and excitement of less efficient markets, they absolutely wallow in obfuscation and complication. After all, how are the hordes of assistant professors ever going to gain tenure if they don't write in stuffy prose and use largely inscrutable mathematical symbols? Thus, after wasting who knows how many reams of paper, financial economists have further refined—perhaps clouded would be a better word—the efficient market theory by splitting it into two.

The two parts of the theory differ in terms of the kind of information that is incorporated into stock prices and the reliability of that information. In a perfectly efficient market, no professional investors are able to do better than a rank amateur since a company's stock already reflects whatever is known about the company.

In financial economics speak, the narrow (or weak) form of the theory holds that no analysis of past stock price patterns provides a path to the "smart money" and extraordinary returns. Charts are for decoration only and, for those who like modern art, they can provide some interesting squiggles. In an inefficient market, dicey behavior such as stock price manipulation exists, and smart traders can pick up such behavior by examining stock charts depicting patterns of past price movements. This theory is not called narrow (or weak) for nothing; while it works well in many developed markets, it does not survive practical application in some emerging markets, where examples of price manipulation are all too common.

Financial economists have also widened their horizons and come up with a broad (or strong) form of the efficient market theory. This version states that even basing investment decisions on fundamental factors—such as a company's earnings, dividends, and prospects for future growth—will not help one iota since all fundamental information, good or bad, is already reflected in the stock price. In other words, the narrow form says past stock price information is useless and the broad form says fundamental information doesn't help either. Both forms assume that no hanky-panky is going on—that the books are not being fudged and that share prices are not being manipulated. And both argue that picking individual stocks is dangerous. For the record, neither Warren Buffett nor Peter Lynch is or ever was a financial economist.

In defense of the efficient market concept, however, let it be noted that many people willingly trade the excitement of the wild swings and bets on particular stocks for the steady, moneymaking long-term growth of the market. The burgeoning number of index funds in all international markets as well as the popularity of exchange-traded funds (ETFs), which are basically index funds that trade on a stock exchange, is a testimony to the view that indexing is a profitable way to avoid the perils of choosing individual stocks. Index funds and ETFs are far easier and less expensive to own, and evidence accumulated over several decades suggests that their performance (net of management fees) exceeds the net returns available from actively managed mutual funds. Indeed, one test of the efficiency of markets is to compare the returns of market indexes with those achieved by professional "active" managers who believe they can obtain higher returns by confining their purchases to stocks that they consider undervalued.

There is another important implication of stock price behavior in an efficient market. Stock prices will behave in a random and unpredictable fashion in a highly efficient market. Paradoxically, such random behavior does not imply that the market is capricious. On the contrary, efficiency means that when news arises, share prices reflect it immediately—not slowly over time. Thus, future stock prices cannot be predicted on the basis of past stock prices. Prices will change when news arises, of course, but true news is by definition unpredictable. Events such as the discovery of a new oil field, the discovery that a company's management has been stealing company resources, and all the other news items that cause stock prices to change cannot be predicted on the basis of past stock prices or past news stories in a highly efficient market. Thus, past stock prices offer no guidance for predicting future prices and no stock price patterns will emerge that might be of use to investors.

Contrast an efficient market with one where insider trading or stock price manipulation exists. Suppose the geologist responsible for the discovery of the new oil field runs out and buys shares in the company that owns the field. The next day, he tells his family members, then later his friends, and eventually his bosses at the company, all of whom buy shares when they hear the news. The stock price in such a scenario will rise slowly and consistently over time so that by the time the discovery is made public, the price may have completely adjusted and the geologist and his family and friends are all eating Beluga caviar and drinking expensive champagne.

Consider another scenario where a group of traders deliberately try to manipulate the price of a stock. Imagine that the authors of this book formed an investment pool. After obtaining an initial position in the (imaginary) stock of Mei Real Estate Company, Patricia sells some of the pool shares to

Burton at a price of 100 yuan. Burton then sells the same shares to Jianping at 101 yuan and Jianping resells them to Rui at 102 yuan. Rui then sells the shares back to Patricia at 103 yuan per share. Note that all these trades are not real trades—the shares simply move back and forth among the pool members. (These are called "wash" sales and are illegal in most markets around the world.) What they cause is a systematic daily increase in the price of the shares. Such an uptrend is likely to attract the attention of public investors who may believe that the rising price indicates Mei Real Estate Company will soon announce very favorable news. With the public now doing the buying at continuously rising prices, it is time for the pool members to "pull the plug." They sell their original position that had been purchased at far lower prices, and leave the public holding the shares at artificially inflated prices.

With regard to the Chinese market, we can test for the existence of insider trading or the kind of market manipulation described above by looking at the sequence of its stock prices. Do prices develop haphazardly, as would be expected in reasonably efficient markets? Or do price changes very often occur in a single direction and are prices at least somewhat predictable on the basis of past price changes? Pay attention now: this is where the narrow and the broad forms of the efficient market theory come into play. We call tests based on the sequence of share prices over time "narrow form" tests of the efficient market hypothesis. If markets are narrow form efficient, chart readers cannot fashion a trading strategy that will earn above-average returns. Tests that ask if markets are sufficiently inefficient for professional security analysts and portfolio managers to beat the dart throwers, or more realistically the index investors, are called "broad form" tests of the efficient market theory. We will cover both kinds of tests in this chapter for both local A shares and shares fully accessible by international investors.

Tests of Chinese Stock Manipulation

If information is not fully and immediately reflected in market prices, as was the case for our hypothetical geologist, then stock prices will only gradually adjust to new information. In such a case, future prices will be predictable on the basis of past prices, and profits can be earned by identifying such predictable patterns and making trades to exploit them. Perhaps, then, the simplest test of the narrow form of the efficient market hypothesis is to look explicitly at whether a stock price change today can be predicted on the basis of stock price changes yesterday or on previous days (or from week to week, month to month, etc.).

Continuous movements of stock prices in the same direction may also reflect the existence of manipulation, such as that in our author investment pool. Very efficient market prices will behave much like a "random walk," where price changes are uncorrelated from period to period. Moreover, it will be impossible to predict the future price of a stock by examining how prices changed in the past. In the United States, market prices from period to period are for all practical purposes uncorrelated.

We will not burden you with an academic review of the variety of statistical studies that have tested for patterns in the development of Chinese stock prices and that suggest the possibility of price manipulation. The references associated with this book can be accessed by interested readers who desire a full description. Here we simply state the conclusions that result from this work. The Chinese A-share market often fails the test of narrow form efficiency. In plain English, this means that professionals can use trading strategies to beat the market. While we also find that the H-share market has been narrow form inefficient in the past, there is some indication that it is reasonably efficient at the present time.

THE DICEY BEHAVIOR OF CHINESE STOCKS

Examples abound of fraudulent accounting and stock manipulation in China. In a truly daring move, branch officials of the Agricultural Bank of China issued $10 billion in phony letters of credit in 1993. Shen Taifu had a better idea. As a senior officer of the Great Wall Machinery and Electronics Scientific and Technological Industry Company, he duped 100,000 hardworking Chinese into investing over $170 million in securities touting a 24 percent annual interest rate. After collecting the money, Shen tried to leave China on a phony passport. He was caught and eventually shot, once again proving the old adage that "you can't take it with you." These two cases, plus numerous other examples, spurred the Ministry of Finance to conduct a study. In 1999, the ministry released data showing that a whopping 89 percent of the companies listed on the Chinese exchanges had cooked their books.

In a typical example, two mainland Chinese—Zhu Huanliang, a major market player, and Lu Liang, a journalist— hatched a scheme reminiscent of the pools that operated in the United States during the late 1920s prior to the establishment of the SEC. The story begins in 1998, when the China Venture Capital Group was listed on the Shenzhen Stock Exchange and sold at a price of around 10 yuan per share. The two men pooled their resources and slowly accumulated holdings that eventually amounted to more than half of the tradable shares of the company. In the spring of 1999, *Securities Market Weekly* (a Chinese investment journal) published the first of four articles written by a Mr. K (Lu's pseudonym) that touted the riches to be made from ventures exploiting the new technological revolution. Having cleverly whetted the public's appetite, Lu then inflamed it in August 1999 with an unsigned article in *China Securities Daily* that described how the China Venture Capital Group was poised to become the Berkshire Hathaway of China.

As the articles went to press, the two men were busy engaging in a series of "wash" sales. Zhu would sell some shares to Lu at 10 yuan and then buy them back at higher prices. The share price quickly rose from 10 to 13 yuan and the game took off. And what a game! For the next twenty-six months, the shares of the China Venture Capital Group sold at increasing prices. Leaving nothing to chance, an impression of active interest in the stock was maintained by continuing a series of "wash" sales at increasing prices. The Shenzhen market is an electronic crossing market so Lu had to ensure that orders from pool members were entered simultaneously. The brokers were instructed either to buy or sell on the basis of telephone orders. His traders would talk into two telephones at once and when the trader said, "Fifty thousand shares at thirty yuan," the brokers understood that one account was to be the buyer and the other the seller. University of Houston professor Guojun Wu has amassed a unique set of unpublished data on all the transactions over the period and was able to identify all the accounts controlled by the manipulators. He found that during many months in 1999 and 2000, "wash" sales of the stock accounted for as much as 90 percent of the daily trading volume. At its height, more than 1,500 stock-trading accounts in more than 20 Chinese provinces were participating in the scheme, and the stock hit a high of 84 yuan. All told, the manipulators pocketed over $640 million of their investors' funds.

No manipulative scheme can be maintained indefinitely. Various "traders in the loop" began to realize that they might be able to take advantage of the pool. Zhu was among them and sold out, double-crossing his partner and leaving Lu with a spectacularly bursting bubble, as shown in Exhibit 5.1. The fortunes of one hundred companies and many co-conspirators who were also involved in the scheme burst as well. Lu recouped a bit by selling his "confessions" to a magazine reporter. In the end, Lu and Zhu were put under house arrest; perhaps the monies from Lu's confessions and Zhu's selling out early were helpful in enabling both to somehow elude their guards. Although six of their cronies were sentenced on April 1, 2003, by a Beijing court to jail terms ranging from two to four years, the two initiators of the scheme have yet to be found.

Many other examples of price manipulation support the

EXHIBIT 5.1   *The Price of Chinese Venture Capital Group Stock, July 1998–July 2001*

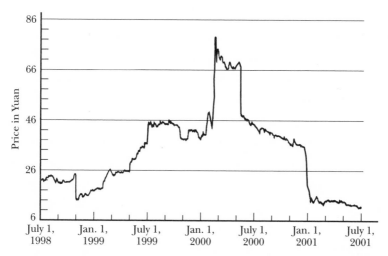

SOURCE: Guojun Wu, University of Houston, working paper, "Manipulative Trades in Equity Markets" (2007).

conclusion that the Chinese share market has been far from efficient. One example from the mid-1990s concerns a very mundane company—Dalian Beida Auto Stock Company Ltd. The company, which was simply called Beida Auto, was primarily in the business of repairing automobiles. In an attempt to boost the price of its stock, management changed the company name to Beida Tech and claimed that the company was among the leading technology companies in China. Based on nothing but its confused identity (the company itself was unprofitable), the stock soared during the late 1990s, only to collapse during the early 2000s. Investors in the United States will remember, however, that several U.S. companies added ".com" to their names during 1999 and early 2000 to capitalize on the Internet fever that was sweeping world financial markets.

A similar scenario involved Haihong Chemical Fiber Company, which was in the business of making textile fibers, and consistently losing money. Changing its name to the more opaque Haihong Holdings, the company announced that its business now included the more glamorous digital entertainment business. During one period, the price of the stock rose 5 percent (the daily price limit on the Shenzhen Stock Exchange) for twenty-three consecutive days. The price of the stock increased ninefold over the period despite the fact that the company was losing money. Later, the stock fell almost as quickly. Still another example was the stock of Shanghai Meilin, a money-losing producer of canned food. The company announced it would enter the E-business market and chose a Web site address: 85818. As we have seen, eight is a particularly lucky number for the Chinese, and the Web site sounded like "lucky-me-lucky-I'll-be-lucky" in Shanghainese. The E-business operation was never significant, but the promoters who sold their stock to the public at wildly inflated prices were "lucky" indeed. The public investors lost their shirts. But Americans cannot be smug. Over $5 trillion of market value evaporated when the Internet bubble deflated during the early 2000s. The U.S. stock markets, while undoubtedly the most efficient in the world, do not always efficiently price stocks either.

And the beat goes on. The Chinese government gave new regulatory powers to the China Securities Regulatory Commission in January 2006 and doubled the maximum penalty for stock manipulation to ten years in June 2006. As a result, the summer of 2006 provided many juicy headlines. Two weeks after receiving its new powers, the CSRC went after the Tang brothers. The government charged the two brothers, who had banking and government connections, with fraudulently raising more than $5.6 billion from the public between 2001 and 2004 in a breathtaking scheme that involved 2,500 organizations and 32,000 individuals. Auditors discovered $100 million missing from the accounts of Ocean Grand Holding, a Hong Kong–listed chemical maker with extensive China operations. A spokesperson for Guangdon Kelon, the country's largest refrigerator maker, said that an investigation into alleged fraud by its former chairman had resulted in restating its 2005 results to reflect a nearly $400 million loss. And trading in shares in the state-controlled Shanghai Electric was suspended after newspapers reported that one of its directors was suspected of obtaining $400 million in illegal loans from a city pension fund.

In summary, the mainland Chinese stock markets are not narrow form efficient. They are marked by price manipulation as well as instances of outright fraud in issuance of financial statements. Fortunately, the Chinese government recognizes the importance of cleaning up these unsavory practices, and continued improvement is likely.

THE EFFICIENT ROLE OF ARBITRAGE

But here is what we think is an interesting and potentially profitable tidbit: Even if the Shanghai and Shenzhen markets were squeaky clean, they would still be considered—in financial economics terms—inefficient. How can we say this? Easy. Several of the companies trading as A shares are listed on other exchanges in Hong Kong or New York and their A shares typically trade at premiums over the values in the other exchanges. Thus, if you paid the equivalent of $15 for a share on the Shanghai exchange, you would probably cry when you learned that the same stock was selling for $10 a share on the Hong Kong market. At times, the A shares have sold at nearly double the prices of those listed in overseas markets. On one day in January 2007, as shown in Exhibit 5.2, Sinopec shares on the Shanghai market sold at a 66 percent premium to the

EXHIBIT 5.2   *The A-share Premium: Sinopec Shares, Dec. 18, 2006–*
Jan. 18, 2007 (daily price differential on A market
versus N market)

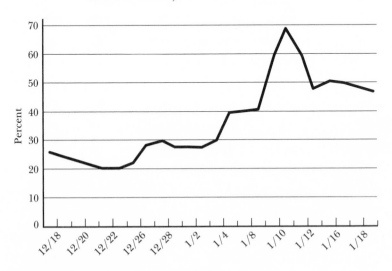

SOURCE: Bosera Asset Management Co.

same Sinopec shares traded on the New York market. In addition, when both A and B shares (remember both are available only on mainland exchanges) exist for the same companies, the A shares typically sell at a premium. This is hardly evidence of an efficiently functioning stock market.

Most analysts blame arbitrage—or rather, the absence of it—for this situation. Just what is arbitrage? Why does it ensure that stocks are appropriately priced? A generally accepted definition of arbitrage is purchasing in one market for immediate sale in another at a higher price. Let's see how it might work in practice. Suppose PetroChina was selling at $100 per share in New York and at (the equivalent in U.S. dollars) $110 per share in Hong Kong. The arbitrageur could buy a share of PetroChina in New York and simultaneously sell the share in Hong Kong, pocketing the $10 difference as pure profit. As long as there was any discrepancy between the prices of PetroChina in the two markets, such a trade would be both riskless and profitable. Therefore, we would expect that such arbitrage trades would continue until the prices were identical in both markets. The existence of arbitrage makes competitive markets quite efficient. If PetroChina is selling at $100 in New York, it will sell at (the equivalent of) $100 in Hong Kong and in any other market where arbitrage is possible. This is what is called the Law of One Price.

But what if PetroChina traded at a higher price in Shanghai than in Hong Kong and in New York? The arbitrage trade cannot be undertaken because of trading restrictions on both Chinese and international investors and because the Chinese yuan (the currency in which PetroChina is traded in Shanghai) is not readily converted into international currency. Thus, because arbitrage is impossible in this case, the same stock can (and, in fact, does) trade at different prices in the local Chinese and in the international markets. As a result, investors can usually buy shares of a stock that is traded locally and internationally at a lower price in the Hong Kong and New York share markets.

The natural arbitrageurs who keep freely accessible markets reasonably efficient are hedge funds. As soon as any anomaly appears—say a stock is selling at $100 per share in New York and $110 in Hong Kong—a hedge fund will swoop in to buy the New York shares and then immediately sell them in Hong Kong. The profit, in this and every similar case, goes to the swiftest. For as soon as word spreads about the cheapness of the PetroChina shares in New York, others will rush in to buy, thereby driving the share price up to the point where it is the same as that in the Hong Kong market. The bottom line: While people can argue until they're blue in the face that open markets with reliable information are not efficient, the existence of hedge funds as arbitrageurs can help make them so. And where hedge funds are not allowed to go, the market will never be able to attain a reasonable efficiency, either the narrow form described above or the broader form to which we now turn.

MAINLAND CHINA FUNDS AND THE HOMEGROWN ADVANTAGE

It's time to move on to the second component of the efficiency test: the broad form of the efficient market theory. Remember, if you can—and we have already recognized that much of this material is sleep-inducing—that one of the clearest tests of broad form market efficiency is to compare the performance of professional investors with the returns from holding a broad-based index, an index that simply buys and holds all the stocks in the market. If all information is properly reflected in stock prices without delay, then one stock should represent just as good a buy as another. Almost everyone has heard the expression, "Mother knows best." In a reasonably efficient market, "The market knows best," and the wisdom of the entire group of investors turns out to be better than the views of any individual investor. In such a market, no professional investor or guru is able to beat it consistently over time. In the United States and in most developed countries in the world, the evidence is unmistakable that professional investment managers certainly do not earn—though most certainly they do enjoy—their exorbitant salaries when their performance is compared with that of low-cost index funds. The question we examine here is whether Chinese fund managers can see in their own market what U.S. fund managers cannot in theirs.

It turns out Chinese mainland fund managers can and do beat the mainland market. In Exhibit 5.3, we show the results of our examination of the returns of all the professionally managed investment funds in China and how they compare with the returns of the Shanghai and Shenzhen stock indexes. To be scrupulously fair in performing the test, we took only the equity portion of the managed fund portfolios (managed funds in China—unlike anywhere else—are required to hold a part of their portfolios in bonds). We see from the figure that managed funds restricted to buying A shares have in most recent years and on average been able to far outdistance the indexes of A shares from 1998 through 2006. We conclude that the Chinese A-share market is broad form inefficient. Thus, the A-share market is not one where investing in index funds represents the optimal strategy, demonstrating yet again the uniqueness of the Chinese stock market.

One can argue—and we do—that investment managers in the Chinese stock market have a homegrown advantage that professional managers in other markets do not. Unlike stocks

EXHIBIT 5.3 *Managed Equity Funds in China Have Usually*
Outperformed Local Share Indices

YEAR	RETURN OF MANAGED FUNDS* (%)	RETURN OF SHANGHAI STOCK INDEX (%)	RETURN OF SHENZHEN STOCK INDEX (%)
1998	-9.50	-3.97	-29.52
1999	45.73	19.18	14.25
2000	70.60	51.73	41.05
2001	-33.04	-20.62	-30.03
2002	-19.47	-17.52	-17.03
2003	31.68	10.27	26.11
2004	-0.63	-15.40	-11.85
2005	-1.28	-8.33	-6.65
2006	102.69	130.43	132.12
AVERAGE RETURN	20.75	16.20	16.20

*Return is measured by the return of the equity portion of the managed fund portfolio. Included in the calculation are the returns from all open- and closed-end funds that are restricted to buying local shares.

SOURCE: Bosera Asset Management Co.

anywhere else in the world, some of the listed Chinese companies are in fact owned and held by an unlisted parent group.
Consequently, the earnings of the listed company are subject
to the needs of the parent company. For example, if a listed
company is not doing well, the parent company can make
sure that the ailing firm has profitable dealings with other
companies under the parent's control; similarly, the earnings
of the listed company can be skimmed off and thus decreased
by the parent company. Homegrown investment managers
have the knowledge and contacts to investigate the undercur-
rents of the listings on the Chinese stock exchanges, and they
use that inside information to their considerable advantage.

In the English-speaking world, there is an old adage that "it is not what you know, it is who you know"; in recent times, that adage has been simplified to the word "networking." In Chinese, there is a similar concept, and it is known as *guanxi*, literally, "relationships." This concept dates back millennia and is broader than the English word "networking." It entails a long-term commitment to the well-being of another and requires a sense of obligation between people. Professional investment managers in China have grown up with this concept and they know how to use it to navigate through the multiple layers and connections in Chinese business entities. Their results, as reflected in the table above, show how successful they are in utilizing *guanxi*.

There is one further indication of the inefficiency of the Chinese A-share market that we will try exploit when we develop practical investment strategies later in the book. Closed-end funds hold investment portfolios as do the more common open-end mutual funds. But open-end funds accept new monies and redeem outstanding shares at the net asset value per share of the fund. Closed-end funds differ from open-end mutual funds in that they neither issue nor redeem shares after the initial offering. To buy or sell shares, you have to go to the stock exchange.

The price of closed-end fund shares depends on what other investors are willing to pay for them; however, unlike shares in an open-end fund, this price is not necessarily related to net asset value. Thus, a closed-end fund can sell at a premium above or at a discount from its net asset value. There have been times in the United States market where closed-end funds sold at substantial discounts from net asset value, and analysts took this to be a sign of inefficiency. Large discounts no longer exist in the United States. But closed-end funds in China have recently sold at discounts of 25 percent or more from net asset value. As you will read in chapter 9, we consider these funds to be attractive investments at this discount level for local investors.

CHINA SHARES ON THE HONG KONG AND NEW YORK MARKETS

It is not surprising that the A-share market for Chinese stocks shows signs of being highly inefficient. The market is isolated from the flows of international capital, and arbitrage trades that could bring prices in line with fundamental values are precluded. By contrast, the H-share market in Hong Kong is open to all international investors. Similarly, shares traded in New York, London, and other international markets are open to international capital flows. Listing standards are strict in these markets and regulation is better developed, so we should expect a more efficient market for shares of Chinese companies traded in Hong Kong and elsewhere.

EXHIBIT 5.4 *Actively Managed, U.S.-Domiciled China Mutual Funds versus FTSE/Xinhua 25 Index (FXI), 2000–07**

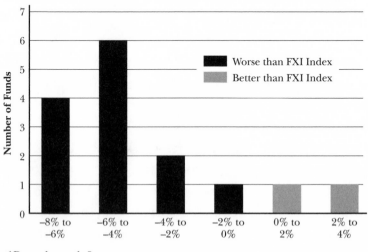

*Data through June 2007.

SOURCE: Authors' calculations.

Let's review the broad form efficiency of the Hong Kong H-share market for Chinese stocks. As a result of our narrow form tests, we found that the H-share market appeared to be inefficient during the late 1990s and early 2000s, especially during the 2003 SARS scare, and concluded that some manipulation may have taken place. But since 2003, there has been a dramatic increase in the capitalization of the H-share market, and more recent tests have failed to confirm that the H-share markets are inefficient. Similar tests of the U.S.-based N-share market also suggest general efficiency. Prices of mainland China shares traded on U.S. stock exchanges do not show evidence of manipulation. We conclude that both the H- and the N-share market appear to be narrow form efficient as of this writing.

Even stronger evidence exists to suggest broad form efficiency in the market for Chinese stocks traded in international markets. Exhibit 5.4 compares the investment results for fifteen actively managed open-end investment funds with the returns from a market index of H shares. These fifteen funds were domiciled in the United States but the actual management usually took place in Hong Kong. The funds held both H and N shares. The index used is the FTSE/Xinhua Index of 25 H-share companies. The index itself also forms the basis for an exchange-traded index fund on the New York Stock Exchange traded under the ticker symbol FXI (described in greater detail in chapter 9). On average, an investor who purchased the index fund would have earned a substantially higher return than would have been achieved by the typical actively managed fund. Moreover, Exhibit 5.4 shows that only two funds have outperformed the index funds during the time frame. Most funds underperformed the index—some by a substantial margin.

An additional study covered the twenty-five-month period from November 2003 through December 2006. The records of twenty-three funds domiciled in Hong Kong and invested in "China companies" were examined. Even before expenses, few managed Hong Kong funds succeeded in beating the FXI Index. Exhibit 5.5 presents the results. As we shall indicate in Section III of this book, indexing the Chinese stocks traded in international markets does appear to be a serviceable investment strategy.

EXHIBIT 5.5 *Actively Managed, Hong Kong–Domiciled Funds Invested in Chinese Companies versus FXI, 2003–06*

ANNUALIZED RETURNS VERSUS FXI BEFORE FEES

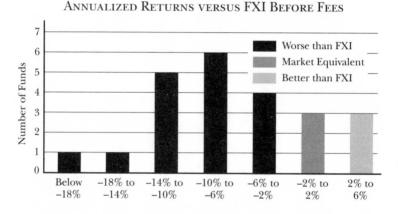

ANNUALIZED RETURNS VERSUS FXI AFTER FEES

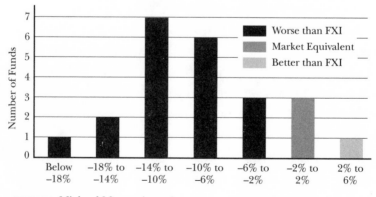

SOURCE: Michael Massey (2007).

A Summing Up

In nonacademic English. Though manipulation and fraud have been rampant in stocks listed on the Chinese markets, there is now a concerted government-backed effort to change that situation. Still, local Chinese investors would do well to seek and follow the professional investment advice of local firms with proven track records. Those outside China who wish to invest directly in the booming economy will find that Chinese shares listed on foreign markets are reasonably efficiently priced and can easily be acquired through exchange-traded funds.

In academic English as spoken by economists. Strong evidence exists that the local A-share Chinese stock market is inefficient. The market has been highly volatile and subject to waves of speculation. In addition, both the anecdotal and the statistical evidence suggests that manipulation and fraud occur with some frequency. Moreover, professional investment managers have substantially outperformed the broad stock market indexes of the Shanghai and Shenzhen markets.

There is, however, some evidence that the market is becoming more efficient over time. With increasing openness to international investors and a better regulatory framework, the markets do seem to be adhering to international standards of openness and accountability. Nonetheless, professional investors were able to outdistance the market until 2006, and an indexing strategy does not appear to be useful in the A-share market.

While there is also some evidence of narrow form inefficiency in the H-share market prior to 2005, statistical analysis suggests that there have been marked improvements since then. Moreover, professional investors do not seem to be able to outperform the H-share index of stocks of Chinese companies that are traded in international markets.

We will make use of these findings—thankfully, in nonacademic English—when we develop optimal investment strategies to exploit the continued growth we anticipate for the Chinese economy in the years ahead.

NOTE: *In August 2007, after this chapter was set in type and ready to go to the printer, China took a potentially significant step toward relaxing the limits on mainland citizens from making investments abroad. On a trial basis, Chinese citizens will be allowed to open accounts at the Tianjin (Tientsin) branch of the Bank of China whereby yuan may be exchanged for Hong Kong dollars. The dollars may then be used to buy shares on the Hong Kong Stock Exchange. If policies are adopted that allow such exchanges without limit, some of the anomalies we have discussed in this chapter may no longer hold true.*

CHAPTER 6

The Attractiveness
of Chinese Stocks

*I am a big fan of buzzword investing, and there
isn't a bigger buzzword out there than China.*
— KEVIN KENNEDY, *FIDELITY SELECT REPORT*

THE LAST CHAPTER DESCRIBED THE BAD NEWS; this chapter contains the good news. We are extremely optimistic that the extraordinary growth of the Chinese economy will continue and that you—and we—can earn attractive returns from this growth. While it is not reasonable to think that 9 to 10 percent growth rates can continue indefinitely, we are quite confident that high single-digit growth rates can be sustained over the next two decades and that China will prove to be the fastest growing major economy in the world. By the end of that second decade—when adjusted for purchasing power—China's GDP is likely to surpass that of the United States.

We are not alone in our assessment of China's growth prospects. In 2006, Goldman Sachs reported that China's GDP will far exceed that of the United States by the middle of the current century. And hand-in-hand with China's growing economy are its corporations, many of which are poised to become major world players. That same year, the Boston Consulting Group prepared a report on one hundred companies in rapidly emerging economies, companies that the Group believed are destined to become major global players. China, with forty-four companies, led the list, distantly trailed by India in second place with twenty-one.

ECONOMIC GROWTH, ALAS, DOES NOT ALWAYS EQUAL STOCK MARKET GROWTH

But will rapid economic growth generate significant returns for investors in Chinese equities? While we believe the answer is yes, there have been many cases where stock markets in rapidly growing economies performed no better than the equity markets of slower growth economies. In other words, a growing economy does not always lead to stock market riches. Elroy Dimson, Paul Marsh, and Mike Staunton of the London Business School, in an important study, confirmed this.

The three examined more than a century of data comparing real (inflation-adjusted) economic growth and real stock market returns for fifty-three countries over the period from 1900 through 2004. This time span presented two special problems. First, stock markets for most of the countries in the sample were not in existence over the whole period (the United States stands out in having a stock market in continuous existence for more than a century). Second, the time period of stock market observations for emerging markets is typically quite short.

Dimson and his colleagues tried to overcome these hurdles by performing tests over a variety of different time periods and for a number of individual countries. The results surprised many investment professionals: There was essentially zero correlation between GDP growth and investor returns. In plainer English, this means that you don't necessarily make a lot of money in the stock markets of economies with the most rapid output and income growth.

Many factors explain the lack of correlation between investor returns and real growth. First, earnings and dividends do not always grow at the same rate as general economic growth. Second, in some cases, exchange rate losses have offset positive stock returns in local currencies. Third, even if earnings grew, a contraction of price-earnings multiples has sometimes eroded stock market returns. And finally, in economies where corruption is unchecked, profits are often siphoned off to managers, family, friends—anybody but the shareowners.

China Stocks Disappoint—At First

The China domestic share market's performance, at least through 2005, points out the importance of the Dimson et al. findings. Returns earned by investors in Chinese securities traded on the local Shanghai and Shenzhen stock exchanges were, to put it mildly, dismal. Despite real economic growth proceeding at rather steady 9 to 10 percent rates from 2001 through 2005, and despite falling interest rates, investors in local Chinese shares lost money—big time. Although earnings and dividends of individual companies did rise, Exhibit 6.1 shows that China's market indexes fell by almost 50 percent from 2001 through 2005. The Chinese stock market looks like the poster child for the Dimson results.

Why was there such a disconnect between investor returns and economic growth in China? We believe the answer will not only explain the poor 2001–05 performance but also has important implications for the future. But first let's examine some popular explanations for the shortfalls that do not seem to hold water.

EXHIBIT 6.1   *A Case Study of Disastrous Investment Returns: Shanghai and Shenzhen Stock Markets, 2001–05*

YEAR	RETURN OF SHANGHAI STOCK INDEX (%)	RETURN OF SHENZHEN INDEX (%)
2001	-20.62	-30.03
2002	-17.52	-17.03
2003	10.27	26.11
2004	-15.40	-11.85
2005	-8.33	-6.65
CUMULATIVE 2001–05	-44.02	-39.76

SOURCE: Bosera Asset Management Co.

CULPRITS THAT ARE EXCUSED

In many instances, the Dimson results were caused by a disconnect between the growth of the economy and the growth of corporate earnings. Indeed, they show that earnings and dividend growth are only weakly correlated with real output growth. That was not the case in China. The earnings of local Chinese A shares not only grew but also recorded a very respectable annual increase of almost 10 percent during the early 2000s. Dividends paid to shareholders grew at roughly similar rates. The failure of Chinese equities to provide returns commensurate with the growth of the economy during the 2001–05 period was not caused by the lack of earnings growth.

We do believe that some profits may well have been siphoned off by corrupt managements and that many state-owned enterprises have not been managed with shareholders' interests primarily in mind. Nevertheless, inadequate profit growth could not have been the explanation for the negative shareholder returns. Moreover, the exchange rate of the Chinese yuan was pegged during this period and there was no depreciation relative to the U.S. dollar.

It's the P/E, Stupid!

We believe that the principal explanation for the poor performance of Chinese equities during the first five years of the twenty-first century rests in a major change in valuation relationships in the Chinese stock market. In other words, though earnings (E) were going up, the (P/E) multiple of those earnings declined. U.S. investors faced a similar situation in the dot-com crash of 2000. This crash, still vivid in many investors' minds and empty wallets, saw the overall market P/E ratio decline by more than one third, going from well over 30 to below 20, with the P/Es of high-tech stocks sinking at twice that rate, if they had earnings at all. China's crash in valuations was even more dramatic than that of the dot-com bust.

When Deng Xiaoping told his people that to be rich is glorious, many were convinced that the new stock markets provided the avenue to riches. The new Chinese market promised to become the largest in Asia, and investors were convinced that if they got in on the ground floor, riches were sure to follow. Speculative trading dominated, and the markets in Shanghai and Shenzhen became little more than legal gambling casinos. Institutional participation in the market was limited and valuations in the A-share market became completely divorced from reality. Stocks traded in the Shanghai and Shenzhen markets at far higher valuations than similar stocks traded in the international markets.

Manipulative schemes were common, and market price-earnings multiples reached triple-digit levels in the 1990s. Even in the early 2000s, price-earnings multiples of about 50 were typical in the A-share markets. Such levels were well above the multiples of comparable companies traded in world markets and well above the prices at which the same Chinese companies sold in international markets. Chinese stocks sold at essentially "bubble" levels throughout the late 1990s; and even in 2001, the market—selling at about 50 times earnings—was extremely overvalued by world standards.

As Exhibit 6.2 shows, price-earnings multiples for Chinese stocks declined drastically during the first five years of the 2000s. It was the collapse of multiples that prevented Chinese stock prices from reflecting the growth in earnings that was actually taking place. Think of a stock earning $1 per share and selling at a price-earnings multiple of 60, or $60 per share. Now suppose that earnings double to $2 per share, but that the price-earnings multiple falls to the average world level of 15. The stock will then sell at $30 per share. The stock has fallen by 50 percent even though the earnings have doubled. This simple illustration shows why Chinese stocks were such a bad investment during the early years of the new millennium.

But by the start of 2006, when price-earnings multiples had adjusted to the high teens, consistent with world levels, there was no reason to believe that equity returns would continue to be unsatisfactory. Once valuations had adjusted by the end of 2005, one might assume there was every reason to believe that future earnings growth would be reflected in rising stock prices. Indeed, as shown in Exhibit

EXHIBIT 6.2 *One Table Tells It All: Price-Earnings Multiples Stocks on the Shanghai Stock Exchange, December 2001–December 2005*

	2001	2002	2003	2004	2005
Shanghai A Shares	48.30	41.25	32.98	21.03	18.42

SOURCE: Bosera Asset Management Co.

6.3, the Chinese stock market did produce outstanding returns during 2006 (as well as the first half of 2007), making up all the losses of the preceding five years. Furthermore, there is now greater reason to believe in the validity of the earnings reports. In 2007 (as we saw in chapter 4), China required all companies listed on the Shanghai and Shenzhen stock exchanges to adopt international accounting standards for their financial reports. This has proven to be a boon not only for the international accounting firms hired to ease the transition but also for domestic investors (companies listed overseas are required to use the international standards).

EXHIBIT 6.3 *Chinese Stocks Bounce Back in 2006*

- Shanghai Stock Exchange Composite Index +130%
- Shenzhen Stock Exchange Index +132%
- FTSE/Xinhua H Share Index +79%

SOURCE: Bosera Asset Management Co.

Chinese A shares during August of 2007 sold at price-earnings multiples that were well above world averages. The A-share market was no longer cheap. P/Es in the A-share market rose to well above 40 during 2007, suggesting that there is certainly a risk of another downward leg of the roller-coaster Chinese stock market. But P/E multiples for H shares were only about 18, and one index of N shares, which we will discuss later, had a P/E ratio of only 14. Moreover, Chinese H and N stocks were still reasonably priced in relationship to their growth rates. Hence, price-earnings to growth ratios, the criterion we will describe below, were still attractive relative to world equities. Chinese stocks, at least those traded in international markets, still promised relatively generous future rates of return.

MANY CHINESE STOCKS IN EARLY 2007 WERE POISED TO PROVIDE GENEROUS RETURNS

Whenever the term "great investor" comes up in conversation, two people immediately enter the discussion: Warren Buffett and Peter Lynch. Buffett has enjoyed a stellar long-term record—over forty years with an average annual return of 25 percent—in running Berkshire Hathaway. Lynch's record is shorter. He ran Fidelity's Magellan Fund for only thirteen years, racking up an average annual return of over 29 percent, and then retired while he was ahead of the game at the ripe old age of forty-six. Buffett and Lynch are similar, however, in that they both consider themselves "value" investors. "Value" investors look to invest in stocks or businesses that are modestly priced in terms of their earnings, asset values, and future prospects.

Buffett was a disciple of Benjamin Graham, co-author of *Security Analysis*, the bible of security analysts. Graham's chief criterion for buying a stock was that its share price must be lower than the stock's fundamental value. That "value" is determined by multiplying the earnings actually achieved by the company by a modest price-earnings multiple—one that is not greater than the historical market multiple. Thus, if a stock is earning $2 per share and has a P/E of 14 (which is just below the historical, long-term average for the U.S. market), a share price below $28 would indicate a buy. If, on the other hand, the stock was selling for $55 a share, Graham and Buffett would probably avoid it. Buffett also takes into account the value of a company's assets, and if a stock is priced in line with such asset value, it may be deemed a good buy, despite an above-average current P/E.

Lynch came up with another criterion—one that took into account the concept of growth—to spot good buys. For

Lynch, the best stocks to buy were those that not only had good growth prospects but were also relatively unrecognized by the market and thus still sold at modest valuations. He looked for stocks for which substantial long-term growth was expected but that sold at reasonable price-earnings multiples. The best kind of stock to buy was one that had high expected growth and a low P/E. He would then calculate the ratio of the P/E to the growth rate. He might have called the resulting measure the P/E to growth ratio, but thankfully he simplified it to the PEG ratio. If he could find a stock for which 15 percent growth was expected, but which sold for only 15 times earnings—a P/E to growth ratio or PEG of 1—he would buy the stock for his fund. Eschewing stocks with PEG ratios of 3, 4, or higher, Lynch filled his portfolio with stocks that had ratios as close to 1 as possible. We will use the Lynch PEG criterion as a shorthand method to buttress our thesis that valuations of many Chinese equities were still reasonably priced as this book went to press.

Now we all know—or should know—that the future cannot be reliably forecast and, thus, neither can growth rates. As Niels Bohr, a Nobel laureate in Physics, put it: "Prediction is very difficult, especially if it's about the future." The professionals who earn their living forecasting the performances and growth rates of individual companies are called security analysts. They typically specialize in an industry, poring over industrywide as well as individual company statistics—past earnings growth, overall economic conditions, investment plans, competitive strategies for further growth, and so on. In the compiling of page after page of statistics, these analysts, Buffett's mentor Graham wrote, remind us of Gilbert and Sullivan's erudite Major General with his "many cheerful facts about the square of the hypotenuse." While the facts may be cheerful, the mistakes—on the analysts' part—can sometimes be egregious.

Although growth projections are often wrong, we do acknowledge that growth rate estimates are needed to make sense of different P/E multiples in the market. Ford Motor Company, for example, had a low P/E and a hefty dividend payout in the early 2000s. Even a cursory look at the company's growth prospects, however, would have warned investors that Ford was definitely not a buy. On the other hand, Google in the United States and Baidu.com in China sell at P/E multiples that are much higher than that for the market because stock buyers expect these companies to grow much faster than the economy as a whole. So, while we recognize that the growth rate estimates of professionals can be and often are highly imprecise, we must use them to make any sense out of stock market valuations. In what follows, we

EXHIBIT 6.4   *Price Earnings ÷ Growth Ratios (PEGs) for Various Chinese Security Indexes, Spring 2007*

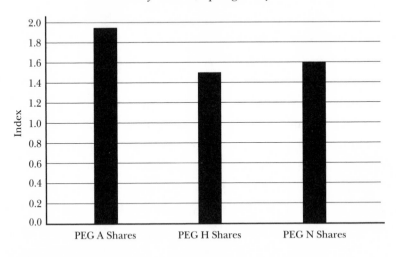

The PEG for the U.S. market is about 2.

SOURCE: A-share data from Bosera Asset Management Co. earnings forecasts; H-share and N-share data from Bloomberg and the Institutional Brokerage Estimate Service.

will use a consensus of analysts' estimates—an index of estimates, if you will—to create PEGs for the Chinese stock market.

Exhibit 6.4 presents estimated PEG ratios for three types of Chinese stocks: The A shares traded in Shanghai and Shenzhen; the H shares of Chinese companies traded in Hong Kong; and the N shares traded in New York as American depository receipts (ADRs). While the U.S. market had a PEG ratio around 2 when this book went to press, the PEGs for many Chinese stocks were lower, especially those traded on international markets. The PEG for the Chinese A shares, during early 2007, was comparable to those of U.S. stocks; valuations for the H and N shares, which were nearer to 1.5, were more attractive. Based on the Lynch PEG valuation criterion, the stocks of Chinese companies traded in international markets still appeared reasonably priced.

ADDITIONAL MEASURES OF ATTRACTIVENESS

The comparison above can be faulted for not comparing apples with apples. The composition of Chinese share indices often differs from indices in world markets such as the United States. Take the H-share index, for example. H-share indices such as the FTSE/Xinhua 25 Stock Index are heavily weighted with energy companies and financial firms—companies that traditionally sell at low P/E multiples, thus making the Chinese stocks seem artificially cheap. Moreover, the weighting of the companies in the index is not representative of the Chinese economy as a whole. A true apples to apples comparison should involve a comparison of Chinese companies in a broad set of industries compared with similar companies that are traded in international markets.

To obtain a more accurate comparison between the relative

valuations of the stocks of Chinese companies and those in the
United States, we conducted a "matched pairs" study. We
reviewed a wide variety of different industry sectors in China
and matched the leading Chinese companies within each
industry with a similar U.S. company. For example, taking integrated oil companies, we matched China's national oil company CNOOC with ExxonMobil in the United States. In all, we
used over two dozen firms in the sample of Chinese companies
traded in the H-share market and matched them with a similar
number of companies domiciled in the United States. The P/E
and consensus earnings growth estimates for U.S. firms were
derived from Bloomberg and I/B/E/S (the Institutional Brokerage Estimate Service). Those for Chinese firms were provided mainly from Bosera Asset Management Company's
internal research, with some additional estimates provided by
I/B/E/S. Exhibit 6.5 presents the results—anticipated growth

EXHIBIT 6.5   *Comparative Spring 2007 Valuations of Chinese and U.S.*
Companies

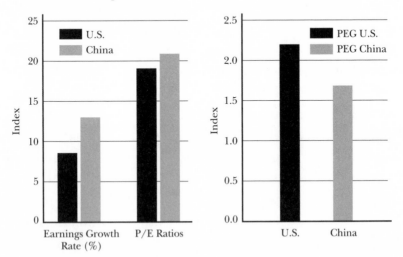

SOURCE: Bloomberg; Institutional Brokerage Estimate Service; and Bosera
Asset Management Co.

rates are higher for the Chinese sample than for the comparable U.S. companies. Although the Chinese companies had slightly higher P/E multiples, their PEG ratios at under 2 were more favorable than those for the U.S. firms which were over 2. The bottom line: Despite the sharp rise in price in the price of Chinese equities during 2006, valuations were still reasonable in 2007.

Other valuation metrics confirm the attractiveness of Chinese equities. Chinese H and N shares, also sell at modest multiples of their sales and their cash flows. The investment firm Goldman Sachs estimated that the enterprise value of Chinese companies (that is, the combined value of their equity and whatever debt they have outstanding) was low in relation to "EBITDA." This last term is Wall Street gibberish for "earnings before interest, taxes, depreciation, and amortization," and it gives a measure to the gross cash flows that run through the firm during a given year. Chinese stocks were among the best performers in 2006 and 2007, following years of disappointing returns. Even after such a stellar performance, by this metric, those shares available to international investors still offered attractive opportunities for future profit in the summer of 2007.

THE YUAN STARTS TO FLUCTUATE

There is a further reason for optimism about Chinese equities. Strong, rapidly growing economies tend to have strong currencies, especially those that have demonstrated strong export competitiveness. Consider the behavior of the Japanese yen during Japan's rapid growth phase in the 1970s and 1980s. As is shown in Exhibit 6.6, the yen appreciated from over 350 yen per dollar during the 1960s to just over 100 yen per dollar during the 1990s. South Korea also experienced

EXHIBIT 6.6 *The Yen-Dollar Exchange Rate, 1960–2007*

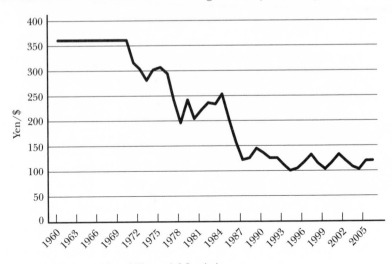

SOURCE: International Financial Statistics.

an appreciating currency during its rapid growth phase in the 1990s. We believe China will be under increasing pressure to allow the yuan to appreciate as it continues to enjoy rapid growth, increased exports, and sizable trade surpluses.

To our eyes, the yuan is significantly undervalued. An amusing (but hardly scientific) method to show the relative purchasing power of different currencies has been devised by *The Economist*. The magazine prices an identical product—in this case a McDonald's "Big Mac"—in many different countries to achieve an estimate of "purchasing power parity." Using current official exchange rates to value the product, a Big Mac sells for $3.22 in the United States and only $1.41 in China. On the basis of the "Big Mac Index," the Chinese yuan would appear to be almost 60 percent undervalued relative to the U.S. dollar.

We do not expect that China will let its currency appreciate sharply against the U.S. dollar over the short term. It took

EXHIBIT 6.7   *The Big Mac Index: 2007 Estimates of Purchasing Power Parity*

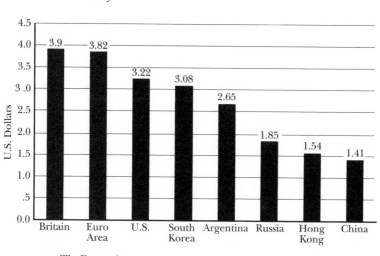

SOURCE: *The Economist.*

more than thirty-five years for the Japanese yen to appreciate from 350 yen/dollar to about 100 yen/dollar. Because of their large labor force, Chinese leaders wish to maintain an undervalued currency to make China's exports competitive. But we believe that large and growing trade surpluses are not politically sustainable in the long run. During 2005, China allowed its currency to appreciate by 2 percent versus the U.S. dollar; the following year, the pace quickened so that by the end of 2006 it had risen almost 6 percent in total. The appreciation continued in the first half of 2007, appreciating more than 3 percent. We expect this trend to continue as China will be under heavy pressure from the United States and the European Union to adjust its currency as a means to rein in its growing trade surplus. Any appreciation of the yuan will produce additional returns for investors outside China.

As an example, suppose a Chinese company had profits of 10 yuan per share and sold at 10 times earnings. If the exchange rate was 8 yuan to the dollar, the firm would earn $1.25 and sell for $12.50 in the U.S. American depository receipt market. Now if the yuan appreciates to 7 yuan per dollar, the 10 yuan of earnings per share (EPS) exchanges into an EPS of $1.43 per share, and at a P/E of 10, the share price will rise to $14.30, an increase of almost 11 percent.

One caveat: If the company in question was in the export business and faced strong price pressure, the company's earnings would probably suffer from the appreciation. However, a Chinese company making goods for the domestic market should suffer no earnings harm. Indeed, if the company needed to import raw materials in its production process, its profits would be enhanced, since a stronger yuan would enable it to save on all raw material costs whose dollar prices remained unchanged.

Standard Valuations Model Also Makes Chinese Stocks Look Attractive

Let's use another model to compare prospective equity returns in China with those in developed economies like the United States. Named after its inventor, a Canadian financial economist, Myron Gordon, the Gordon Model posits that the long-run rate of return from equities can be estimated by adding the dividend yield at the time the shares are purchased to the long-run growth rate of earnings and dividends. The dividend yield is simply the dividend paid by an individual stock (or the dividends paid by the stocks in a broad index) divided by the price of the stock (or the stock market index). The growth rate is simply the average annual rate of increase of the earnings and dividends of the individual stock or the stock index. The Gordon Model is not only a theoretical model—based on the belief that any asset should be valued as the discounted value of the future cash flows it provides; it's also a very practical technique that can explain past returns. For example, we know that in the more than eighty years from 1926 to 2007, the U.S. stock market provided average annual returns slightly under 10.5 percent. The dividend yield at the start of the period was just under 5 percent and the growth of earnings and dividends was close to 5.5 percent. Adding the two numbers together produces a number that approximates the nearly 10.5 percent that investors actually earned.

What can we say about future returns? We can use the Gordon Model to compare the U.S. and Chinese markets as of early 2007. Projections for the U.S. market are shown in Exhibit 6.8.

The Gordon Model indicates bad news for U.S. stock investors in 2007. With dividend yields of about 2 percent and an expected 5.5 percent growth rate, the long-run equity return of 7.5 percent is substantially below the historical gain of 10.5 percent.

By contrast, the same calculation for the Chinese market produces a much higher estimated future rate of return. While the dividend yield for Chinese stocks trails the U.S. at 1.5 percent, a conservative estimate of the Chinese long-run growth rate of 7.5 percent is substantially higher. Note that the 7.5 percent estimated future earnings growth rate is considerably lower than past rates. It is also well below the economy's past growth rate and the security analysts' estimates

EXHIBIT 6.8 *U.S. Market Estimated Rate of Return from Common Stocks, 2007*

Dividend yield	= 2.0 %
Growth rate	= 5.5 %
Estimated rate of return for investors	= 7.5 %

EXHIBIT 6.9 *Chinese Market Estimated Rate of Return from Common Stocks, 2007*

Dividend yield	= 1.5 %
Growth rate	= 7.5 %
Estimated annual rate of currency appreciation	= 2–3 %
Estimated rate of return	= 11–12 %

used in earlier exhibits. Therefore, 7.5 percent must be considered very conservative. Adding the two numbers, we arrive at an estimated long-run return of 9 percent. But Chinese equities have another advantage that is likely to enhance their returns even further: an appreciating currency. If the value of the Chinese currency increases by 2 to 3 percent, then so will the value of all Chinese assets, including common stocks. Thus, the prospects for Chinese stocks are far brighter then are the prospects in the United States (as well as those for all developed financial markets).

China Stocks Add Diversity, and That's a Good Thing

There is another important reason for investors to include Chinese stocks in their investment portfolios. Chinese stocks are extraordinarily volatile. They swing up and down more than twice as much as U.S. equities. Indeed, the volatility of Chinese stocks is even higher than the volatility of stocks in highly unstable emerging markets such as Brazil. But, paradoxical as it may seem, adding Chinese stocks to an investment portfolio could give investors the nearest thing to a free lunch that investment markets offer. Chinese stocks may both increase the return and *decrease the risk* of an internationally diversified investment portfolio.

A simple example from Malkiel and Mei's *Global Bargain*

Hunting illustrates the potential benefits from diversification. Suppose we have two contiguous countries: Sun Country, located at the bottom of a mountain, and Ski Country, on the top. Tourism is the main business of both. Sun Country has sparkling beaches, tennis courts, swimming pools, and golf courses. When the weather is dry and sunny, its economy booms. Unfortunately, in some years it rains continuously, and the country's resorts suffer badly. Ski Country features majestic mountains and superb alpine skiing. When Mother Nature cooperates with abundant snow cover, the resorts of Ski Country are full and business is brisk.

Now suppose that half the years are sunny and dry and the other half are snowy and wet, and that the fortunes of both economies are entirely dependent upon the weather. During sunny years, Sun Country booms and stocks in its industries produce 50 percent rates of return. During rainy seasons, however, travelers stay away and investors lose 25 percent of their stakes. If half the seasons are dry and half are wet, Sun Country's investors will earn an average return of 12.5 percent per year. Investors putting up $200 will make $100 in dry seasons, while they lose $50 in wet ones. On average, they will receive a net income of $50 every two years, or $25 per year, which is 12.5 percent of their $200 investment.

The situation is exactly the same for investors in Ski Country, except that the years are reversed. During wet years, Ski Country will have abundant snow and investors will make 50 percent profits, but when ski conditions are poor, they will lose 25 percent. Again, on average, investors will earn a 12.5 percent average annual rate of return.

Concentrating one's investments in either country is very risky. There could be several dry seasons in a row and investors in Ski Country could lose their shirts, or several wet seasons in a row could ruin investors in Sun Country. Yet even though investing in a single entity is very risky, that risk is completely eliminated by diversifying across countries. No matter what the weather, by spreading investments over both countries, an investor is sure of making a 12.5 percent return each year. Suppose an investor puts $100 into Ski Country and $100 into Sun Country. If the season is wet, the investor earns $50 from the Ski Country investment but loses $25 from investing in Sun Country. On average, the total $200 investment makes $25 or 12.5 percent. If the season is sunny, exactly the same net return is earned except that the returns from the two countries are reversed. The trick that makes the game work is that while both countries are risky (their returns are highly variable from one year to another), they are affected differently by climate. (In statistical terms, the two companies have a perfect negative correlation.)

The benefits of diversification are unlikely to be as tidy in practice as they are in the illustration above. World economic conditions often affect all countries, at least to some extent. But even in an integrated world economy, the same event has a different effect on various national economies. For example, increases in oil, mineral, and other raw prices have positive effects on nations rich in natural resources such as Australia and negative effects on many developed countries with manufacturing bases.

Analysts employ correlation coefficients to measure the extent to which different markets hit their peaks and valleys at different times. A perfect positive correlation (a correlation coefficient of +1) indicates that two markets are in lockstep, moving up and down at precisely the same times. A perfect negative correlation (a correlation coefficient of −1) means that two markets always move in opposite directions: whenever one zigs, the other always zags. When two markets have a perfect negative correlation—as was the case in our two mythical resort economies—an investor can eliminate risk completely by diversifying. But perfect negative correlation is not needed to achieve risk reduction through diversification. What is necessary is that the economic conditions in different national markets are not always perfectly synchronized. Exhibit 6.10 shows the crucial role of the correlation coefficient in determining the extent to which diversification can reduce risk.

EXHIBIT 6.10 *The Correlation Coefficient and Diversification's Ability to Reduce Risk**

CORRELATION COEFFICIENT	EFFECT OF DIVERSIFICATION ON RISK
+1.0	No risk reduction is possible
0.5	Moderate risk reduction is possible
0	Considerable risk reduction is possible
-0.5	Most risk can be eliminated
-1.0	All risk can be eliminated

* The less correlated stocks in different markets are, the greater the risk reduction benefits of diversification.

We can profitably translate these principles into practice with Chinese equities. Exhibit 6.11 looks at the correlations over time between Chinese A shares and the U.S. market as measured by the Standard & Poor's 500 Stock Index. The correlations shown are calculated each month based on the preceding thirty-six months of data (we refer to such calculations as "rolling three-year correlations"). The exhibit shows that the correlations of the Chinese A shares with the U.S. market have fluctuated above and below zero from the late 1990s through 2006. On average, correlations of the S&P 500 with both the Shanghai and Shenzhen indexes have been around zero.

We show in Exhibit 6.12 that Chinese stocks traded in Hong Kong (measured by the Hang Seng Composite Index)

EXHIBIT 6.11   *Rolling Three-Year Correlations of Chinese Stocks versus S&P 500 Stock Index, 1993–2007*

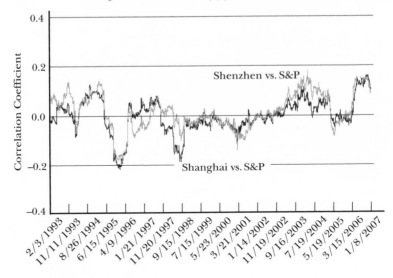

SOURCE: Bosera Asset Management Co.

are somewhat more highly correlated with the U.S. market. This should be expected. After all, the A-share market, almost completely restricted to local Chinese investors, is not open to significant flows of international capital. The Hong Kong market is open to those flows and, therefore, is more likely to be influenced by the optimism or pessimism of world investors. The U.S. and Hong Kong markets are far from perfectly correlated, however. Correlations have typically measured 0.6 or less. These correlations are low enough so that moderate risk reduction is achievable by adding Chinese mainland stocks traded in Hong Kong to a portfolio that includes U.S. equities. Also shown is the correlation coefficient of the S&P 500 and the Goldman Sachs Commodity Index. These correlations have actually been around zero or negative during the early 2000s. Thus, we find in practice two classes of assets (commodities and U.S. stocks) that behave in

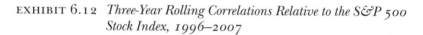

EXHIBIT 6.12   *Three-Year Rolling Correlations Relative to the S&P 500 Stock Index, 1996–2007*

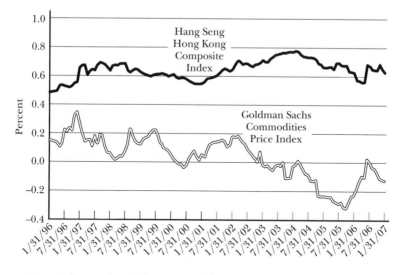

SOURCE: Bosera Asset Management Co.

a somewhat similar fashion to the hypothetical Sun Country and Ski Country returns. We will use these insights in the investment strategies found in Section III.

THE 2008 OLYMPIC BOOSTER EFFECT BEARS WATCHING

Behavioral finance specialists emphasize the importance of the psychological as well as the logical elements that drive the behavior of stock markets. Among these specialists, the proposition is often stated as follows: "What is the catalyst that will make some particular stock or group of stocks catch the fancy of the investing public?"

On Wall Street, the question is, "Where's the next home run or four bagger?" (The last term refers to stocks whose prices increase more than fourfold.) There is an obvious catalyst—a bagger effect, if you will—for Chinese securities: the 2008 Olympic Games in Beijing. This event has spurred China to spruce up Beijing, ameliorate its pollution, and improve its infrastructure and facilities. It is all part of an effort to increase international awareness of the strides that China has made over the last three decades. The Olympic Games are also likely to focus the attention of world investors on Chinese equities and their substantial growth prospects.

The Games may serve too as a benchmark for China's economic and stock market development. Goldman Sachs has argued that in many ways China resembles Japan in 1964 (when Tokyo hosted the Olympics) and South Korea in 1988 (when the Games were held in Seoul). There are similarities in the development models of all three countries, with substantial government as well as private participation, and there are strong cultural similarities as well. By this benchmark, China lags Japan by about forty years and South Korea by about twenty years in its stage of economic development and its per capita income levels.

Per capita income projections for China are consistent with the forty- and twenty-year lags suggested above. The projections suggest that in forty years, China will have a GDP per capita that surpasses Japan's figure today. In twenty years, GDP per capita in China should exceed the level in South Korea today, and these projections allow for China's growth rate to fall well below the current 9 to 10 percent figure. Nevertheless, China's stage of economic development today suggests that the country is not at the end of its high growth period. Rather, China is still in the early stages of a growth period with a full-fledged consumption boom ahead of it.

In the twenty years after Japan hosted the Olympic Games, its Nikkei Stock Index produced average annual returns of 9 percent. From 1985 (when Seoul began preparations for the

1988 Olympics) through 2005, Korea's KOPSI Index produced returns of over 10 percent per year. If we are correct that the Chinese equity markets are quite similarly situated to those in Japan and Korea when they hosted the Games, investors should be well rewarded over the next decades. The 2008 Beijing Olympics could well be the signature event that brings to the attention of world investors the opportunity we see for Chinese investments.

THE GOLD MEDAL BAROMETER

Goldman Sachs has also devised a fanciful approach to gauging the Olympic effect on China's economy. Starting with the Los Angeles Olympics in 1984, the firm calculated the compound annual growth rate for both China's gold medals and its nominal GDP. It turns out, as shown in Exhibit 6.13, that the growth rate in gold medals has been an accurate predictor of the economy's growth: 16.4 percent for the former and 16.8 percent for the latter over the 1984–2004 time period. Though China won its most ever gold medals at the 2004 Athens Olympics—thus raising the bar for the 16.4 percentage rate to continue—the country is going all-out in training athletes for the 2008 Olympics.

According to the Gold Medal Barometer, if China significantly increases its gold medals in the 2008 Olympics, the economy should follow suit. With the government's increasing emphasis on corruption crackdowns and improving both the governance and reporting standards of companies, the Gold Medal Barometer could well point the way to increased profitable returns for those investing in Chinese equities. Yet, as with all fanciful measures—particularly the classic "hemline indicator," which purports to predict the direction of the Dow by the increases or decreases in hemlines dictated by

EXHIBIT 6.13   *The Gold Medal Barometer (in terms of compound annual growth rate)*

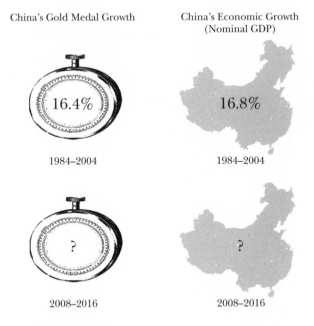

SOURCE: Goldman Sachs.

fashion—the Gold Medal Barometer might only predict good fortune for the athletes winning the medals rather than for those investing in the country.

INDEED, THE BOOSTER EFFECT HAS ALREADY STARTED

We believe the Olympic booster effect has already started, as shown in Exhibit 6.14. Chinese stocks, represented by an H-share index of Chinese stocks trading as an ETF in New York under the ticker symbol FXI, burst out of their doldrums during 2006. Without question, savvy investors have already taken note of the attractiveness of Chinese equities. We caution investors, however, that the FXI exchange-traded fund

EXHIBIT 6.14 *Chinese Share Index (FXI) versus S&P 500 Index, 2005–07*

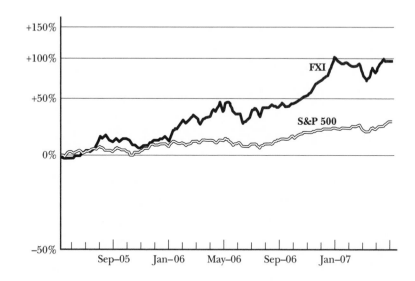

SOURCE: http://finance.yahoo.com.

has a different composition than the Chinese economy in general. FXI is heavily weighted with energy and financial stocks. With a cooling off of the hot energy and real estate markets, these sectors should not be expected to enjoy as robust a performance in the future. As exhibit 6.14 shows, the performance of FXI during the first four months of 2007 was quite volatile.

SOME FURTHER REASONS TO BE OPTIMISTIC

We have developed a case for double-digit returns for Chinese equities on the basis of an extremely conservative forecasted 7.5 percent earnings growth rate. That growth rate is below the historical earnings growth rate for the A-share index, whose companies grew at rates slower than the H- and

N-share indexes. The rate is also far below the mid-teens earnings growth forecasts of security analysts. While analysts are often too optimistic and guilty of rosy forecasting, the situation in China has been different. Forecasts for the growth of Chinese companies have regularly turned out to be too conservative and have had to be revised upward. With reasonable current valuations of earnings and cash flow, this growth is likely to be reflected in future stock returns. Any currency appreciation of the Chinese yuan will further enhance the returns for non-Chinese investors.

Returns may also be enhanced by improved corporate governance. As state-owned enterprises are privatized, and as more and more Chinese companies are listed on international stock exchanges, we can expect better corporate governance and far more attention paid to the rights of minority shareholders than has existed in the past. There is growing evidence of an increase in the numbers of independent directors and their membership in audit and compensation committees. Management quality is improving, and we would even regard the growth of performance-based compensation arrangements (such as executive stock option plans) as positive. When properly used, stock options can align the interests of managers and stockholders. Finally, as discussed in chapter 5, we can continue to see increasing transparency in Chinese accounting statements. We are well aware that accounting and governance problems still exist, but the direction of change is unambiguously positive.

A WARNING FOR INVESTORS

We must again stress that Chinese stocks are notoriously volatile. Even if they may be attractive as this book goes to press, there is no guarantee that they will be so as you are reading it. As we write these words, prices of the stocks of Chinese companies, whether traded on the mainland or in international markets, have risen sharply. Book publishing is a painfully slow process. It can take a full year between the submission of a manuscript and its publication. As you read this book in 2008, or later, there is only one absolute certainty about the Chinese stock market. "It will fluctuate," as J. P. Morgan remarked when asked about the direction of the U.S. stock market during the volatile 1920s. Chinese stocks could be even more attractive than at the start of 2007; but the opposite could also be true. Bubble valuations have existed in the past and there is no reason to deny that the same thing could happen again. Investors should definitely take the temperature of the Chinese stock market at the time they wish to invest.

There is no sure way to conclude that a stock market reflects reasonable valuations. But the metrics suggested in this chapter are a good place to start. Price-earnings multiples and expected growth rates provide excellent benchmarks. If you can buy Chinese stocks at around 20 times earnings or less, you will likely be rewarded in the long run. If you buy stocks that are growing rapidly at double-digit rates, that is, at PEG ratios well below 2, we believe you will gain generous returns. As we will describe in the chapters that follow, you should be widely diversified, and that means buying funds rather than a few individual stocks. You can further reduce your risk by making your commitments in increments over time rather than all at once. And we will recommend that you can further reduce your risk by using indirect as well as direct strategies to benefit from the growth of China.

A Summing Up

China is very likely to be the fastest growing economy in the world over the next two decades. In July 2007, Chinese stocks traded in international markets appeared to be moderately priced relative to other equities around the world. Individual investors could reasonably anticipate long-run double-digit returns by purchasing them. Bonds and stocks in the developed world sold at relatively low yields and thus were likely to produce only single-digit returns. While Chinese stocks are highly risky, they tend to be good diversifiers that can play a role in smoothing out the fluctuations in a global investment portfolio. When their earnings multiples and PEG ratios are reasonable relative to those in the developed world, we believe you should include exposure to Chinese securities as part of any well-diversified portfolio.

CHAPTER 7

Real Estate, Art, and Bonds

The individual investor should act consistently
as an investor and not as a speculator.
—BENJAMIN GRAHAM

ALTHOUGH FEW CHINESE ARE SUPER-RICH by Western standards today, China nevertheless has well over 300,000 millionaires—a clear sign that the recent economic growth has been creating wealth in the country at an incredible pace. Backed by these newly affluent Chinese, and by foreign investors eager to cash in on China's boom times, there has been an increased interest in real estate, art, and bonds. All can be useful instruments for portfolio diversification. This chapter considers the suitability of these assets as investments and also singles out several areas of opportunities. While we realize that such assets are too specialized for most investors, no book on Chinese investments would be complete without a discussion of their merits.

REAL ESTATE: THE LURE OF OWNING MORE THAN YOUR OWN HOME

Over time, real estate has consistently proven to be a good investment—one that provides generous returns and excellent inflation-hedging characteristics. The first time most people in the United States make a real estate purchase is when they buy their own home. This is considered less as an investment and more as a core foundation of one's assets. Real estate *investments* are a means of diversifying the risk in one's portfolio, and lately throughout much of the world, and within China in particular, real estate investments have been particularly lucrative. As a *Forbes* magazine headline recently put it: "If you are tiring of real estate in Florida, New York and California, you might want to get a piece of an Asian office building."

Mainland China's real estate market has been driven by the country's strong fundamental growth, particularly in urban areas where the population increase borders on exponential. According to one United Nations study, by the end of 2015, Shanghai and Beijing alone will have experienced a 50 percent population increase and will be home to over 20 million inhabitants each. And under the new "harmonious society" concept, announced in spring 2006, there will be a greater emphasis on urbanization in the western, more rural areas of the country, with a resulting increase in industrialization in these areas as well as marked improvements in their infrastructure.

It is no surprise, then, that investment in new office buildings, apartments, and shopping centers in China is running at an annual rate of well over $200 billion and is continuing to grow. Spurred by the prospect of the Beijing Olympics in 2008 and the Shanghai World Expo in 2010, the government has approved a plethora of additional real estate endeavors in order to present a national image of a major world power. According to the China National Bureau of Statistics, over 1.5 billion square feet of new space will be built per year through the five years ending in 2010, easily ranking China first in the world for real estate development. No wonder international visitors to China often joke that the national bird is the construction crane.

This huge development has put tremendous pressure on urban land prices—all kinds of land. A standard burial plot with tombstone in the Ba Bao Shan cemetery outside of Beijing has increased at an annual compound rate of 21 percent over the past twenty years. This is well above the rate of inflation and the returns from stock and bonds over the same period. Moreover, the newly sold plots are not as desirable in location, or Feng Shui, as many Chinese believe.

The government's investments in infrastructure and environmental quality have also helped to increase real estate values. Driven by the 2010 World Expo, the Shanghai municipal government has spent huge sums to relocate industrial factories to the suburbs and has cleared large areas of land for public parks. It has built three elevated ring roads and several bridges throughout the city. Attracted by its easygoing business and living environment, an estimated 600,000 expatriates are now working in Shanghai. Their demand for housing, comparable to the demand for single-family apartments and homes in Western countries, has also made Shanghai the most expensive Chinese city to live in.

Chinese entrepreneurs have been quick to take advantage of soaring real estate prices, with the result that those working in private real estate firms have made more money on average than those in other industries. According to the *Forbes* "China's Richest List," the majority of China's wealthiest citizens have amassed their fortunes through real estate ventures. And, as a 2006 Crédit Suisse report noted, real estate is also one of the most important assets in the hands of China's local governments: "Private companies are usually closely related to local government, which positions them well to obtain cheap land and earn huge profits."

While many have made fortunes in Chinese real estate investments, the opportunities for individuals are very limited. Most real estate funds—such as the $500 million plus Rockefeller Group Sinolink Greater China Fund—are privately held. In addition, the entry price into these exclusive investment vehicles is quite high. For example, the Wanyuan–New China Land Fund, a Cayman Islands five-year unit trust that opened in 2006, had a minimum subscription of $5 million for institutions and $1 million for individuals. Yet some readers might be unknowingly, albeit indirectly, participating in China's real estate boom: the New York State Teachers' Retirement System, for example, has invested $50 million in the ING Real Estate China Opportunity Fund. Many pension funds have similar types of investments. The bottom line, however, is that most individuals and many institutions lack the expertise to evaluate Chinese property investments as well as to navigate through China's complicated legal system. Poor liquidity and high transaction costs also make it very difficult to turn a property into cash if funding needs or investment prospects change.

Real estate investment trusts (REITs)

Real estate investment trusts, known as REITs and pronounced "reets," are a relatively new, potentially safe way to invest in real estate. They were first introduced in the United States in the early 1960s, but didn't attract much interest until the 1990s. Since then, they have proven to be very popular investment vehicles. The professionally managed trusts package real estate ownership interests into marketable stocks that are then traded on stock exchanges. Apartment houses, office buildings, and shopping malls are usually included in the trusts, and the rental income from these properties is converted to a steady stream of dividend payouts. REITs enable individuals to add commercial real estate to their portfolios and are an excellent means of diversifying assets. They are not without risk, however, particularly in the volatile Asian economies.

Many Asian exchanges, notably Korea, Singapore, and Japan, introduced REITs in the early 2000s. These securities are quite turbulent, falling in value during periods of rising interest rates and rebounding when rates come down. Nevertheless, both the income yield and the long-run price appreciation of these financial instruments have been quite attractive, so much so that risk-tolerant investors have invested heavily in them. With the economic growth in China and the subsequent increase in real estate wealth, there has been much demand for this type of investment vehicle in China. As this book goes to press, however, there is no REIT-enabling law in mainland China; thus, REITs cannot be listed on either the Shanghai or the Shenzhen stock exchanges. Hong Kong, on the other hand, has responded to the demand and in November 2005 introduced the Hong Kong Housing Authority LINK REIT. This was followed in December by the Prosperity REIT, which also consisted of Hong Kong properties.

The advent of REITs on the Hong Kong Stock Exchange was a major event—investors finally had a relatively safe way to invest in Hong Kong's booming real estate. On December 21, 2005, Guangzhou Investment Company (GZI) took the Hong Kong market one step further. On that day, this Hong Kong–listed company brazenly introduced a REIT consisting of mainland China properties that it owned. In effect, GZI had circumvented the ban on mainland REITs. Given the governmental hurdles GZI had to leap, this was truly an extraordinary event. A 2006 research report by CB Richard Ellis noted, however, that GZI had links to the municipal government in which the properties were located. Such connections undoubtedly helped facilitate the resolution of various title issues and "may have contributed to the REIT's ability to obtain special approval for the repatriation of rental income offshore without delay."

The GZI REIT attracted hordes of investors. Its subscription rate was 496 times its Hong Kong public offering and 74 times the international offering. At the end of the day it had raised $230 million. As a spring 2006 issue of the official journal of the Hong Kong Securities Institute noted, "the launch of GZI REIT represents a significant development in the markets of REITs in Hong Kong." Another significant development occurred soon after when the Chinese government, in a widely lauded effort to restrain possible overinvestment in real estate development, instituted new measures to discourage speculation and overbuilding. These effectively squelched all proposed Hong Kong–listed REITs composed of mainland China properties.

When more REITs are issued in Hong Kong and dual-listed in both Hong Kong and New York markets, they will be ideal mediums for overseas investors since they provide liquidity, diversification, enhanced oversight, professional management, and growth potential. At present, it is difficult as well as expensive for U.S. investors to directly buy shares listed only on the Hong Kong exchange. Should the Chinese government approve the listing of mainland REITs, these will be excellent vehicles for both domestic investors and those with QFII quotas, since they will be packaged by professionals who know the shortcomings of the various properties and will thus offer a high yield and a relatively stable income alternative to the low-yield, fixed-income products currently available.

Until then, foreign investors may best be served by indirect investment plays in China's real estate. Rapid growth is causing land values to increase not only within China but also throughout countries on its periphery. And where there is profit, there quickly follows a means to tap into it. UBS, the Swiss financial conglomerate, projects that there will be $75 billion in such REITs (excluding Japan) by 2010. In response to the demand, one U.S.-based firm, Cohen & Steers, has created one of the first NASDAQ-listed, Pacific Basin REITs, Asia Pacific Realty Shares; about one third of its property holdings are in Hong Kong. In addition, slightly over one third of the holdings of the EWH Exchange Traded Fund, which is listed on the American Stock Exchange, are in Hong Kong and China real estate. The EWH diversified ETF is probably the safest way for individual investors to gain exposure to Chinese real estate.

Property development companies

Where a REIT owns various buildings and uses the rental income from the buildings to pay dividends to its shareholders, a property development company buys land, constructs buildings on it, and then either sells the finished buildings or pockets the lucrative rental income. Given the poor corporate governance of most domestically listed development companies and currency restrictions, we advise investors to be particularly cautious when considering investing in property development companies listed on the Shanghai and Shenzhen exchanges. Hong Kong–listed Chinese property development companies, on the other hand, do offer attractive opportunities. Although earning almost all their revenue from mainland developments, the fact that they are listed in Hong Kong subjects them to more stringent exchange oversight as well as more rigorous disclosure standards.

The most valuable asset held by these companies is their land bank properties, which they have acquired over time as a land reserve for future development. With land in mainland China quickly appreciating in value, the land banks have become increasingly valuable. Here's the kicker: they are typically carried at book value, defined as their original purchase price. Several property development companies listed on the Hong Kong Stock Exchange sold in early 2007 at discounts to their actual net asset value after taking their land bank holdings into account. As the following examples demonstrate, however, investors should be careful when buying shares in these companies.

Guangzhou R&F Properties listed on the Hong Kong exchange in July 2005 at an IPO price of HK$10. Sixteen months later, its share price had quadrupled and its profits doubled. The holdings in R&F's land bank—over 145 million square feet—are primarily located in the fast-growing cities of Beijing, Tianjin, and Guangzhou. In 2007, it still sold at a discount to the value of its assets, though whether this will be true in 2008, 2009, or later is anybody's guess. And in many ways it is anybody's guess as to how to determine the current value of the land bank.

Shimao Property particularly illustrates the difficulties individuals may encounter when looking to invest in China's real estate market. On the surface, Shimao Property looks enticing. The company is run by Xu Rongmao, whose name in Chinese means "Wealth and Success." He started the company after the Asian financial crisis in the late 1990s by purchasing a collection of distressed properties in Shanghai. He then began a huge riverfront development in the city's Pudong district, where some apartments now sell for more than $4 million. By 2010, Shimao Property is expected to complete about 145 million square feet of property building, more than the entire 120 million square feet that Chicago's Sam Zell, the biggest individual property owner in the United States, controlled until he sold his Equities Office Properties to the Blackstone Group in 2007. Xu, the *New York Times* commented, "is no Donald Trump, Sam Zell, or Mortimer Zucker-man. He's bigger."

While Xu will likely profit handsomely in his property development, it is not clear that individual investors will do so. Xu controls three listed companies. And some stock analysts feel he has diverted profits from these companies for private gains. This could be one of the reasons why Shimao Property has traditionally sold at a lower P/E multiple and higher discount to net asset value compared with Guangzhou R&F Properties.

A third major property company, Cheung Kong Holdings, represents a real estate play on both Hong Kong and mainland China. When we stayed at the Beijing Grand Hyatt, we were amazed to learn that not only the hotel but the entire block of gleaming commercial and residential buildings was owned and developed by Holdings and other members of the Cheung Kong Group. The block almost surpassed Manhattan's Rockefeller Center, although it was missing the famous skating rink and the statue of Prometheus. And this massive urban development is but a literal drop in the bucket for the company, which is also extremely active in Shanghai and other major mainland China cities.

To read about Cheung Kong Holdings is to enter a maze of Chinese business connections, a maze headed by Li Ka-shing, Asia's richest man. Cheung Kong Holdings is, as the company itself says, the flagship of the Cheung Kong Group. Hutchison Whampoa, China's equivalent of General Electric, is part of the Group, which operates in fifty-four countries and employs close to 250,000 people. The Holdings is the property development and strategic investment arm and its shares are traded as a separate entity. About one in twelve residences in Hong Kong have been built under the auspices of the Holdings. It is also one of Hong Kong's largest commercial and industrial real estate developers.

As with Guangzhou R&F Properties and Shimao Property, Cheung Kong Holdings has a large land bank and was selling at a substantial discount to its asset value in early 2007. Sadly, it is not an easy company for investors to buy. It is listed on the Hong Kong Stock Exchange under a ticker symbol of 0001 and has two separate listings on the U.S. over-the-counter pink sheets market: CHEUF.PK and CHEUY.PK. Neither listing generates much trading activity, and there is often a large spread between "bid" prices, at which you can sell, and "asked" prices at which you can buy. Furthermore, some U.S. brokerage firms tend to shy away from the pink sheets and often are unable to quickly provide information on how to buy such shares. Under the right circumstances, investing in China's real estate market can be extremely lucrative, but it is neither for the ignorant nor for the financially faint of heart. This is why we favor indirect methods for ordinary investors to gain some exposure.

ART: THE TEMPTATION TO MAKE MONEY FROM A PRIZED POSSESSION

The wealthy and the powerful have long distinguished themselves by owning art—expensive art. The artworks not only provide (or should) significant aesthetic enjoyment but also serve as status symbols. Thus, as an economy grows and individual wealth increases, the demand for art picks up as well. And with that demand comes an increase in price for individually created and unique artworks.

The no-no words: Art as an investment

According to a 2005 study by two New York University professors, Jianping Mei (a co-author of this book) and Michael Moses, fine art in the United States has provided returns comparable to those from common stocks during the last fifty years. Using sales data from public auctions at Sotheby's and Christie's, Mei and Moses created a fine art index which showed that fine art provided an annual compound return of 10 percent over the 1955–2004 period, just about equal to the 10.3 percent return generated by the S&P 500 common stock index. Since stocks of listed companies constitute an important part of world wealth, especially the wealth of U.S. collectors, Mei and Moses concluded that the performance of fine art over the last fifty years demonstrates that the prices of fine art increase with the wealth of its collectors.

Mei and Moses also made a surprising discovery. They found that while Impressionists such as Renoir and Monet often commanded the highest prices for their paintings in the auctions, it was the less auspicious American paintings that produced the highest returns during the last fifty years (see Exhibit 7.1). Although this result may seem counterintuitive, it nonetheless reveals an important shift in taste as the American economy grew to be a superpower.

Fifty years ago, in the aftermath of World War II, few self-respecting wealthy families in the United States had American art prominently displayed in their collections. Only the old masters such as Rembrandt and Rubens, and the Impressionists, such as Gauguin and Van Gogh, were included in important collections. Thus, American paintings were cheap and underappreciated while old masters and Impressionists sold at price premiums. However, as America grew stronger and increasingly exerted its political and cultural influence around the world, its homegrown artworks became popular among wealthy collectors. As a result, American art appreciated more than the blue chips of the art world.

Despite these findings, no one in the art world—and we have interviewed many experts—recommends that people buy art as an investment. Beauty, after all, is in the eye of the beholder, and the concept of what is and what is not attractive is fickle

EXHIBIT 7.1   *Fine Art: The Mei-Moses American, Impressionist, and Old*
Master Indices, 1955–2006 (1955 = $1)

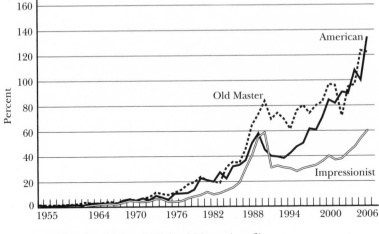

SOURCE: Jianping Mei and Michael Moses (2006).

and changes over time. Thus, adhering to the standards set by
major art dealers, auction houses, and scholars, we will refrain
from suggesting that readers of this book consider Chinese art
as an investment—and this despite the fact that we believe the
relative value of Chinese art is now analogous to that of American art at the end of World War II. Certified Financial Planner
Oliver B. Taylor adds a further caveat: Art is taxed differently
from many other investments. Long-term capital gains on
stocks, for example, are currently taxed at 15 percent for most
investors in the United States; long-term capital gains on art
and other collectibles are taxed at 28 percent.

The proper term: Art as a collectible

Having declared that art should not be viewed as an investment, we will now discuss art in terms of collecting, which we
define as purchasing for pleasure rather than monetary gain.
And Chinese art, both modern and traditional, is—as the saying

goes—very hot. It's hot not only in China, where an abundance of cash among newly minted millionaires is changing the entire scope of the market, but also throughout the Asian periphery, particularly in Hong Kong and Taiwan, where collectors are buying Chinese art in a big way. As headlines have proclaimed record-setting, multi-million-dollar auction prices and as major exhibitions have been mounted at museums throughout Europe and North America, collectors in these areas have joined the fray. For example, in announcing that it was opening a branch in Shanghai, France's Georges Pompidou Centre stated that "China is destined to become a major player on the world artistic scene" and that it was "vital for the Pompidou Centre to have its finger on the pulse of this movement."

When we interviewed Ken Yeh, deputy chairman of Christie's Asia in Hong Kong, he told us that there are currently some distinct differences among buyers of Chinese art. Mainland Chinese are generally acquiring works reflecting their heritage, such as porcelains and traditional classical painting. Buyers of contemporary Chinese art, he said, primarily hail from outside mainland China. The end result is that Christie's Hong Kong office has seen its activity expand dramatically in recent years, to the point where it is now third among Christie's worldwide offices in sales.

Laura Zhou echoed this observation when we visited her at the trendy ShanghART Gallery, located in a former manufacturing area of Shanghai that has now become an arts center. Among the works featured during our visit to the gallery were Wang Guangyi and Yu Youhan's political Pop art of Red Guards and Mao; Zhou Tiehai's acrylic paintings of the Joe Camel advertising icon with a bare bottom and similarly unadorned female breasts; and Xu Zhen's sawed-off snow peak from Mount Everest (enclosed in a specially constructed, temperature-controlled installation). Zhou said that interest in contemporary Chinese art has soared and that prices have increased three- to fourfold over the past five years. Almost three fourths of ShanghART's sales are to overseas buyers, including private collectors, museums such as the Tate in London and the Whitney in New York, and large corporations like UBS and JPMorgan Chase.

All forms of Chinese art—scrolls, bronzes, furniture, ceramics, and paintings—have received increased attention from collectors and dealers; but it is the last two areas that have gained the most headlines in recent years.

Ceramics. When a Chinese porcelain jar sold for $27.2 million at a Christie's London auction in summer 2005, the world sat up and took note. Of course this was not just any old jar; it was an exquisite Yuan dynasty blue-and-white vessel from the mid-fourteenth century. Sotheby's Hong Kong auction, held a few months later, could not quite match the price set at Christie's London auction, but it did represent the fourth time in four years that a new world record had been set for Qing porcelain: A pheasant vase sold for $14.9 million. One of our favorite stories occurred soon afterwards. A small New Hampshire auction house had put an estimate of $400 to $600 on a pair of Chinese *famille rose* porcelain vases; when the auctioneer's hammer came down on the last of some dramatically competitive bidding, the vases had sold for $545,000.

The tug-of-war between the Chinese bidding offensive to buy back their heritage and Western collectors eager to enrich their holdings acquired an interesting twist when it came to the auction of an extremely rare, fourteenth-century Ming vase. The material used to create the copper-red color was said to have been so difficult to work with that potters asked the royal court to limit orders. This beautiful, pear-shaped work of art somehow found itself in Scotland, where it was used as a lampstand by its owners. When it was offered to Christie's as part of an estate sale, the firm's China art experts immediately recognized its value and helped to propel its 1984 auction price to $588,000, which was a world record for Asian art at the time. In slightly less than two decades, Steve Wynn saw to it that the value increased almost twentyfold when he put in his winning bid for $10,122,000 in a May 2006 auction in Hong Kong. Wynn promptly donated the vase to a Macao museum "so that it can be seen by all Chinese people." Perhaps it is a coincidence, but in September 2006, Wynn Resorts Ltd. opened a $1.2 billion casino in Macao. Chinese poured into the place, and while they might have been in Macao to view the vase, they also provided $900 million in chip sales in the casino's first thirteen days of operation.

Paintings. Paintings within mainland China are priced according to what we believe is a unique system: sales are reported by square foot rather than for the entire piece. Thus, a 2 by 2 painting (4 square feet) and an 8 by 8 painting (64 square feet) could have similar value reports if each sold for $100 per square foot; by Western standards, the larger painting would be deemed to have sold for a significantly higher sum ($6,400 vs. $400). But whether one views the sale of Chinese paintings in terms of square feet or by the artwork itself, prices have been dramatically increasing in recent years.

The market for Qi Baishi (1863–1957), one of the most prominent and revered traditional Chinese painters, provides an illustrative example. Born into abject poverty and initially working as a carpenter, Qi eventually mastered an extraordinarily beautiful minimalist painting skill, one in which he would use a few strokes of his pen or brush to make fish, shrimp, and other creatures come to life. Qi's work was not recognized until quite late in his life. Though he used to sell his paintings from street corners to provide for his family, his fortune changed when his works were exhibited in Europe. After seeing them in Paris, Picasso was quite impressed and joked that "I am afraid of going to China because there is a great impressionist master—Qi Baishi."

Even with Picasso's endorsement, one could still buy a simple fish scene by Qi for a few thousand dollars during the 1990s. And then China's economy took off. In a recent auction, a set of three works fetched $1.8 million. As shown in Exhibit 7.2, both the price and sales volume of Qi's paintings more than doubled in the period 2000–06. This exhibit also graphically illustrates how quickly tastes in the art market can change. In the year ending December 2006, both the price and the sales volume of Qi's paintings declined dramatically—although both were still much higher than six years earlier.

Wu Guanzhong (1919–) represents a bridge between Chinese traditional painting and Western abstract expression-

EXHIBIT 7.2 *Annual Turnover Volume of Sales and Average Price per Square Foot for Qi Baishi*

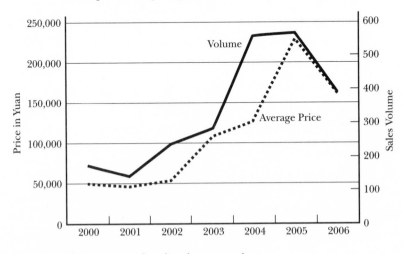

SOURCE: Artron.net and authors' computation.

ism. As a young man, he studied in Paris, and then, in a classic case of bad timing, returned to China in 1950 to serve his homeland. Denounced a few years later during an antirightist campaign, he survived the next decades by teaching character sketching. Unlike Qi, Wu has lived long enough to see his creations gain great popularity. He is the first living Chinese to have his work featured in a solo exhibition at the British Museum, and he currently holds the record auction price for a living Chinese artist's work: an impressionistic painting of birds by Wu sold for $3.7 million in 2005. His works are particularly popular among newly wealthy Chinese collectors.

Qi and Wu are known as modern artists, because they created their works in the twentieth century. Paintings created today are known as contemporary art, and the world is looking quite favorably on current Chinese creations. When the results of a spring 2006 Asian contemporary art auction exceeded the highest pre-auction estimates by 65 percent, Henry Howard-Sneyd, Sotheby's managing director in Asia and Australia, jubilantly declared: "It was a market waiting to happen."

The painting that garnered the most headlines was by Zhang Xiaogang, a young Chinese artist who had painted a dreamy portrait of a dazed-looking comrade. The buyer, an anonymous Singapore resident, paid $979,200 for the piece, more than twice Sotheby's highest estimate of $350,000. In November 2006, at a Christie's sale in New York, Zhang showed that he can hold his own with established American and European contemporary artists. At that auction, Zhang's work again sold for more than the highest estimate when his *A Big Family Series No. 16* fetched $1.36 million. That sale, however, paled in comparison with the results from an art auction in Beijing in November 2006, where China's newly rich bid up a painting by Liu Xiao-dong, known as a "cynical realist," to $2.7 million, a record for a contemporary Chinese artist.

Provenance is one of the many reasons contributing to the current popularity of contemporary Chinese art. The authenticity of the work is easy to confirm since the artists are still living or have just recently died. Note, however, that many Chinese artists today deliberately omit their names on their work; rather, they are expert forgers who create copies of older styles and traditions. This leads us to the concluding section in our discussion of art.

The most important phrase: Let the buyer beware

In September 2006, Sotheby's put a pre-sale estimate of $500,000–$700,000 on a beautifully colored bronze sculpture of a tapir. After viewing the sumptuously prepared catalogue, a leading international dealer cautioned two wealthy Americans who were interested in the piece that its authenticity as an antique was questionable. Upon hearing this, Sotheby's withdrew the tapir, and subsequent lab tests confirmed the dealer's judgment. As the art expert Souren Melikian wrote in the *International Herald Tribune*, "If a reminder was needed that one should never buy an object on the strength of a catalogue description, this is it."

So, what is a potential buyer of Chinese art to do? First, if you're not spending a lot of money—say less than $1,000— and you really like a piece, buy it because you want to enjoy it. After all, just one night at a ballgame can now cost several hundred dollars and you'll be able to view your new artwork for years. If you want to have some fun while literally seeing what kinds of Chinese art are for sale and for what price, check out iGavel.com. This online auction, with its heavy emphasis on Asian art, was started by Lark E. Mason, Jr., an *Antiques Roadshow* regular and a former senior vice president of Sotheby's Chinese Department. You can easily click on a piece, see what the pre-sale estimates are, and then track the bidding over a set period—all from the comfort of your own home and without the competitive presence of a live auction. It's fun to see what does attract buyers and also educational to view the variety of work on offer.

If you're a serious collector, however, a reputable dealer is your best guide to locating and buying the works that you want. How to find such a dealer? The super-rich need not ask such a question. If you're less than super-rich, independent appraiser Judith Applegate suggests visiting long-established antique shows; dealers at these events are all vetted by the sponsors.

BONDS: THE PROMISE OF FIXED INCOME

"Gentlemen prefer bonds," Andrew Mellon is said to have declared. At the time, a century ago, the rich were often known as "coupon clippers." The paper coupons were literally attached to bonds and were clipped periodically to redeem promised interest payments, thus assuring a steady, reliable stream of income. Today, "bond" is often regarded as a four-letter word—something to be avoided not only in polite society but also in a portfolio. Why? Inflation has reared its ugly presence in recent years and when it increases at a faster pace, the bond holder loses out on two fronts: the sale value of the bond prior to redemption decreases, and the fixed-interest payments decline in purchasing power with each successive inflation hike.

In mainland China, investors have few options beyond bonds. Unlike most Western countries, where mutual funds can and do consist entirely of equities, such funds in China must include both bonds and equities in their portfolios.

With the official interest on savings held at an abnormally low rate, many Chinese by default own bonds either outright or through ownership of mutual fund shares. Thus, with the increasing wealth of the country, China's domestic bond market has expanded rapidly in recent years.

The total market value of China's outstanding bonds increased from 230 billion yuan in 1997 to 9 trillion yuan by 2007. These financial instruments included Treasury bonds, financial bonds (issued by large domestic financial institutions), corporate bonds, convertibles, repurchase agreements (known as repos), commercial paper, and asset-backed securities (known as ABS). The maturity of these bonds ranged from one day to thirty years.

The main driver of Chinese bond yields is the government's response to the threat of inflation. Over the last few years, the Chinese government has been trying hard to keep the economy from overheating by periodically increasing its benchmark interest rates. To date, the government's performance is stellar. Chinese inflation has been reasonably contained, and we expect it to remain restrained. There seems to be a consensus among top Chinese bankers that inflation is public enemy number one and that a low and stable inflation environment means more economic growth.

Although Chinese bonds may have unattractive yields, dollar investors can expect an additional return of perhaps 3 percent per annum from anticipated currency appreciation. Between July 2005 and the end of 2006, the yuan appreciated from 8.27 yuan per dollar to 7.82 yuan per dollar, a 5.75 percent appreciation in seventeen months. Given the surge of China's currency reserve to over $1 trillion, and America's large budget and trade deficit, we expect the Chinese yuan to continue to appreciate against the dollar in the long term.

Chinese bonds also offer the benefit of diversification.

Studies show that Chinese interest rates have a low correlation with the U.S. and European markets and almost zero correlation with the Japanese market. Adding Chinese bonds to an international bond portfolio could substantially reduce risk. But here's the catch: government controls make it difficult—indeed, pretty much impossible—for individual investors to buy Chinese bonds directly. Selected institutional investors, however, can buy Chinese bonds through QFII quota allowances. Given the low correlation with bonds in other currencies, the benefits of portfolio diversification, and China's continued opening of its financial borders, we expect specialized Chinese bond funds to be available to global investors in the near future. At that time—but certainly not now—they will be worth consideration.

A Summing Up

Real estate. "Land is about the only thing that can't fly away," the British novelist Anthony Trollope once wrote. The problem for individual investors outside China is that they have to fly to see the land they own. One of the few means for outsiders to buy China properties is through REITs or property development companies listed on either the Hong Kong or U.S. stock exchanges.

Art. Remember the words of the publishing magnate Walter H. Annenberg: "Being moved is what collecting is all about." Treat art pieces as things to be enjoyed rather than as investments. On the other hand, given the growth of the Chinese middle and upper classes and their increasing interest in acquiring objets d'art, it appears likely that any authentic, high-quality Chinese art you buy will not decrease in value over the next several years. And if you have some porcelain, a rose medallion tea set, or some scrolls that a great ancestor brought back from China decades or centuries ago, it would be wise to have them reappraised for insurance purposes.

Bonds. With the Chinese government, for all practical purposes, putting a freeze on the outside purchase of bonds, gentlemen should stick to blondes (brunettes, jet blacks, and redheads are also attractive) and investors should seek other opportunities.

Section III

THE
STRATEGIES

Armed with the information contained in the first two sections of this book, you are now ready to review various investment strategies for profiting from China's growth. We start this section with a chapter appropriately titled "The Preparation." Here, we guide you through the very necessary process of knowing how to evaluate your capacity for risk and how to allocate your assets. The next three chapters describe markedly different approaches for investing in China: a diversified approach utilizing investment funds dedicated to China companies; a lower-risk approach through buying funds and other instruments that are organized outside of China but that profit from China's growth; and a very risky but potentially lucrative approach utilizing the purchase of individual Chinese stocks. In the last chapter, we present our recommendations for a mixed strategy that provides what we consider the best balance of potential reward and risk for investors.

CHAPTER 8

The Preparation

To be prepared is half the victory.
—MIGUEL DE CERVANTES

BEFORE UNDERTAKING ANY INVESTMENT, investors need to understand something about what they are buying and how that investment fits in with their risk level and the allocation of their wealth. In the case of investing in China, a country that has undergone a remarkable and yet unique transformation over the past three decades, such understanding is crucial.

CHINA: WHAT YOU ARE BUYING

There is no historical precedent for the enormous economic success story that has played out in China since the economic reforms instituted by Deng Xiaoping. Now well into its third decade, China's real growth rate has been a relatively steady 9 to 10 percent per year and was proceeding beyond that rate as this book went to press. Undoubtedly, the rate will slow—but we believe that China will continue to experience exceptional growth in the coming decades, and at rates well above those of any other large country in the world. We believe that every investment portfolio should have some exposure to the growth of China.

Similarly, there is no historical precedent for the kind of stock market that has evolved in China. It is one still dominated by state-owned enterprises and open to private firms started by entrepreneurs. Within the investment community, there is a great debate as to which kind of enterprise one should invest in: the SOE or the private firm. Those who favor SOEs point out that with the government in control, the companies will never fail.

SOE skeptics point to China Petroleum and Chemical Corporation. A petrochemical refining and production company, this SOE ranks among China's most profitable companies and has both a low P/E and PEG ratio. So what's the catch? To begin with, even trying to define this company is difficult. It was established as a joint stock limited company in 2000 under the Company Law of the People's Republic of China with Sinopec Group Company as the sole shareholder. Thus, many refer to the company as Sinopec; its ticker symbol on the New York Stock Exchange is SNP. The company is an SOE because the government holds 70 percent of its shares. There are more than eighty subsidiaries associated with the company, and some of these, such as Shanghai Petrochemical Co. Ltd. (SHI), also trade on the New York Stock Exchange.

The Chinese government not only owns the company but also has a very heavy hand in Sinopec's operations. While the government allows crude oil prices to move in line with international markets, it controls the price of refined oil products, like gasoline. In times of high and rising crude oil prices, the government holds refined oil prices artificially low in keeping with its goal of creating a harmonious society and avoiding civil unrest. In the period between late 2004 and late 2006, for example, Sinopec lost money for each barrel of oil its subsidiaries refined. While major international oil companies were raking in money during this period, Sinopec sold its products at below cost. Even though the government partially compensated for this by giving the company subsidies, Sinopec's profits nevertheless failed to reflect the growing demand for its products. Furthermore, the parent company can shift—and has shifted—monies from one subsidiary to another to improve balance sheets. In the end, when you buy shares of China Petroleum and Chemical Corporation or any other SOE, you really cannot have a clear picture of the company in which you are investing—even if the financial press is touting its profitability and attractive dividend.

How about private enterprises? Certainly, owners of these companies do not run them for the benefit of the state or to further the goal of a harmonious society. On the other hand, some do not run them for the benefit of shareholders, either. Rather, many privately run enterprises are controlled by extended families—and these folks often look after their own rather than their shareholders' interests. And then there are the newer start-ups, companies like Baidu.com, the Chinese version of Google and Yahoo. The brainchild of Robin Li, a Chinese national who emigrated to the United States as a computer science student and then worked as a programmer before returning to China, Baidu.com went public on the NASDAQ exchange on August 5, 2005, at $27 a share and closed at the end of the day at $122. While the share price leaped to three digits, so too did the P/E multiple—and therein lies the problem with many of the new, private Chinese companies that are being listed on U.S. exchanges. Although average valuations for some stocks may be moderate, such is not the case for all Chinese equities.

If you plan to buy individual Chinese stocks, you will be

buying either an SOE or a private company. Familiarize your-self with the risks associated with each kind of corporate structure before you do so. As we will point out below, this implies that investors need to be broadly diversified, and that most should consider only diversified portfolios of Chinese stocks rather than individual companies.

A SHORT PRIMER ON MUTUAL FUNDS

We believe that most investors will be better off participating in Chinese investments through mutual funds. These vehicles are very popular in the United States—an estimated 70 percent of all shares on U.S. exchanges are held by pension funds or institutions. Although most investors in the United States own whatever domestic stocks they may have through mutual funds, it is nevertheless appropriate at this point to review the different kinds of funds and their costs. Understanding the basic aspects of mutual funds will give you a clearer picture of the reasons behind some of our recommendations in the chapters that follow.

All mutual funds package together a portfolio of stocks and then sell shares that represent interests in that portfolio. According to the Investment Company Institute, close to 8,000 different mutual funds are offered for sale in the United States and their total value is close to $10 trillion. They are wonderful instruments, giving even small investors an opportunity to buy fully diversified portfolios that can easily be bought and sold. Trying to sift through so many offerings, however, can make picking the limited number of Chinese funds seem like a piece of cake! Fortunately, all mutual funds—including the 200 or so with a China component—can be further narrowed down by analyzing their structure, focus, and costs.

Structure

One important distinction between investment funds concerns whether they are "open-end" or "closed-end." Open-end mutual funds issue and redeem shares in the fund at the net asset value of a share at the close of the market on the day of the transaction. They are "open" because the number of shares in the fund can increase indefinitely. When more money comes in, the managers use the funds to buy more stocks and thus create more shares in the fund. Open-end funds are not traded on stock exchanges; rather, the purchase and redemption of shares are all handled directly by the sponsoring company.

Closed-end funds are listed on exchanges and are bought and sold—like other stocks—at any time during trading hours. The manager of the fund can trade stocks within the fund, but usually does not issue new shares after the initial offering. Thus, the term "closed-end" refers to the fact that once the fund is created and listed on an exchange, the number of shares in the fund is constant, as opposed to open-end, where the number fluctuates. Furthermore, shares in open-end funds are priced at net asset value, while the price of closed-end fund shares depends on what other investors are willing to pay for them, and thus can be either above (known as a "premium") or below (known as a "discount") net asset value. The Web site www.etfconnect.com provides daily updated data on the premiums and discounts of closed-end funds. (As the name suggests, it also provides data on exchange-traded funds, which are described below.)

Focus

Mutual funds, both open and closed, come in all sizes and shapes. There are some that concentrate on large "growth" stocks, others that specialize in small "value" stocks, those that concentrate on commodities, and those that highlight specific industries or regions. Name just about any arena in which to invest and there is probably a mutual fund dedicated to that area. For our purposes, there are geographical mutual funds that cover all emerging markets; mutual funds that specialize in Asia; mutual funds dedicated to each country surrounding the China periphery; and mutual funds dedicated solely to China. There are also mutual funds that cover energy, gold, and raw materials.

Costs

It is important to recognize that most mutual funds are created for the benefit of the sponsoring companies and not for the buyers of the fund. The sponsoring companies have made a lot of money from these funds—so much so that many fund management companies have actually gone public and sold shares in their operations. Open-end mutual fund managers generally reap riches by charging customers in two ways: by assessing a fee known as a "load fee," and by charging annual management and transaction fees, as well as marketing fees known as "12b-1" charges. These management costs make up the fund's expense ratio, which shows the annual percentage of a mutual fund share price that is devoted to covering the expenses of the sponsoring firm.

With the publication of numerous books and articles, including *A Random Walk Down Wall Street* in 1973, the general public in the last quarter of the twentieth century became aware of the onerous nature of the load fee and began to switch to no-load funds because they do not charge an initial fee. Both load and no-load funds, however, do assess annual management charges. The amount and extent of these charges vary dramatically from fund to fund. Some fund expense ratios can be as much as ten times that charged by other mutual funds. While closed-end funds, because they are traded on exchanges, do not assess a load fee (you do have to pay a broker's commission to buy them), they do have management expenses that affect the net returns of the shares.

When those mutual funds that had been collecting great rewards through their loads saw their profits evaporate as customers switched to no-load funds, they came up with a clever scheme to partially disguise their loads. They created classes of shares known as A, B, or C shares; depending on which class you buy, you can be charged either an up-front sales fee or a redemption fee when you sell, or both. The combined effect of all these charges means that mutual funds—over time—are rarely able to provide better results than the overall market. Indeed, our advice is to prefer funds that have no sales charges. Moreover, we favor funds that have relatively low annual expense charges.

Management fees, as well as the transaction costs of buying and selling stocks, tend to be considerably higher for international funds (and especially emerging market funds) than they are for funds specializing in U.S. stocks. It is far less costly to research the major companies in the United States than it is to conduct similar studies in foreign markets. Researching Chinese stocks poses particular challenges, and making transactions in small Chinese companies is far more difficult than trading shares of General Electric or ExxonMobil. Hence, the expense ratios for emerging market funds tend to be higher than for U.S. domestic funds. This is even true for the low-expense index mutual funds and ETFs described below.

Index Funds and Exchange-Traded Funds

Index funds are similar to open-end mutual funds in that they are not traded on exchanges but rather sold and redeemed by the sponsoring company. They differ markedly from open-end mutual funds in that they usually (but not always) have extremely low management costs and therefore relatively low expense ratios. Index funds, in fact, are often referred to as passive funds in that once a benchmark—such as the Standard & Poor's Index of 500 Stocks—is chosen, and a portfolio of the shares in that index is put together, there is for all intents and purposes no further management involvement as far as stock selection goes.

The first index fund was introduced by Vanguard in 1976 and mimicked the performance of the S&P 500. Since then, investors have flocked to index funds, plunking down hundreds of billions of dollars in these instruments over the years. Right after the index concept caught on, however, some investors began to quibble, pointing out that the S&P 500 only covered about three quarters of all stocks traded in the market. What about the remaining 25 percent, they asked, those future Microsofts and Googles that could be just starting out but were too small to make the top 500? More indexes rushed in to fill the gap. Today, there are indexes covering the entire market (the Dow Wilshire 5000), most of the market (the Russell 3000), market sectors (technology, financials), commodities (gold, energy), broad categories of companies (value, growth, high-dividend-paying), size of companies (corporate behemoths known as large caps and smaller firms called small caps), and more. None are traded on exchanges and all can only be redeemed at net asset value at the close of a trading day.

This last caused a wrinkle. When stock markets were plunging, holders of index mutual funds could not get their money out until the end of the day when the losses had really piled up instead of at the beginning when the decline started. Enter the exchange-traded fund (ETF). This is very similar to an index fund in that it is a low-expense, passively managed grouping of shares selected to meet specific criteria. The key difference, as the name implies, is that these funds are traded on exchanges, which means you can buy and sell them at any time during a trading day. The first ETF was introduced in Toronto in 1990. Three years later, the first ETF traded in the United States appeared on the American Stock Exchange and, as with the first index fund, was based on the S&P 500. Since then, almost 500 ETFs have been listed on U.S. exchanges.

ETFs are somewhat similar to closed-end funds in that they can sell at a premium or a discount to their net asset value. There is a mechanism, however, that prevents large premiums or discounts from occurring. Unlike regular closed-end funds, the number of shares in an ETF can be decreased or increased by redeeming the portfolio shares in kind or by delivering the basket of stocks making up the fund in exchange for ETF shares. Say that again? Even if we did, it would still be complicated. Those who like to keep things simple should just jump to the next paragraph; detail-oriented readers may wish to read on.

ETFs are created by institutional investors who deposit a specified group of securities into the fund. In return for this deposit, the investor receives shares in the fund, shares which can then be traded on stock exchanges. The institution can exchange the fund shares for the original securities or create new shares (called a creation unit) in the fund at any time. The privilege is not cheap. Just one creation unit for the China-centered ETFs discussed in this book ranges from 50,000 to 100,000 shares—and there are redemption or creation fees tacked on as well. Retail investors, those who buy the ETF shares on the market, are not entitled to the exchange privilege. It is this creation and redemption of ETF shares that tends to keep the ETF selling at net asset value. For example, suppose the ETF sold at a premium over the value of the shares in the fund. An investor could then sell short the ETF shares and present the constituent shares (which had been purchased at lower prices) to obtain new ETF shares to deliver against the (short) sale position. Such an arbitrage would produce a guaranteed profit. A similar arbitrage is possible if the ETF sold at a discount from net asset value. This is the mechanism that tends to keep the ETF selling very close to net asset value.

In addition to being traded at any time during market hours, ETFs have another advantage over mutual funds in that they tend to be more tax-efficient. As with index funds, there are all kinds of ETFs, and they cover a range of areas, including broad markets, single countries, market sectors, and commodities. We feel ETFs dedicated to China represent very attractive investments.

The Managed versus the Self-Directed Approach

If you've read this far and feel a headache coming on, you may well ask yourself: "Do I have time for all of this?" Or, perhaps, "Do I *want* to spend any time on this?" Since you're reading this book in the first place, it is a given that you are interested in investing in China. How far you take such interest is up to you and your priorities.

If you feel that you have neither the time nor the inclination to follow through on our recommendations in the chapters that follow, you will have to hire a financial adviser to do the work for you. And even here you are not scot-free as far as time and certainly money is concerned. Advisers expect to get paid for the work they do for you. All good advisers should first review your capacity for and attitude toward risk, and then recommend an asset allocation. If they don't, fire them and get an adviser who can guide you through these essential activities before you begin investing. The remainder of this chapter will help you get started with these important first investment steps.

THE CRUCIAL MATTER OF KNOWING YOUR RISK LEVEL

There's a saying that risk has its reward, and this is certainly true in investing. The more risk you take on, the more money you can make—or lose. Hundreds of years of investment experience stand as evidence of that essential truth. Common stocks have provided considerably higher returns than traditionally staid bonds. The riskiest common stocks—such as those of smaller and start-up companies—have provided higher returns than those of larger, more established firms. But these higher returns have come at the expense of far greater risks. For example, portfolios of large U.S. companies (such as those making up the S&P 500 Index) might, in a bad year, decline by 25 percent or more. Portfolios of smaller companies could lose 50 percent or more during bear markets. If you have accepted our argument that at least some China investments should be in your portfolio, you need to assess the degree of risk you are willing to assume, or, to put it in more sober tones, the amount you can afford to lose and still maintain your financial and mental health.

Capacity for risk

Risk capacity involves the amount of risk you can assume without endangering either your financial stability or your ability to maintain your accustomed lifestyle. An individual's capacity for risk depends crucially on age. A thirty-year-old with a well-paying job can afford to suffer investment reverses for two major reasons. First, her lifestyle will not be affected by investment losses because her employment income will continue to provide the money needed for living expenses. Second, the thirty-year-old investing for retirement will have many years to ride out the ups and downs of stock prices. She won't have to liquidate portfolio assets during a bear market in order to fund necessary living expenses.

Contrast the situation of the thirty-year-old with that of a retired seventy-year-old, who has some health problems, and who is counting on the investments in his retirement nest egg to provide for living expenses. For people meeting these criteria, investment reverses will undoubtedly affect their living standards. They have neither employment income nor long periods to ride out market reverses. They have very limited capacity for risk.

Attitude toward risk

Attitude toward risk has led many people astray because they can only think of the reward side of the equation. Let there be no illusions about the returns from equities. They come at the expense of considerable volatility. In October 1987, the U.S. stock market sank by 23 percent on a single day; in the first nineteen days of the month, almost $1 trillion was lost. In a relatively short period afterwards, from March 2000 to October 2002, the overall U.S. market declined by 40 percent. You think that's bad. Smaller companies, high-tech firms, and emerging market stocks did even worse. In general, emerging markets tend to be twice as volatile as the U.S. market.

There are investors who literally get sick when experiencing such volatility and the loss (even if it is temporary) of a significant share of their investment portfolio. As the old saying goes, if you can't stand the heat, get out of the kitchen. If watching your portfolio decline at times by 30 to 40 percent or even more is unbearably painful, then cut back your alloca-tion to equities. A friend of J. P. Morgan's once asked for advice about what to do with his stock portfolio because it was so volatile that he could not sleep at night. Morgan's response was swift and succinct: "Sell down to the sleeping point."

A real-life example

An actual example of how an investment in a successful Chinese mutual fund would have fared over a ten-year period provides a realistic picture of the riskiness of Chinese stocks. The fund is called the Templeton China World Fund and is run by Mark Mobius, an authority on investing in emerging markets in general and China in particular. The fund invests up to 80 percent of its assets in "China companies"—defined as companies that derive at least 50 percent of their revenues from goods sold or produced in China, or have 50 percent of their assets in China. The companies may have their offices in the People's Republic of China or in Hong Kong or Taiwan. As China funds go, this fund is conservatively run.

Suppose you invested $100 in the Templeton China World Fund on January 1, 1997. By January 1, 2007, you would have been holding an investment worth over $250 assuming that all dividends and distributions had been reinvested in the fund. Your average annual return would have been very close to 10 percent per year—certainly an attractive return. But you would have endured a roller-coaster ride along the way. Two years after you made your investment, you would have lost almost half your money. It took six and a half years before you broke even. Only if you had the financial capacity to ride out the storm and the stomach to endure consistent losses for months on end would you have been able to enjoy the benefits of the investment. Unfortunately, most investors probably did not earn the generous 10 percent return the fund provided over

EXHIBIT 8.1   *Results from a $100 Investment in the Templeton China World Fund (dividends and distributions reinvested)*

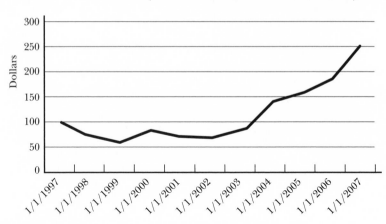

SOURCE: Templeton China World Fund annual reports.

ten years because like the majority of stock buyers, they rushed to put their money in after a big price rise and sold out after a big decline. Exhibit 8.1 charts the results of a $100 investment made on January 1, 1997. Don't invest in China unless you are prepared to accept similar volatility in the future.

THE IMPORTANCE OF ASSET ALLOCATION

Once you've matched your capacity for and attitude toward risk, it is time to review your asset allocation. This involves looking at the entire spectrum of your investments—stocks, bonds, real estate, and cash—and then deciding what percentage each should occupy within your total net worth.

Asset allocation by investment categories

Generally, asset allocation guidelines are constructed by four or five age categories, with people in the younger groups being able to take on more risk than those who are older. We present an even simpler scheme in Exhibit 8.2, in which we divide those with assets into two groups: the *accumulators*, who are generally salaried, younger adults; and the *spenders*, who are generally older adults dipping into their retirement nest eggs. Many of the latter are, in fact, required by law to take withdrawals from their tax-deferred retirement plans. The basic idea behind these allocations is that the risk capacity for the accumulators is far greater than that for the spenders. Accumulators, for example, can own growth stocks that don't pay dividends. Spenders, those living off their nest eggs, need steady income; their equity portions should be tilted in the direction of common stocks that pay dividends. Obviously, different individual circumstances require adjustments to these guidelines. A seventy-five-year-old man with substantial assets may wish to give his assets to his children and grandchil-

EXHIBIT 8.2 *Broad Age-Related Asset Allocation Charts*

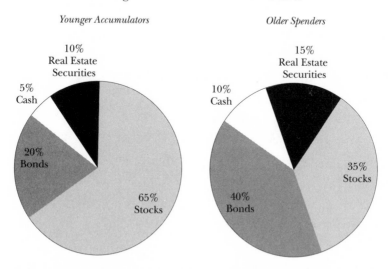

Bonds include a diversified portfolio of corporate as well as Treasury Inflation Protection Securities.

SOURCE: Authors' recommendations.

dren. His investment period will tend to be a long rather than short one, resulting in a larger concentration of equities. A couple who are both in their thirties may be saving to make a down payment on a house in a year or so, and thus a large concentration in equities would be inappropriate. Monies set aside to fund major purchases such as a house or college tuition should be invested in safe bonds with a maturity that matches the date when the funds will be needed. In short, you should consider the allocations in Exhibit 8.2 as rough guides that need to be adjusted for your needs and circumstances.

How China fits into the asset allocation picture

For all practical purposes, stocks are the only reasonable investment vehicle for those wishing to profit from China's booming economy. Currently, bonds are restricted to mainland residents, and the real estate investment opportunities are not only quite limited (as we saw in chapter 7) but also generally speculative. The critical question we now need to address is, What percentage of the stocks in a portfolio should be invested in China? Again, the fundamental principle of valuation must inform the answer: Risk has its reward. We believe Chinese equities can provide higher returns than those available from stock markets in the developed world. But Chinese stocks are extraordinarily volatile—soaring up and plunging down more than twice as fast as U.S. stocks. Chinese market gyrations make the fluctuations in North American and Western European markets look tame in comparison. How would you feel if the portion of your portfolio devoted to China declined by 50 percent? A thirty-year-old with a stomach for risk taking might reason, "I can ride it out—the long run looks rosy." But the seventy-year-old, dependent on his portfolio for living expenses, is unlikely to accept such a risk.

What follows are broad guidelines that present our suggestions for the proportion of an equity portfolio that should be devoted to China. Remember that these are stated in terms of the proportion of equities—not the proportion of the total portfolio. Thus, if a portfolio consists of 50 percent equities and 50 percent bonds and we recommend that 10 percent of the equities be devoted to China, then only 5 percent of the total portfolio will be invested in the China market. And we define "the China market" broadly so that both China-based companies and funds and non-China-based firms and funds that profit from the nation's growth are included.

EXHIBIT 8.3 *Percentage of Equities That Should Be Allocated to a China Strategy*

	CAPACITY	
ATTITUDE	Low risk capacity (%)	High risk capacity (%)
Willing to assume the risk	5–10	15–20
Very risk-adverse	0–5	5–10

A mixed strategy of direct and indirect investments somewhat reduces the overall risk of including China in your portfolio, as we will explain in chapter 12. Thus, for even the very risk-averse, with little capacity for risk taking, up to 5 percent of the portfolio equities could be devoted to a China strategy. For those who have a high capacity for risk, 20 percent of the equities in their portfolio can be devoted to China. Indeed, we are sufficiently bullish on China that we believe the greatest risk to any portfolio is to exclude China altogether.

A SUMMING UP

China is the investment place to be, and we believe that those who invest now will be generously rewarded in future years.

But before you commit your money to Chinese enterprises, you need to have some basic understanding of their structure. That's what we have attempted to do in this chapter. Never forget that Chinese companies march to a different tune than American companies. Many are controlled by the government and others are beholden to closed circles of family members. Still, there is and has been a lot of money made from these firms. Most important of all, become aware of your risk tolerance and how your assets are allocated. Perhaps it might also be wise to remember the Wall Street adage: "There are bulls and there are bears, but pigs get slaughtered." If you think Chinese investments are the way to get rich quick, with all gain and no pain, you may be in for a rude disappointment.

Now that you have completed the necessary preparations for investing in China, it's time for us to describe specific investment strategies to meet your personal objectives and situation.

CHAPTER 9

The Homegrown Strategy

"There's no place like home."
—LAST LINE IN THE MOVIE *THE WIZARD OF OZ*

HUNDREDS OF MILLIONS OF DOLLARS: these are the amounts that major corporations are pouring into China to profit from the country's ever-expanding economy. They are also the staggering profits that many institutional investors have made by investing in initial public offerings (IPOs) and by taking equity positions in China's companies four and five years ago. Goldman Sachs's record in this regard is hard to beat; it reaped billions—that's billion with an "s"—for its role in taking the Industrial & Commercial Bank of China public in 2006. Without question, the most profitable way to tap into China's riches is to invest directly in the country and its enterprises, and that's what the so-called "big guys" are doing.

But, as we have repeated time and again throughout this book, risk has its reward. While large corporations routinely make bad investing decisions, they can employ battalions of public relations specialists to put a positive spin on such losses or bury the bad news in a wad of statistics that are appended to annual reports. Individual investors, the so-called "little guys" like us, do not have such options. For the individual, investing directly in China is fraught with peril—the peril of losing a lot of money.

We have taken two approaches to investing directly in China. In this chapter, "The Homegrown Strategy," we cover a range of funds that own shares in Chinese companies. Because of the diversification that these funds offer, we believe that this is the most prudent way for individuals to make direct investments in Chinese securities. In chapter 11, "The Go for Broke Strategy," we describe how investors with iron-clad stomachs for assuming risk might purchase stocks in individual Chinese companies.

In light of the unique nature of the Chinese stock market, we have divided this chapter into two major parts. The first section presents our investment recommendations for those with access to the Shanghai and Shenzhen markets. The second section describes how to profit from China's economic boom through ownership of Chinese equities listed outside mainland China.

SHARES TRADED ON THE SHANGHAI AND SHENZHEN MARKETS

Both open-end and closed-end investment funds are available in mainland China. Open-end mutual funds are not traded on stock exchanges but are rather sold by a sponsoring company at a price equivalent to the net asset value of the shares at the end of the trading day. All sorts of fees—detrimental to your profits—can be attached to such funds. Even so, within the mainland China exchanges, open-end mutual funds investing in A shares—those listed on the Shanghai and Shenzhen stock exchanges—have handily beaten broad market indices. We attribute this to the indigenous knowledge of the Chinese fund managers as to which companies are corrupt and particularly risky and which ones are not. Because the local markets are far from efficient, we strongly prefer active management to access portfolios of A shares. A look at the statistics makes our point. In the years 1998–2006, managed funds posted an average annual return of 20.75 percent; the Shanghai and the Shenzhen exchanges came in at 16.20 percent.

It is unfortunate that many individual investors in China have considered—not without reason—their stock markets to be little more than gambling casinos, with speculation the main performance feature. The taint of corruption has also been associated with several fund managers. This is changing, with increased monitoring by the exchanges themselves and with regulatory crackdowns, yet selecting a good mainland-based mutual fund still can be a bit tricky. In Exhibit 9.1, we present a sample of actively managed, open-end mutual funds that have enjoyed excellent records and have scandal-free managements. Several are jointly managed by local companies and well-known international financial institutions, like JP Morgan Chase, Invesco, and ABN Amro. We believe that individual investors in China will be better served by owning a managed fund than by attempting to pick stock market winners for themselves.

There is, however, an even better strategy available for investors with access to the A-share market. When available at substantial discounts, managed closed-end investment companies are the best vehicles to extract profit from the A-share market.

Closed-end funds are bought and sold on stock exchanges and can sell at a premium or a discount to their net asset value. We highly recommend buying closed-end funds at a discount because any time an investor can buy a portfolio of

EXHIBIT 9.1 *Selected Chinese Open-End Equity Mutual Funds Holding A Shares*

FUND NAME	2005–06 TRAILING GROWTH (%)	MORNINGSTAR RATING (JAN. 2007)
Fuguo Tianyi Value (Code 100020)	167.43	★★★★★
E Fund Strategy Growth (Code 110002)	151.28	★★★★
Shanghai Trust–JPMorgan China Adva (Code 375010)	169.99	★★★★★
Invesco–Great Wall Domestic Growth (Code 260104)	182.20	★★★★★
Harvest Growth (Code 070001)	125.78	★★★
Guangfa Jufu (Code 27001)	129.74	★★★
Fortis–Haitong (Code 519011)	118.13	★★★
ABN Amro–Teda (Code 162202)	137.82	★★★★

SOURCE: Bosera Asset Management Co.

common stocks at a discount, that investor can potentially obtain a return that will exceed the return earned by the portfolio. Although this does not hold if the discount widens, it is true even if the discount does not disappear or narrow. Suppose an investor bought a common stock portfolio worth $100 and paying a $3 dividend but could buy the portfolio for only $60—a discount of 40 percent. Even if the discount stayed at 40 percent until the time the investor sold the shares, such an investment would earn an enhanced return. Buying the fund at $100 net asset value would produce a 3 percent return from the $3 dividend. (We ignore any growth in the value of the shares.) But the buyer of the discounted fund at $60 gets an augmented 5 percent dividend yield: $3/$60 = 5 percent.

The advantage of buying mainland China closed-end funds at a discount is even greater. The funds we recommend have provisions to be liquidated at a specified future date. When the fund is liquidated, it will sell all its holdings (or become an open-end fund) and redeem the outstanding shares at net asset value. Several funds in the table below have liquidation dates as early as 2014. Thus, investors buying them at a discount will not only get the advantage of a higher dividend yield, but also the extra return when the fund is liquidated at full net asset value. In Exhibit 9.2 we show a number of heavily discounted, large closed-end funds run by reputable investment management companies. For mainland Chinese or those international investors who can exercise QFII quotas, these funds represent an extraordinarily good buy.

A warning is in order, however. Investors should be aware that the discounts on these closed-end funds are highly variable. When Malkiel, Mei, and Yang first recommended the strategy of buying discounted closed-end funds at the end of 2005, the discounts ranged between 40 and 50 percent. At

EXHIBIT 9.2 *Chinese Closed-End Funds Selling at Deep Discounts (Jan. 1, 2007)*

FUND NAME	SCHEDULED LIQUIDATION DATE	DISCOUNT (%)	MARKET CAP (100M YUAN)	INVESTMENT OBJECTIVE
Hongyang	12/9/2016	-29.15	25.00	G&V*
Tongqian	8/28/2016	-28.04	25.00	Growth
Jinghong	5/5/2014	-27.09	29.68	Growth
Hanxing	12/20/2014	-26.47	33.48	G&V
Tongsheng	11/5/2014	-26.45	40.14	Value
Jingfu	12/30/2014	-25.60	43.35	G&V

*G&V = Growth & Value

SOURCE: Bosera Asset Management Co.; Lipper.

the time this book goes to press, discounts range between 25 and 30 percent. One of the paradoxes of investment advice is that when people act on a recommendation, they tend to diminish its value. No purchase of these closed-end funds should be made unless the discounts remain substantial. Investors who buy closed-end funds at small or zero discounts run the risk of losing money if the discount widens in the future.

This is true both for mainland and for international investors. In September 2006, for example, Morgan Stanley used its QFII quota to introduce a closed-end fund on the New York Stock Exchange that consisted primarily of equities sold on the Shanghai and Shenzhen exchanges. This was the first time that outside investors could easily access the mainland China stocks through a U.S. exchange. At the time the fund came out, news about the meteoric rise of the mainland markets was just beginning to spread. The Morgan Stanley China A Share Fund (ticker symbol CAF) took off two months after its inauguration and rose 50 percent within three months. At the start of 2007, however, investors became nervous about the steep rise in the mainland Chinese markets, and widespread selling took place. Within the space of a week or so, CAF lost 10 percent of its value. In its first nine months of existence, CAF gyrated from a premium of 16 percent of net asset value to a discount of 16 percent. This fund should not be purchased by U.S. investors unless it is selling at a substantial discount from its net asset value.

This leads us to a second warning. The Chinese stock market is extraordinarily volatile. In 2006 and 2007, the market was one of the best performing in the world. However, the market also had several quite sharp corrections. Markets are subject to inexorable tendencies to revert to the mean. This means that eventually they balance out to their true value;

thus, overpriced markets will ultimately decline and underpriced markets will rise. A strategy of making commitments to Chinese equities gradually over time (rather than all at once) will lessen the chance that you buy in at the top of a period of euphoria.

Shares Traded on International Markets

Some of the companies that are listed in the A-share market are also listed internationally. Indeed, in 2006, twenty-four companies with a total market capitalization of over 600 billion yuan had shares traded in both the mainland and the Hong Kong share markets. In 2007 the number of companies and the value of shares increased further. Other top-notch Chinese companies are not listed in the mainland exchanges but only in international exchanges such as those in Hong Kong, New York, and London.

There is convincing evidence that the large Chinese companies listed in Hong Kong and New York tend to be stronger and better companies than those only listed in Shanghai and Shenzhen. Exhibit 9.3 supports this finding. The top part of Exhibit 9.3 shows that the average 13.38 percent annual earnings growth rate for an index of A shares, though quite respectable, lagged behind the earnings growth rate of both the Hong Kong traded shares (as represented by the FTSE/Xinhia Index of 25 H Shares) and the shares of China companies listed on U.S. stock exchanges. Both the Hong Kong and the U.S.-listed shares enjoyed earnings growth over three times as fast as the growth rate for the domestically listed shares.

Another way to compare the attractiveness of companies is to look at the return on equity (ROE), which is the ratio of company earnings to the stated value of the equity

EXHIBIT 9.3   *The Better Companies Have Listed in Hong Kong and New York*

Earnings growth has lagged for A shares

DATE	ANNUAL EARNINGS GROWTH OF A SHARES (%)	ANNUAL EARNINGS GROWTH OF FTSE 25 H SHARES (%)	ANNUAL EARNINGS GROWTH OF ADRS (%)
2000–06	13.38	30.73	29.14

Return on equity is lower for A shares

DATE	ROE OF SHANGHAI A SHARES (%)	ROE OF FTSE 25 H SHARES (%)	ROE OF ADR SHARES (%)
2000–06	10.29	14.80	16.00

SOURCE: Bosera Asset Management Co.

invested in the business. The bottom half of the exhibit shows that the ROE for shares listed outside mainland China exceeded the ROE for mainland-listed shares. Without question, the most profitable and fastest growing Chinese companies list in Hong Kong and New York, thus allowing international investors easy access to these companies for portfolio investments.

The bottom line, then, is that dollar-denominated mutual funds focused on China offer a double bonus: they are easy to buy, and they are composed of solidly profitable China companies traded on the Hong Kong and New York markets. As with all mutual funds, they offer investors a diversified portfolio that helps to minimize investment risk. Based on their relatively low expense ratios and reasonable past performance, we have selected seven no-load, open-end U.S. mutual funds for individual investors; these are shown in Exhibit 9.4. The expense ratios are higher than a typical mutual fund investing in U.S. securities because of the added expenses of research in foreign countries and the higher trading costs in buying shares in markets such as Hong Kong.

EXHIBIT 9.4 *Open-End, No-Load U.S. Mutual Funds Investing in Chinese Securities, May 2007*

FUND NAME	MORNINGSTAR RATING	EXPENSE RATIO (%)	ASSETS ($MM)	TRAILING 5-YR AVERAGE ANNUAL RETURNS (%)
AllianceBernstein Greater China	★★★	2.02	112	23.21
Columbia Greater China Z	★★★★	1.47	246	22.84
Dreyfus Premier Greater China	★★★★	1.88	818	26.78
Fidelity China Region	★★	1.08	948	15.23
Templeton China World	★★★	2.06	906	27.83
Guinness Atkinson China	★★★	1.59	154	20.04
Matthews China	★★★★	1.26	1,109	23.18

SOURCE: http://quicktake.morningstar.com/fund; http://finance.yahoo.com.

Although China-focused, closed-end funds listed on American exchanges have neither the set liquidation dates nor the extremely large discounts of the mainland China closed-end funds, they represent an advantageous purchase when they are selling at substantial discounts. These funds often hold shares trading on the Hong Kong Stock Exchange, shares which are extremely difficult and expensive for individual investors to buy through a U.S. broker. As with all funds, closed-end funds also provide diversification benefits. In the case of the Templeton Dragon Fund, for example, you are purchasing not only a portfolio of stocks of Chinese compa-

EXHIBIT 9.5   *Closed-End U.S. Funds, March 2007*

FUND NAME	PRICE ($)	MORNING- STAR RATING	PREMIUM/ DISCOUNT	EXPENSE RATIO (%)	TRAILING 5-YR AVERAGE ANNUAL RETURNS (%)
Jardine Fleming China Region (JFC)	18.95	★★★	-13.5	2.08	23.12
Greater China (GCH)	24.63	★★★★	-9.9	2.09	23.09
China Fund (CHN)	30.55	★★★★	-12.7	1.38	26.91
Templeton Dragon Fund (TDF)	23.16	★★★★	-10.7	1.52	31.73

SOURCE: http://quicktake.morningstar.com/fund; http://finance.yahoo.com.

nies but also a stake in Chinese property development companies when you buy a share of the fund. The www.etfconnect .com Web site presents data on thirteen closed-end funds focused on China, and it daily updates their discount or premium to net asset value. The Closed-End Fund Association at www.cefa.com also provides information on several more funds with large concentrations of Chinese investments.

In Exhibit 9.5, we list four closed-end funds that have been selected on the basis of their past performance, attractive discounts, and relatively low expense ratios. We strongly prefer that you buy closed-end funds when they sell at attractive discounts. These premiums and discounts vary substantially from day to day. If these closed-end funds are selling at only tiny discounts (less than 5 percent) or at premiums, you should buy equivalent open-end funds instead. If the discount widens in the future, your return will suffer.

Index investing: Three popular indexes

Index investing is a passive, low-cost method of profiting from efficient stock markets. The key word is *"efficient,"* and the mainland China share markets have yet to behave efficiently, so we do not recommend indexed investments in the local A-share market. However, the Chinese share markets in Hong Kong and the United States are reasonably efficient. Therefore, index investing, either through mutual funds or exchange-traded funds, is a reasonable strategy for investors looking for a low-cost, diversified method to access the stocks of Chinese companies traded in world markets. As this book goes to press, there are three widely recognized indexes of Hong Kong listed stocks that are the basis for funds that can be bought to tap into the riches of China. Recently, several more indexes, each incorporating mainland China companies trading on U.S. stock exchanges, have been created.

Hang Seng Index. The benchmark of the Hong Kong Stock Market, the Hang Seng Index is one of the best-known indexes in Asia and is widely used by fund managers as their performance benchmark (much as U.S. managers use the Standard & Poor's 500 Stock Index as their benchmark). As this book goes to press, the Hang Seng Index consists of forty companies that account for about two thirds of the total market capitalization of all stocks listed on the Hong Kong exchange. You can check on the daily performance of the index by searching for ^HSI at online financial Web sites such as Yahoo Finance. Generally speaking, when the financial press reports on the Hong Kong market, it is basing its report on the Hang Seng Index.

Some of the companies in the index are not listed on mainland China exchanges. Companies that are listed on the mainland as well as in Hong Kong must have completed their share reform in order to be included. Sinopec, for example, completed its share reform in summer 2006, and was not included in the index until fall 2006. In addition, the financial performance of all companies is carefully scrutinized before they are included. HSI Ltd., which constructs the Hang Seng Index, also offers many other indexes derived from the Hong Kong Stock Exchange. Among these is the Hang Seng Composite Index, which includes 200 companies that account for about 90 percent of the exchange's market capitalization.

Several Hang Seng ETFs trade on the Hong Kong Stock Exchange, but these are not readily available to U.S. investors. The U.S.-based State Street Global Advisors does offer its large clients a Hang Seng Index Strategy in which the firm will purchase each security in the same capitalization weight as it appears in the index. Truly sophisticated investors— some might wish to use the term "high-flying gamblers"—can also buy and sell Hang Seng futures online through www.xpresstrade.com. For the most part, investors wishing to purchase an indexed portfolio of Chinese stocks will have to do so through one of the ETFs described below.

MSCI Hong Kong Index. There is a Hong Kong stock index that is easily accessible for purchase by international investors. Morgan Stanley Capital International, Inc. (MSCI), is an international leader in the creation of market indices. The firm's global equity benchmarks are the basis for an annual $3 trillion in sales, and the company has constructed several for China, Hong Kong, and the China periphery. The one most pertinent to this book is the MSCI Hong Kong Index, which covers most of the stocks traded on the Hong Kong Stock Exchange. It is the basis for the Fidelty China Fund and for the iShares MSCI–Hong Kong Index ETF (ticker symbol EWH) described below.

FTSE/Xinhua China 25 Index. FTSE/Xinhua Ltd. has also created several China-centered indexes. This firm is a joint venture of FTSE, an independent company owned by the *Financial Times* and the London Stock Exchange, and Xinhua Finance Ltd., a Hong Kong–based financial services and media company. One of their indexes, the FTSE/Xinhua Hong Kong Index, is the benchmark for China's Social Security Fund.

Their most widely known index is the FTSE/Xinhua China 25. It is the basis for an ETF traded under the ticker symbol FXI. This consists of the twenty-five largest and most liquid—without regard to share reform—Chinese stocks trading on the Hong Kong Stock Exchange. In a further differentiation from the Hang Seng Index, which is a market capitalization index (the larger the company, the greater its weight), the FTSE/Xinhua China 25 Index caps individual constituents at 10 percent in order to avoid overconcentration in any one stock. The holdings are reviewed quarterly and adjusted accordingly with regard to concentration. Even with this periodic rebalancing, however, FXI is a relatively concentrated index, with the top ten holdings accounting for approximately 60 percent of the index's total capitalization.

Additional China Indexes. With the China market taking off, other companies have sought to profit from creating China indexes. Given the unusual nature of company listings—generally, those on the mainland are closed to outside investors and those on foreign exchanges are closed to mainland citizens—there is a great deal of variety in these indexes.

The Halter USX China consists of all China companies—including some very small and dubious ones—traded in the United States. Created in 1994, this index is the basis of the PGJ exchange-traded fund, described below. A year later, Standard & Poor's and Citigroup Global Markets worked together to created the BMI China Index. This consists of over one hundred companies traded on either the U.S. stock exchanges or the Hong Kong Stock Exchange or both, and is the basis for the GXC exchange-traded fund, described below. The NASDAQ Stock Market institution jumped into the game on May 7, 2007, when it introduced the NASDAQ China Index. In one sense, this is the U.S. ADR equivalent of the FTSE/Xinhua China 25 Index in that it consists of only thirty mainland and Hong Kong–listed China stocks that are traded on the major exchanges in the United States. All are traded heavily and have a market capitalization of $600 billion. As this book went to press, there was no ETF based on the index, although news of such an ETF was expected to be announced soon.

Four ETFs

Exchange-traded funds, described in chapter 8, have proven to be a low-cost, extremely popular vehicle for investing in a wide number of areas. The following section describes four China-centered funds that currently trade on U.S. exchanges. Given the attraction of investing in China, we believe the number of China-dedicated ETFs will increase in the future.

EWH ETF. Introduced on March 12, 1996, this is the oldest of the China-centered ETFs. It is widely known by its ticker symbol, EWH, rather than its long-winded official title of iShares MSCI–Hong Kong Index Fund. That official title, however, tells you the name of the index on which the fund is based. As such, the fund holds China-based companies that are incorporated in Hong Kong, rather than companies that are incorporated in China itself. However, many of the companies in the index, such as Hutchison Whampoa, do most of their business in China. And, yes, that is the Esprit apparel

EXHIBIT 9.6 *Top Ten Holdings of EWH, April 2007*

FUND NAME	% NET ASSETS
Hutchison Whampoa Ltd.	8.74
Cheung Kong Holdings Ltd.	8.35
Sun Hung Kai Properties Ltd.	6.82
CLP Holdings Ltd.	5.62
Esprit Holdings Ltd.	5.39
Hang Seng Bank Ltd.	4.56
Swire Pacific Ltd.—Class A	4.55
Hong Kong Exchanges and Clearing Ltd.	4.32
BOC Hong Kong Holdings Ltd.	3.90
Bank of East Asia Ltd.	3.80
% of Assets in Top 10 Holdings	56.05

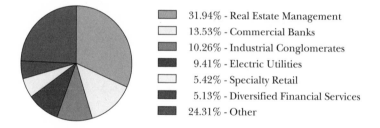

31.94% - Real Estate Management
13.53% - Commercial Banks
10.26% - Industrial Conglomerates
9.41% - Electric Utilities
5.42% - Specialty Retail
5.13% - Diversified Financial Services
24.31% - Other

SOURCE: MarketWatch from Dow Jones.

and housewares company listed among the top ten holdings. A true representative of the global economy, Esprit was founded in San Francisco; is headquartered in Ratingen, West Germany; and is listed on the Hong Kong Stock Exchange (with a secondary listing on the London Stock Exchange), where its Financial and Investor Relations offices are located.

Of the four funds reviewed here, EWH has the highest trading volume—well over 1 million shares a day—as well as the highest dividend payout and the lowest expense ratio (0.54 percent). In contrast to the other ETFs, EWH is heavily concentrated in Hong Kong property development companies, companies which are reaping huge profits from their activities in mainland China. For those who would like to take a conservative position in China's real estate market, this ETF would be an appropriate choice. Indeed, EWH is one of the few feasible ways for international investors to take a position in Chinese property companies.

FXI ETF. On October 4, 2004, Barclays Global Investors introduced the iShares FTSE/Xinhua China 25 Index Exchange Traded Fund. Fortunately for all concerned, this fund quickly became known by its simpler name, the FXI ETF, and indeed, its New York Stock Exchange ticker symbol is FXI. As the name implies, this ETF closely follows the FTSE/Xinhua China 25 Index.

The FXI exchange-traded fund is an excellent way to gain easy access to Chinese shares available to international investors. FXI also allows international investors the opportunity to participate in companies that are only listed on the Hong Kong Stock Exchange. It is extremely difficult, for example, for international investors to purchase shares in COSCO Pacific Ltd., a huge container-related shipping conglomerate, because the company is only listed on the Hong Kong Stock Exchange. When you buy FXI, however, you are buying a piece of COSCO Pacific Ltd., as well as a portion of twenty-four other major Chinese companies.

Note that over 70 percent of the FXI ETF is concentrated in the Financials, Telecommunications, and Energy sectors. This gives it a quite different composition from the EWH ETF.

PGJ ETF. On December 9, 2004, just two months after the FXI ETF debut, the PowerShares Golden Dragon Halter USX China made its appearance. Mercifully, again, this mouthful is widely known by its ticker symbol, PGJ. PGJ differs signifi-

EXHIBIT 9.7 *Top Ten Holdings of FXI, March 2007*

NAME	% NET ASSETS
China Mobile Ltd.	10.13
PetroChina Co. Ltd.	8.75
Industrial & Commercial Bank of China Asia	7.65
China Life Insurance Co. Ltd.	6.24
Bank of China Ltd.	5.82
China Construction Bank	4.48
China Petroleum & Chemical Corp.	4.16
Ping An Insurance Group Co. of China	4.14
CNOOC Ltd.	4.13
China Telecom Corp. Ltd.	3.96
% of Assets in Top 10 Holdings	59.46

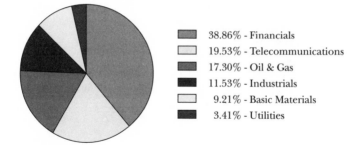

38.86% - Financials
19.53% - Telecommunications
17.30% - Oil & Gas
11.53% - Industrials
9.21% - Basic Materials
3.41% - Utilities

SOURCE: MarketWatch from Dow Jones.

cantly from EWH and FXI in that it only includes U.S. exchange–listed companies that derive a majority of their revenues from mainland China. Thus, you do not own a piece of COSCO Pacific Ltd. or any other company listed only in Hong Kong when you buy PGJ. PGJ also differs from FXI in that it includes over sixty companies in its holdings.

And PGJ differs from the above two ETFs in another, unfortunately detrimental, aspect. PowerShares, the PGJ sponsor, argues that its ETF is a safe way for U.S. investors to get expo-

EXHIBIT 9.8 *Top Ten Holdings of PGJ, May 2007*

FUND NAME	% NET ASSETS
PetroChina Co. Ltd.	6.17
China Mobile Ltd.	5.70
Aluminum Corp. of China Ltd.	5.04
Huaneng Power International Inc.	4.79
China Life Insurance Co. Ltd.	4.70
China Unicom Ltd.	4.67
China Petroleum & Chemical Corp.	4.60
Suntech Power Holdings Co. Ltd.	4.50
CNOOC Ltd.	4.42
China Netcom Group Corp. (Hong Kong) Ltd.	4.33
% of Assets in Top 10 Holdings	48.92

24.11% - Energy
22.54% - Telecommunications
13.10% - Internet
9.04% - Basic Materials
5.80% - Technology
4.70% - Utilities
20.71% - Other

SOURCE: MarketWatch from Dow Jones.

sure to China because it only includes stocks listed on U.S. exchanges. But PGJ has its critics as well. Not all of the PGJ stocks are traded on the New York Stock Exchange or the NASDAQ market; some are thinly traded in the over-the-counter or "pink sheet" markets described earlier. Some of the issues in the index—and indeed the poorest performers—were formed by mergers engineered by Tim Halter, the creator of the index on which PGJ is based. To make matters

EXHIBIT 9.9 *Top Ten Holdings of GXC, March 2007*

FUND NAME	% NET ASSETS
China Mobile Ltd.	12.33
PetroChina Co. Ltd.	6.83
China Life Insurance	5.85
China Construction Bank	5.14
Industrial & Commercial Bank of China Asia	4.59
CNOOC Ltd.	4.07
China Petroleum & Chemical Corp.	4.00
Bank of China Ltd.	3.03
China Shenhua Energy	2.34
China Telecom Corp. Ltd.	1.93
% of Assets in Top 10 Holdings	50.11

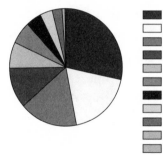

Financials (28.535)
Energy (18.64%)
Telecommunication Services (16.47%)
Industrials (11.32%)
Materials (7.01%)
Consumer Discretionary (6.18%)
Information Technology (4.59%)
Consumer Staples (3.52%)
Utilities (2.72%)
Unassigned (0.87%)
Health Care (0.15%)

SOURCE: MarketWatch from Dow Jones.

worse, financial journalists from *Barron's* and *The Wall Street Journal* have suggested that Halter's firm sold some stocks right after inclusion in the index boosted their prices. While the conflict of interest suggestions are troublesome, the stocks associated with Halter constitute only a small fraction of the total holdings in the index. Halter has also suggested that rules are now in place that will prevent the occurrence of any future conflicts.

GXC ETF. On March 9, 2007, State Street Global Advisors introduced its version of a China-centered ETF under the ticker symbol GXC. Officially titled SDPR S&P China ETF, it consists of both H and N shares and has close to 200 companies in its market-weighted index. This last means that a company's proportion in the index is determined by its relative size to other companies; at the time of its introduction, shares of China Mobile constituted more than 12 percent of the holdings. It differs from FXI, which includes only the twenty-five largest companies traded as H shares and which limits the holdings of any one company to no more than 10 percent of the entire portfolio. It also differs from PGJ in that it does not include low-volume N shares traded on the U.S. pink sheets.

The composition of GXC is reviewed quarterly and adjusted if the market weighting of any one company has changed significantly. This ETF has one of the lowest expense ratios: at the time of its introduction, this was set at 0.6 percent. Because of its low expense ratio and the broad composition of its holdings, we feel this is the best of the China-centered ETFs currently available.

A Summing Up

In this chapter we have presented practical strategies that enable investors to build portfolios of Chinese companies. For those with access to mainland China, managed closed-end funds represent the optimal strategy and are available at substantial discounts. Moreover, the closed-end funds we recommend have maturity dates when the funds are to be liquidated and the discounts will disappear.

Since many of the strongest and most profitable China companies trade on international exchanges, foreign investors have broad opportunities for purchasing attractive portfolios of homegrown Chinese companies. Indeed, Chinese companies that trade in international markets appear to be more efficiently priced than those traded in local Chinese markets, and at least the larger companies appear to be among the strongest Chinese companies available for investment.

Many investors will find that mutual funds and closed-end funds provide attractive vehicles for gaining exposure to Chinese companies. The funds offer broad diversification and easy one-stop shopping. They can also enable the individual investor to gain access to the Hong Kong stock market. Diversified funds are essential for investors who want to moderate the substantial risk involved in buying individual company stocks.

As this book goes to press, the stocks in the four ETFs focused on China sell at price-earnings multiples in line with those on world equity markets, but have considerably better long-run growth prospects. EWH is representative of the Hong Kong market, which includes many companies profiting handsomely from their mainland China activities, and has a large real estate exposure. FXI is representative of the twenty-five largest Chinese companies on the Hong Kong Stock Exchange. PGJ covers a universe of U.S.-listed, China-based companies. While there are some definite issues with regard to the smaller holdings in PGJ, it has nevertheless handily outperformed U.S. stock averages in recent years. FXI's performance has been particularly outstanding. GXC, the newest China ETF on the block, covers both Hong Kong and U.S.–listed China companies and has a very low expense ratio. All four ETFs can play a useful role in giving investors exposure to the Chinese economy.

CHAPTER 10

The Offshore Strategy

*If GE's strategy of investment in China is right,
it is the future of the company for the century.*

—JACK WELSH

DIRECT OWNERSHIP OF CHINESE COMMON STOCKS presents a number of complications and complexities. One of
our most highly recommended strategies, buying discounted
closed-end Chinese investment funds with near-term liquidation dates, is feasible only for local investors and those international investors who have a QFII quota. Moreover, some
investors in the United States and Europe may be reluctant to
venture that far beyond their national boundaries. They may
feel, correctly, that accounting statements in China are still
relatively opaque and that corporate governance is not yet up
to world standards. Nevertheless, even wary investors who are
impressed with the growth of China may well wish to participate in some way. For these investors, indirect methods of
benefiting from China's economy present useful adjuncts to
their overall portfolio strategy.

In this chapter we describe several practical indirect investment strategies whose results are importantly influenced by

economic conditions in China. One plan takes advantage of China's unprecedented demand for raw materials, by purchasing shares in companies that own or produce raw materials. Other indirect investment strategies look to companies domiciled in countries, such as Taiwan and Japan, whose fortunes are closely tied to China. Indeed, countries throughout Asia have benefited substantially from China's success. Finally, we will analyze a subset of companies domiciled in the United States and Europe that are deriving—and will continue to derive—enormous benefit from China's growth.

CHINA SOAKS UP NATURAL RESOURCES

By 2007, China had to a large extent become the manufacturer to the world. In the twentieth century, the United States, home to the largest economy in the world, was the largest exporter of goods. Starting in the late 1980s, however, China's exports took off, and by the last months of 2006 they

EXHIBIT 10.1 *China Exports as a Percentage of U.S. Exports, 1994–2006*

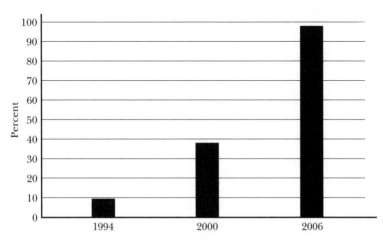

SOURCE: Bosera Asset Management Co.

surpassed U.S. exports in dollar value. Exhibit 10.1 shows the development of China's exports as a percentage of U.S. exports from 1994 through 2006.

China's effect on the prices of manufactured goods is well understood. Manufacturers worldwide are thought to have "limited pricing power" because of competition from China. It is not an exaggeration to say, "If China can make it, its price is unlikely to rise." But the corollary to that statement is even more relevant for us. China imports many of the raw materials it needs in the manufacturing process, which means we can also say, "If China needs to buy it, its price is very likely to rise." We believe that a major factor in the price increases of raw materials since the late 1990s has been China's demand for them.

Both the needs of the country's export sector and the increasing consumption levels of China's huge population have created a growing demand for commodities such as oil, timber, and other raw materials. China already consumes the largest share of the world's copper, using about 20 percent of the global supply—almost one and a half times as much as the United States. China also consumes an equivalent proportion of the world output of wheat, corn, aluminum, and cotton. Growing Chinese demand (as well as increased demand from other emerging economies such as India) has sent the prices of many commodities on a record-breaking upward trajectory for the past twenty-five years. China's need for timber has been particularly strong. In 1998, the country implemented a logging ban on the mainland after previous deforestation caused a major soil erosion problem. Even with the domestic supply of timber constrained, over 100 million square feet of additional housing has been constructed for the 2008 Beijing Olympics alone. Exhibits 10.2 through 10.4 show the growth in the physical volume of Chinese imports of oil, timber, and coal.

EXHIBIT 10.2   *China's Imports of Crude Oil, 1995–2006*

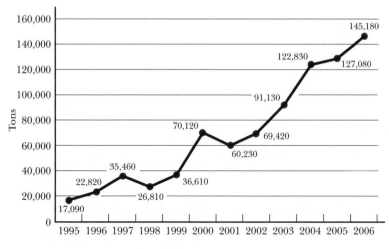

SOURCE: Bosera Asset Mangement Co.

EXHIBIT 10.3   *China's Imports of Timber, 1995–2006*

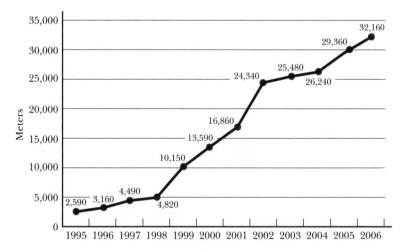

EXHIBIT 10.4 *China's Imports of Coal, 1995–2006*

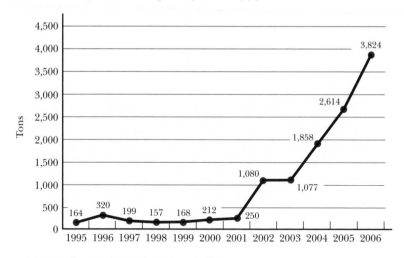

SOURCE: Bosera Asset Management Co.

Exhibit 10.5 uses the Goldman Sachs Commodity Price Index to illustrate the increase in commodity demand, and thus in commodity prices, since the late 1990s. Owning investment instruments that rise with the increase in commodity prices is one indirect way to benefit from China's growth. While commodity prices are extremely volatile, China's continued economic expansion is likely to exert consistent upward pressure on these prices.

Exposure to commodities also provides important diversification benefits. Recall that the lower the correlation between any two asset classes in a portfolio, the greater the potential for risk reduction. The greatest risk reduction comes from adding an asset class that has a negative correlation to an existing portfolio. For a U.S. investor whose holdings are concentrated in U.S. stocks, commodities are excellent diversifiers. During the early years of the twenty-first century, commodities have had a negative correlation with U.S. equities.

EXHIBIT 10.5 *Goldman Sachs Commodity Price Index, 1998–2007*

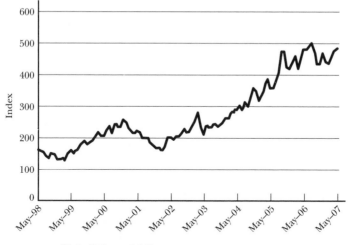

SOURCE: Global Financial Data.

There is a commodity ETF available (trading under the ticker symbol GSC) that tracks the Goldman Sachs commodities index, which has a heavy weight in oil. A somewhat broader commodity ETF (trading under the symbol DBC) tracks the Commodity Research Board (CRB) index of commodities prices. Another ETF (trading under the symbol GLD) tracks the price of gold. We prefer, however, to invest in ETFs that hold shares in the companies that produce the commodities. The fortunes of the producers are largely aligned with commodity prices, and the producers are also profitable businesses that distribute dividends to their shareholders. A sample of commodity producer ETFs is shown in Exhibit 10.6.

Exposure to commodities producers offers an effective indirect way of benefiting from the expansion of China as well as other rapidly developing countries. While commodities and their producers have extraordinarily volatile returns

EXHIBIT 10.6 *Selected Commodity Producer ETFs*

FUND NAME	TICKER	EXPENSE RATIO	TOTAL ASSETS (MM)	DIVIDEND YIELD	TRAILING 5-YR AVERAGE ANNUAL RETURNS (%)
Vanguard Energy	VDE	0.25	601	1.00	N/A
Energy SPDR	XLE	0.24	4333	1.17	20.58
Vanguard Materials	VAW	0.25	263	1.42	N/A
Materials SPDR	XLB	0.24	990	2.12	13.68
iShares Materials	IYM	0.60	637	1.76	12.72
SPDR Metal & Mining	XME	0.36	190	N/A	N/A
Gold Miners Market Vectors	GDX	0.55	612	N/A	N/A

SOURCE: http://quicktake.morningstar.com/fund; http://finance.yahoo.com (May 2007).

and, therefore, are risky by themselves as investments, it is paradoxical but true that they can help reduce the overall risk of a portfolio because of their diversification benefits.

TAIWAN RIDES THE CHINA DRAGON

Despite the acrimonious political rhetoric between the two entities, the economies of mainland China and Taiwan are becoming ever more integrated. Taiwan-owned companies have substantial interests on "the continent," as the Taiwanese refer to the mainland. In 2006, Taiwanese companies accounted for approximately 15 percent of total Chinese exports, with percentages in the information technology hardware sector as high as 60 percent. Taiwanese investment in China now totals over $50 billion, and accounts for almost 70 percent of Taiwan's total outbound investment.

The Taiwanese government's efforts, begun in 2003, to

dampen the massive exodus of capital have done little to halt the flow of money and people out of the island. Approximately 1 million Taiwanese are now living and working in mainland China, and Chinese government statistics indicate that over 70,000 Taiwanese companies have invested there. Thousands more companies in Taiwan have indirect financial interests in China through their investments in enterprises based in Hong Kong and Singapore.

Though Taiwan is the second largest high-tech chip manufacturer in the world, its role is increasingly one of design, management, and finance—with the manufacturing taking place on the mainland. To the Taiwanese government's dismay, more and more design is now taking place there. By expanding into China, many Taiwanese chip makers have achieved a potent mix of technological know-how, worldwide market access, and cheap labor, and they are very well positioned to meet the needs of a growing Chinese market as well as demand from around the world.

We feel that the best way to access the Taiwanese market is through a diversified vehicle rather than by purchasing individual Taiwanese stocks. Two such vehicles worth considering are the Taiwan Greater China Fund and the MSCI Taiwan Index. The first is a diversified, closed-end fund, investing in Taiwan-listed companies that derive substantial profits either from exporting to or operating in mainland China. The fund's ticker symbol is TFC and it is listed on the New York Stock Exchange. As with all closed-end funds, these shares are more attractive if they are selling at a discount from their net asset value. As for the second, the entire Taiwan market can be accessed through the ETF ticker EWT, which tracks the MSCI Taiwan Index, and trades on the New York Stock Exchange.

JAPAN JUMPS INTO THE CHINA BOOM

No student of history can fail to ignore the bitter enmity between China and Japan. To this day, anti-Japanese protests are not uncommon in China, and a residue of ill will continues. But the simple truth remains that the economies of China and Japan are highly complementary and China has become Japan's third-most important trading partner after the United States and the European Union. China is now an important outsourcing center for Japanese companies, as well as an increasingly important domestic market for Japanese products. Contrary to popular belief, domestic demand, rather than net exports, contributed to over 80 percent of China's 10.5 percent growth during 2006, and much of that demand has been for goods sourced from Japanese companies.

The investment research department of AllianceBernstein has estimated that Chinese per capita income will continue to increase on a scale not experienced since the industrialization of the United States, Japan, and Western Europe. Despite the unequal income distribution and concentration of wealth, we believe that currently 100 million Chinese earn an income of at least 50,000 yuan. That figure represents over $20,000 per year in purchasing power. In addition, China's middle class is currently equal in number to the entire population of Japan, and its steady growth has in turn created a significant demand for Japanese products. Moreover, low penetration rates in such products as mobile phones, TV sets, and refrigerators leave room for enormous future growth. Ultimately, Japan benefits from China's advantages both as an important outsourcing center and as an important market for Japan's industrial and consumer products.

Goldman Sachs has put together a "China-Related Japan Stock Basket," which contains those Japanese stocks that

EXHIBIT 10.7 *China-Related Japan Stock Basket Performance (Indexed, Jan. 7, 2000 = 100)*

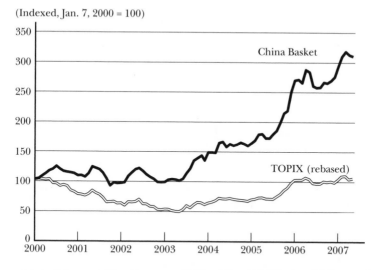

(Indexed, Jan. 7, 2000 = 100)

China Basket

TOPIX (rebased)

NOTE: Prices as of April 9, 2007. Teijin, Mitsubishi Rayon, Oji Paper, Tosoh, Dainippon Ink & Chemicals, Shiseido, Asahi Glass, Nippon Electric Glass, Taiheiyo Cement, Toto, Nippon Steel, JFE Holdings, Mitsubishi Materials, Komatsu, Hitachi Const. Machinery, Daikin Industries, NSK, Sanken Electric, Funai Electric, Fanuc, Honda Motor, Koito Mfg., Ricoh, Yamaha, Itochu, Mitsui, Sumitomo, Mitsubishi, Unicharm, Nippon Express, Nippon Yusen, Mitsui O.S.K. Lines. Equal-weighted.

SOURCE: Goldman Sachs Research calculations.

benefit substantially from sales to China or by doing their manufacturing in China. We believe that the growth of China has been responsible in large part for Japan's recovery from the over-decade-long recession that followed the real estate and stock market bubble of the late 1980s. More than half of Japan's exports to China consist of high-value-added, capital-intensive products, and Goldman Sachs's China basket of Japanese stocks has substantially outperformed the general Japanese stock index.

ALL OF ASIA TAPS INTO CHINA'S WEALTH

In addition to Taiwan and Japan, countries throughout Asia have substantially benefited from China's recent growth. Australia, for example, has had a very strong market during 2005 and 2006, thanks to the Chinese demand for Aus-

EXHIBIT 10.8   *Open and Closed-End Funds and ETFs with Broad Asian Exposure, May 2007*

Open-End Funds

FUND NAME	MORNINGSTAR RATING	EXPENSE RATIO (%)	TRAILING 5-YR AVERAGE ANNUAL RETURNS (%)
American Century Emerging Markets	★★★	2.05	24.15
Fidelity Emerging Markets	★★	1.01	26.82
Vanguard Emerging Markets Index Fund	★★★	0.42	25.79
Vanguard Pacific Stock Index Fund	★★★★	0.27	15.43

Closed-End Funds

FUND NAME	TICKER	MORNING-STAR RATING	EXPENSE RATIO (%)	PREMIUM (+) DISCOUNT (−)	TRAILING 5-YR AVERAGE ANNUAL RETURNS (%)
Asia Pacific Fund	APB	★★★	1.78	-12.15	21.32
Asia Tigers	GRR	★★★	2.20	-10.77	N/A
Greater China	GCH	★★★	1.86	-10.55	25.17
Morgan Stanley Asia Pacific	APF	not rated	1.16	-12.98	18.73
Taiwan Greater China	TFC	★★	2.55	-9.52	6.59
Singapore	SGF	★★★	1.86	-10.84	25.17
Malaysia	MF	★★	1.49	-10.23	16.54
Korea	KF	★★★	0.89	-5.75	23.62

Exchange-Traded Funds

FUND NAME	TICKER	EXPENSE RATIO (%)	TRAILING 5-YR AVERAGE ANNUAL RETURNS (%)
MSCI Hong Kong	EWH	0.54	19.42
MSCI Taiwan	EWT	0.85	-0.33
MSCI South Korea	EWY	0.70	9.45
MSCI Singapore	EWS	0.54	42.99
MSCI Malaysia	EWM	0.54	52.77
MSCI Australia	EWA	0.54	29.76
MSCI Japan	EWJ	0.54	-5.12
iShares MSCI Pacific Ex Japan	EPP	0.50	34.22
Vangard Pacific Index ETF	VPL	0.18	3.32

SOURCE: http://quicktake.morningstar.com/fund; http://finance.yahoo.com.

tralian raw materials and products. Similarly, Chinese growth has benefited South Korea, Malaysia, and Singapore. The Singapore stock market also contains a number of real estate investment trusts that have substantial and profitable property investments in mainland China. Exhibit 10.8 presents a listing of funds (open-end, closed-end, and ETFs) that provide Asian exposure and that have moderately low expense ratios. The broader Asian funds also provide some exposure to India, another emerging market with very attractive growth prospects.

MANY U.S. COMPANIES RELY ON CHINA FOR GROWTH

U.S. corporate profits from operations in China passed $4 billion during 2006, up more than 50 percent from 2005, according to the U.S. Bureau of Economic Analysis. Joseph

Quinlan, chief market strategist at Bank of America, added another perspective on this growth: U.S. companies earned more in China during 2006 than they earned there during the entire decade of the 1990s.

If Wal-Mart were a country, it would be China's fourth largest export market. The company purchased $25 billion of merchandise in China in 2006 and has done more than any other company in the world to make "Made in China" a part of the U.S. retail landscape. Wal-Mart also has a rapidly expanding retail business in China; according to Deutsche Bank analyst Bill Dreher, "China will be as big and as successful a market for Wal-Mart as the United States."

In 2006, Wal-Mart announced a $1 billion acquisition of Trust-Mart, a Taiwanese-owned chain of more than one hundred "big box" superstores in China, all part of Wal-Mart's strategy to grow up with China's middle class, which is expected to quintuple to 200 million by 2015. The company has transformed the way Chinese suppliers operate, replacing a culture based on personal relationships with a supply network based on pricing, delivery, and product quality, made possible by information technology. Chinese suppliers, long accustomed to winning business by wining and dining their customers, have reported being shocked at Wal-Mart's strictly by-the-numbers protocol.

Although China is investing heavily in its transportation infrastructure, its distribution system is still antiquated and inefficient. This gives U.S. companies like UPS and Federal Express significant advantages over homegrown competitors. UPS and FedEx are still making heavy investments in their China networks, and while their businesses in China are not yet profitable, the companies will enjoy significant earnings gains when the networks are up and running.

Americans seem to be losing their taste for Colonel

Sanders's secret recipe for Kentucky Fried Chicken. The growth in same-store sales (the metric favored by retail security analysts) has been relatively flat for KFC's 5,000 plus stores in the United States. The same is true for the Pizza Hut and Taco Bell chains. But the parent company of these fast-food establishments, appropriately called Yum! Brands, has enjoyed high double-digit profit growth from its operations in China, where it opens a new restaurant every twenty-two hours. KFC may be a laggard at home but it is doing a finger-lickin' good business in China. The chain's mascot "Chicky" is far more recognizable in China than the "Ronald McDonald" of their rival. Yum! Brands has also launched a new restaurant chain in China called East Dawning. The restaurants serve chicken prepared with traditional elements of Chinese cuisine in a space designed to resemble a comfortable Chinese home. Income from China is so significant that Yum! Brands breaks it out as a separate item in its annual report. During 2007, profits from China were increasing at greater than a 30 percent annual rate.

A rapidly growing but aging Chinese middle-class population should bring new demand for many U.S. drug and medical equipment companies, such as Pfizer and Johnson & Johnson. The Chinese propensity to save also should benefit asset managers. And while the business is still in its infancy in the country, AIG, Merrill Lynch, and Morgan Stanley have established footholds in China through joint venture companies.

Macao, located thirty-seven miles southwest of Hong Kong, has surpassed Las Vegas to become the largest gaming and entertainment market in the world. Hundreds of millions of Chinese live in an area within a two-hour drive or flight to Macao. Not just a leading destination for mainland Chinese, who simply cross the border, Macao has also become a leading international resort. In 2004, Macao ended the forty-year monopoly over gambling casinos that had been given to Stanley Ho, known in China as "The King of Gamble." Now international companies can enter the market, and two U.S. companies, Las Vegas Sands and Wynn Resorts, have become leading players.

Las Vegas Sands was the first U.S. entrant into the market. The Sands Macao opened in 2005, and the (Sands) Venetian Macao Resort in 2007 on a Vegas-style strip of reclaimed land called Cotai. Thanks to an insatiable Chinese demand for gambling, revenues in Macao now exceed those in Las Vegas. Well over half of Las Vegas Sands resort revenues come from Macao.

Steve Wynn of Wynn Resorts also likes Macao's odds—so much so that he was spending two hours a day on Chinese lessons before Wynn Macao opened in September 2006. Featuring 600 hotel rooms, 100,000 square feet of gambling space, 26,000 square feet of retail space, and seven restaurants, the casino has been adding millions to the firm's bottom line. Wynn Resorts' current expansion plans include an addition to this highly successful mega-casino, as well as a second casino-resort on the Cotai strip. For the flamboyant Steve, it was clearly a big Wynn in Macao. And the future looks even brighter, Wynn opines: "Macao is directly in the path of a huge avalanche of revenues."

Many other U.S. household names are major players in the Chinese market, and they bring their marketing know-how with them to make sure they stay major players. When Procter & Gamble found that low-income women in China only washed their hair once a week, it reformulated its China brand shampoo to keep hair cleaner longer. Goldman Sachs is a leading Asian investment banker. Starbucks projects that China (though it is a nation of tea drinkers) will become the company's largest market outside the United States. Coca-

Cola reports that China is now the company's fourth largest market. Industrial supply manufacturer Honeywell has China revenues that are almost 10 percent of the company's total, and they are growing at 20 percent per year. Motorola enjoys rapidly growing cell phone sales in China. A recent survey by the U.S.-China Business Council reported that profit margins for its members in China were as large as or larger than those in any other part of the world.

One relatively riskless way to profit from the growth of China is to buy the shares of U.S. companies whose earnings stand to benefit from their China-related activities. Exhibit 10.9 presents a broad list of U.S. companies that have substantial interests in China. Exhibit 10.10 plots the returns from these U.S. companies as compared to the Standard & Poor's 500 Stock Index.

EXHIBIT 10.9 *U.S. Companies with Significant Operations in China*

INFORMATION TECHNOLOGY:	Motorola; Honeywell; Microsoft; IBM; Cisco Systems; Oracle; Hewlett Packard; eBay
FINANCE:	Citigroup; Bank of America; Goldman Sachs; Merrill Lynch; Morgan Stanley
CONSUMER:	P&G; American Express
PHARMACEUTICALS:	Johnson & Johnson; Pfizer
RETAIL:	Wal-Mart
INDUSTRIALS:	Du Pont; GE
AUTO:	General Motors; Ford
FOOD:	Coca-Cola; Pepsi; Yum! Brands; Starbucks; McDonald's; Anheuser Busch
ENTERTAINMENT:	Wynn Resorts; Disney; Las Vegas Sands
REAL ESTATE:	ProLogis
TRANSPORTATION:	UPS; FedEx
INSURANCE:	AIG
MATERIALS:	Phelps Dodge; Alcoa

EXHIBIT 10.10   *Performance of U.S. Companies* with Substantial*
China Interests versus S&P 500, 2001–07

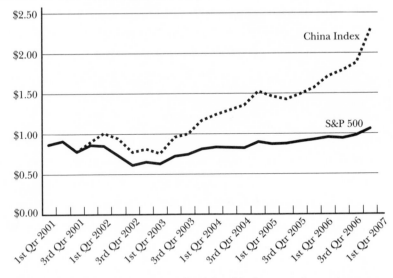

Return on U.S.-China Index and S&P

*The U.S.-China Index is an equal-weighted index assuming an investment
in all the companies listed in Exhibit 10.9.

SOURCE: Authors' calculations.

There are, however, two major concerns with an offshore
method utilizing a basket of U.S. companies that profit from
their operations in China. First, it would be prohibitively
expensive for many individual investors to buy and hold shares
in such a large number of companies. Second, there are
extremely limited opportunities to buy funds that offer such a
strategy. We are familiar with only one such fund, the Alger
China U.S. Growth Fund (ticker symbol CHUSX), and even
this is only a partial play. CHUSX is about evenly divided
between U.S.-headquartered companies that receive significant profits from their China activities and major China companies that are traded on international exchanges. In

addition, this fund carries a hefty load. We feel that U.S. investors would be well served if they were able to buy either an index fund or an ETF consisting of major U.S. companies that have significant earnings from their participation in China's economic boom. We hope such a fund will soon exist.

EUROPEAN MULTINATIONAL CORPORATIONS ALSO LOOK TO CHINA FOR GROWTH

European multinational corporations, many listed as American depository receipts (ADRs) on U.S. exchanges, also offer attractive indirect ways for investors to benefit from the growth of China. An excellent example is the French luxury goods corporation LVMH (Louis Vuitton, Moët, Hennessy). LVMH's sales in China are expanding rapidly in several of its product categories. The company's designer accessories brand, Louis Vuitton, has enjoyed the fastest growth. Louis Vuitton opened its first shop on the mainland in Shanghai in 2004. By the end of 2006, it had over two dozen outlets in China. Yves Carcelle, the head of the design house, identifies China as "the focus of the company's attention" and the area from which "exponential growth" is expected.

By 2006, China accounted for more than 50 percent of the Louis Vuitton brand's sales. The Paris-based Louis Vuitton sold more purses, shoes, and gloves in China (including Hong Kong) than it did in Europe, which accounted for only about one quarter of its sales. *The Economist* reports that Chinese customers for luxury goods constitute "the most rapidly expanding demographic in the Chinese economy." The Chinese nouveaux riches were described as a "huge group of status-conscious, increasingly wealthy people hungry for brands and fanatical about shopping." A sign at the entrance to the Lemon Lake housing development says much about the way rich Chinese are looking to spend: "North American Demeanor: Rich and Strong."

Other European brands have also been extremely successful in China. Armani, Gucci, Hermès, Prada, and Versace are all expanding with great speed. Nokia, the world's largest vendor of cell phones, enjoys the largest share of the handset market in China. As the western part of China develops, there is still considerable room for growth in this area. During the first nine months of 2006, China added about 50 million new mobile phone subscribers, more than the entire population of South Korea. Nokia also keeps selling new and familiar phones to current subscribers. Indeed, by 2012, Nokia estimates the replacement market will constitute 80 percent of total sales.

Consumer goods and food stalwarts like Unilever and Nestlé have considerable sales in China, as does the electronics maker Philips. L'Oréal has been quite successful with its Maybelline line. Volkswagen was an early entrant into the Chinese auto market, and BMW is ramping up quickly. The Swiss electrical infrastructure company ABB continues to win contracts hand over fist to upgrade China's power grid. Companies as diverse as Siemens, Novartis, and Heineken are well-known brand names. Similarly, many multinational financial corporations domiciled in Europe have substantial Chinese interests. Zurich-based UBS, Europe's biggest bank, has made it clear that China is pivotal to the bank's future growth and profit. In 2006, it had a paper profit of over $1 billion from its China activities. Barclays Bank of Britain derives a significant share of its profits from China. HSBC, the huge international financial conglomerate, headquartered in London, got its start in 1865 when it opened as the Hong Kong and Shanghai Banking Corporation. It's no surprise then that the company's financial roots are deep in China, and it is one of the leading foreign institutions developing a consumer financial market in the country. In 2005, HSBC became the first foreign bank to provide local currency services in mainland China.

Clearly, European investors also can tap indirectly into the growth of China. Here again, there are few or no opportunities to do so inexpensively. We feel that a fund or ETF of European companies profiting from their China activities would be an extremely useful tool not only for European investors but also for American shareholders, since many of the European companies are also traded as ADRs on U.S. exchanges. Perhaps a fund company will create "the best of the best"—an index of both U.S. and foreign companies for whom business in China is a significant factor in their operations.

A SUMMING UP

Of course, indirect investments in United States, European, and other Asian companies that seek to gain exposure to China's growth are not pure plays. While these companies will enjoy rapidly growing opportunities in China and are lower-risk investments, their China activities will account for only a percentage of overall revenue. Moreover, U.S., European, and Japanese companies are subject to overall market movement in their own home countries, and thus offer fewer diversification benefits than more direct investment in companies that do most of their business in China. But for the white-knuckle crowd, who see the potential growth of China but do not dare to stray from those local investments with which they are most comfortable, the indirect offshore method has much to recommend it.

CHAPTER 11

The Go for Broke Strategy

*It is not the return on my investment that I am
concerned about; it is the return of my investment.*

— WILL ROGERS

THIS IS THE CHAPTER FOR GAMBLERS—for those who like
to play even when the odds are stacked against them. If they
do win, however, the jackpots can be large. Here we take you
through the labyrinth of how to buy individual Chinese stocks
and give you some idea of where financial gurus are placing
their bets as this book goes to press. In order to keep you out
of too much trouble, we first present a few basic stock-picking
guidelines.

THREE STOCK-PICKING GUIDELINES

Let it be noted at the outset that while these guidelines are
valid for buying individual stocks on your own in large, efficiently functioning markets, they acquire special Chinese
characteristics when applied to mainland China companies.
These characteristics are described under each guideline.

#1. Buy stocks that are expected to have above-average
earnings growth for at least five years

Future earnings growth is the basic criterion for picking
any stock. Throughout history, all the hugely successful company investments have been characterized by extraordinary
growth in earnings per share. Let's say a stock is selling for
$15, earns $1.00 per share, and thus has a price-earnings
(P/E) multiple of 15 (about the long-run market average in
the United States). The next year, the company's earnings
increase by 15 percent, boosting the per share earnings to
$1.15. If the already low P/E remains constant, the stock will
now sell for $17.25. Of course, the market could get excited
about the company's earnings growth and feel that it should
have a higher P/E multiple. Let's say, the market feels the
company's stellar earnings growth should be conservatively
rewarded by assigning the company's stock price a P/E multiple of 18. Bingo! By multiplying the $1.15 per share earnings
by 18, you now have a share price of $20.70—an increase of
38 percent in just one year. Not bad.

Earnings per share of offshore listed Chinese companies
have been growing at rates well above an annual 15 percent
increase for the past several years. The problem, of course, is
what constitutes earnings for a Chinese company. As we saw in
chapter 8, the earnings of state-owned enterprises are often
subject to the whims and policies of the government. Furthermore, the books of privately owned companies can be murky,
to say the least.

#2. Buy stocks with P/Es that are low relative
to their growth prospects

If you buy a stock whose earnings are growing rapidly and
whose P/E is at or below the overall market P/E, you may

have found a deal. The financial world uses the term "PEG ratio" to describe the relationship of price to earnings growth; this ratio is widely regarded as a handy tool for picking stocks—the lower the ratio, the better. Alas, everyone is looking for this kind of stock and it is the rare individual who can spot it before the hundreds of other stock pickers. In the case of China stocks, the P/E data can be suspect, and the intervention of the government can drastically alter any widely accepted growth prospects. And there is another problem. You often cannot obtain any P/E data on individual China stocks, and consensus estimates on earnings growth are frequently not accessible to individual investors. We, for example, had to rely on the Bosera Asset Management Co. to obtain the growth estimates for our calculations.

#3. Buy stocks with glamour stories

Now here is where China stocks really shine. There is glamour everywhere, or so it seems. The country's economy is the fastest growing in the world, and stories abound about the growth of the consumer class and the eagerness of major firms throughout the world to cash in on it. The point to remember here is that all that glitters is not necessarily gold. As we have said repeatedly throughout this book, the Chinese are just as clever as Americans were during the heyday of the dot-com boom in coming up with creative corporate names in order to entice buyers. Tiens Biotech Group (TBV on the American Stock Exchange), for example, has nothing to do with biotech; rather, it sells nutritional supplements and personal products.

The bottom line is that even if you follow these eminently sensible and practical guidelines, you will find that picking and then buying individual stocks in emerging markets such as China's is fraught with danger to your financial well-being.

As *Motley Fool* contributor Will Frankenhoff has noted, purchasing Chinese stocks can be categorized as a manic-depressive activity.

THE ELUSIVE IDEAL OF THE TEN BAGGERS

Glamour, growth—who can resist it? Peter Lynch, the famous investor and co-author of *One Up on Wall Street,* created the term "ten bagger" to describe the lucrative potential of such stocks. Borrowing from baseball slang, in which a single hit gets a runner to first base or the first bag, a "ten bagger" is the equivalent of two home runs and a double. For the stock buyer, it means that the value of her purchase has gone up ten times, or by 1,000 percent. By one means or another, many Chinese stocks look like they are multiple "baggers," and some have been home runs. At least one, as shown in Exhibit 11.1, was actually a ten bagger.

Is there a catch to Exhibit 11.1? Sadly, yes. Only mainland Chinese or institutions with QFII quotas were able to buy these stocks as they are listed only on the Shanghai and Shenzhen stock exchanges. What about investors who don't live in China? U.S. residents have many options—not all of them

EXHIBIT 11.1 *Home-Run Stock Returns and More on Mainland China, 1999–2006*

COMPANY	SECTOR	TOTAL RETURN (%)	ANNUALIZED RETURN (%)
Financial Street	Real estate	1,411	49.6
Rocket	Machinery equipment	848	39.6
Yunnan Baiyao	Pharmaceutical	715	36.5
Lake Chemical	Salt/Potash	634	34.4
OCT	Tourism/Real estate	518	31.0

SOURCE: Bosera Asset Management Co.

easy—when it comes to buying Chinese shares that are listed on exchanges outside of mainland China.

A Primer on How to Buy Chinese Stocks Outside China

With regard to U.S. stock exchanges, Americans can buy Chinese companies in the form of ADRs (American depository receipts) or ADSs (American depository shares). They can also buy ADRs and ADSs on what is known as the "pink sheets." And, finally, they can also—with some difficulty and often a great deal of expense—buy shares directly on the Hong Kong Stock Exchange.

ADRs and ADSs on U.S. stock exchanges

As dollar-denominated, negotiable U.S. securities, ADRs provide the easiest way for U.S. investors to buy shares in foreign companies and thus obtain global portfolio diversification. First created in 1927, ADRs did not come into their own until the past quarter century or so, when globalization took root in the world economy. There are three levels of ADRs. Level I is regarded as the entry-level ADR, and these shares are generally traded as "pink sheets", which we discuss below. Level I ADRs are not required to meet SEC disclosure policies. Level II and Level III ADRs must meet all Securities Exchange Act requirements, which include the detailed filing of financial statements and corporate information. The major difference between the two is that ADRs at Level III, the most stringent of all, can raise capital via public offerings in the United States.

Many familiar international firms trade on U.S. exchanges as ADRs; among them are Nokia and British Petroleum. Chinese ADRs on the New York and NASDAQ exchanges are either at Level II or Level III and are often referred to as N shares. As we saw in chapter 4, in order to make an ADR share price somewhat reasonable by American standards, the ADRs often represent bundled shares. Thus, one Sinopec ADR on the New York Stock Exchange is the equivalent of 100 Sinopec shares traded on the Shanghai Stock Exchange. ADRs and ADSs are often thought to be the same, and in one sense they are, in that the requirements for listing are the same. Technically, however, an ADS is an actual share that is being traded and an ADR consists of a bundle of ADSs. For example, the Shanghai Petroleum Company Ltd., the wholly owned subsidiary of Sinopec, trades as an ADS on the New York Stock Exchange, and one share on that exchange is the same as one share on the Shanghai Stock Exchange.

Pink sheets

The term "pink sheets" is a holdover from the days when quotes for stocks listed here were actually printed on pink paper. Today, it's an area that, in one sense, represents the underworld of stock trading in the United States, the place where bankrupt companies are banished. When Delphi—the motor parts company—went bankrupt, its stock was delisted on the New York Stock Exchange and sent to the pink sheets. It's also a place where companies who do not want to open their books prefer to list. Not all such companies are sleazy, fly-by-night operations—the giant Swiss firm, Nestlé, is listed on the pink sheets. And it is also the place where several Chinese companies, particularly the property development companies, prefer to list.

Though pink sheets are known for being thinly traded—which means you could wait several days before finding a buyer for the pink sheet shares that you want to sell—some of the companies, such as the Cheung Kong Holdings property development company, have an average daily trading volume of over 60,000 shares. This large volume is possible because in 1999, a limited liability company with the very appropriate name of Pink Sheets LLC introduced an electronic quotation service that displaced the old pink sheet system. Even with this service, however, it is extremely difficult to find relevant information on any pink sheet shares. Sometimes, because the shares are so thinly traded, you can only track down a quote that is several weeks old. For more active shares, you generally have to wait at least an hour after the market has closed to obtain information on your share's price. For those wishing to buy shares of foreign institutions that do not open their books to public scrutiny, pink sheets can provide a means—though frequently not an efficient one—of buying such shares in dollar-denominated securities.

Hong Kong Stock Exchange

Many foreign institutions forego the bother of listing on foreign exchanges. Staying on their host country's exchange is good enough for them. Thus, the only way individuals can buy the shares of many Chinese firms is to purchase them on the Hong Kong Stock Exchange. This is not as easy as it sounds.

Let's say, for example, that you wanted to buy 100 shares of COSCO Pacific Ltd. This is a Chinese container-related conglomerate and represents an interest in all the shipping into, out of, and within China. The U.S. accounting firm PricewaterhouseCoopers audits the books, and major U.S. firms, including Merrill Lynch, Goldman Sachs, Morgan Stanley, and Citigroup, track its performance. At the time this book went to press, shares in this company were only sold on the Hong Kong Stock Exchange.

As an experiment, we set out to find firsthand how we could purchase shares in COSCO Pacific Ltd. We called a number of major, widely respected brokerage firms. Some frankly admitted they had no idea how to purchase Hong Kong stocks. Others said they would only do so with a minimum order of $20,000. Still others said they would check with their international desks and try to get back to us within the week. The bottom line: Though it is not impossible to buy Hong Kong listed stocks, you will find that many U.S. brokerage firms are not prepared to quickly and efficiently handle individual, noncorporate requests for such transactions.

By default, then, most investors wishing to purchase Chinese stocks on their own rather than through mutual or exchange-traded funds must do so on their home country stock exchanges. This severely limits the universe of available purchases. In the United States, the number of domestic listed stocks goes well into the thousands whereas the number of Chinese companies that are listed on U.S. stock exchanges barely reaches the hundreds. And of those listed in the United States, many are on the pink sheets and thus do not come under strict regulatory scrutiny and are often very thinly traded.

CHINESE SECTORS — AND STOCKS — DEEMED HOT

Still, this is a chapter for gamblers, for those who like to experience the manic-depressive instability of picking individual stocks. As far as investments in China go, there are many companies that appear exceedingly beguiling. Stock analysts and financial gurus were touting stocks in the following areas as offering substantial future growth and moderate price-earnings multiples as this book went to press.

We want to make it perfectly clear that we do not recommend any of these stocks. They are hot as we write but they could be stone cold as you read about them now. You might have fun comparing their performance from the time these words were written—February 2007—to now when you are reading these words. To track performance, simply go to any one of the Internet financial sites—Reuters, CNN Money, MarketWatch, MSN Money, Yahoo! Finance, Google Finance —type in the stock symbol, and then click on the chart that gives you price comparisons over time. Many of these sites also allow you to compare how well or how poorly the individual stock performed over the designated period versus other stocks or other benchmarks.

Consumer companies

The Y generation—those twenty- and thirtysomethings—is coming into its own in China. These young adults are major consumers, and heavily influenced by Western culture. They like to spend, and to set the standard for those following in their footsteps. As a result, the level of personal savings is starting to flatten and consumption expenditures, spurred by this generation, are steadily rising. Crédit Suisse predicts that by 2014, Chinese consumers could well replace American consumers as the engines of global economic growth. The market potential within China for a broad array of consumer products is simply the largest in the world.

- COFCO INTERNATIONAL LTD. Operating in Hong Kong and throughout mainland China, this major food-processing and trading company also engages in wine-making and the distribution of chocolate products. It strikes a chord with Chinese consumers not only because of the quality of its products but because it is a mainland company and not an outside one. Though the basic story isn't glamorous, its earnings and overall growth have been excellent. Listed on: Hong Kong

Stock Exchange (0506.HK); four German exchanges—Berlin (CFH.BE), Frankfurt (CFH.F), Munich (CFH.MU), and Stuttgart (CFH.SG); and U.S. pink sheets (CFITF.PK).

• MENGNIU DAIRY. "Look at the management rather than the financial reports," one Chinese mutual fund manager told us, and both he and several major U.S. brokerage firms highly praise Mengniu president Niu Gensheng. Under Niu's leadership, this privately held company has become one of the leading dairy product manufacturers in China. In 2001, the government started a program requiring all pupils to drink a cup of milk daily; Mengniu's Flying Cow brand is now a staple in schools throughout the country. Clever marketing—building on national pride—has also propelled earnings for this company: China's astronauts drank its milk, U.S. basketball star Yao Ming is a spokesman, and Olympic medalists back it. With the government's increased emphasis on health and education, Mengniu is expected to prosper—especially as the western part of the country develops. Listed on: Hong Kong Stock Exchange (2319.HK); three German exchanges—Berlin (EZQ.BE), Munich (EZQ.MU), and Stuttgart (EZQ.SG); and U.S. pink sheets (CIADF.PK).

• MINDRAY MEDICAL INTERNATIONAL LTD. Established in 1991, Mindray Medical is an example of the growing marketing and technical sophistication of Chinese companies. With offices in twenty-nine major cities throughout China and in the United States, United Kingdom, Canada, Turkey, and Hong Kong as well, it develops, manufactures, and markets medical devices across three business segments—patient monitors, clinical laboratory instruments, and ultrasound imaging systems. Listed on: New York Stock Exchange (MR).

- LI NING COMPANY LTD. One of the leading sporting goods enterprises in mainland China, Li Ning Company designs, brands, manufactures, and retails sports footwear, apparel, and accessories. It is expected to benefit not only from increasing consumer purchases in the coastal areas but also from the economic growth forecast for the western part of the country. Listed on: Hong Kong Stock Exchange (2331.HK); three German exchanges—Berlin (LNL.BE), Frankfurt (LNL.F), and Munich (LNL.MU); and U.S. pink sheets (LNNGF.PK).

Financial firms

Chinese bank SOEs have undergone massive cleanups in recent years. All the major financial institutions are buying in—Morgan Stanley, Goldman Sachs, Bank of America, Citicorp, Barclays Bank, and so on. The big international banks are buying into the China banks because of the huge potential for banking services throughout such a vast country. Credit card ownership, in just one example, more than quadrupled in the decade ending 2006 and yet still has millions to go. Service fees on the cards can be extremely lucrative. Unfortunately, Chinese financial shares cannot be considered unrecognized. They sell at a considerably higher P/E ratio than do the U.S. major international banks and insurance companies.

- CHINA MERCHANTS BANK. Under the astute leadership of President Ma Weihua, CMB had a successful initial public offering in fall 2006, and continues to rack up impressive results, particularly in the area of corporate governance. The first and only large commercial bank not owned directly by the Chinese government, CMB is a major domestic credit card issuer and is known for its high asset quality. Listed on: Shanghai Stock Exchange

(600036.SS); Hong Kong Stock Exchange (3968.HK); and U.S. pink sheets (CIHHF.PK and CIHKF.PK).

- CHINA LIFE INSURANCE. Operating out of mainland China, Hong Kong, and the British Virgin Islands, China Life Insurance is a major underwriter of reinsurance. It is also active in issuing direct life insurance and in property investments. Listed on: New York Stock Exchange (LFC).

- PING AN INSURANCE. Another hydra-headed Chinese firm with, as its name implies, major involvements in the insurance industry, the company also owns a major and lucrative stake in the all-service commercial and retail Shanghai Pudong Development Bank, which is only listed on the Shanghai Stock Exchange (600000.SS). Listed on: Hong Kong Stock Exchange (2318.HK) and U.S. pink sheets (PIAIF.PK).

Infrastructure corporations

As Merrill Lynch declared in a report on trends in China to 2010, the biggest infrastructure boom in history is in the making. In the Five-Year Program covering the years 2006–10, the government is committed to spending $480 billion to upgrade the country's transportation infrastructure. Of that, over $150 billion will be invested in railways. Deutsche Bank analysts have called the Chinese railway industry a "must own." In addition to transportation expenditures, billions of dollars will be spent on upgrading the water supply and on waste water treatment, as well as on infrastructure-related projects in rural areas. Two companies that are widely expected to benefit from the infrastructure boom are Daqin Railway and China Railway Tielong Container Logistics; unfortunately, for those outside China, these are only listed on local exchanges. The following, however, are listed outside mainland China.

- ANHUI EXPRESSWAY COMPANY LTD. The company should benefit from the government's major investments in both expansion of the western region and transportation infrastructure. Anhui Expressway owns and develops toll roads in China's (central) Anhui Province. State entities hold controlling interest in the company. In addition, because this is after all a Chinese company and is therefore Byzantine in its structure, Anhui Expressway also owns a majority stake in Kangcheng Pharmaceutical, a research and development firm. Listed on: Hong Kong Stock Exchange (995.HK) and U.S. pink sheets (AUHAF.PK and AUHEF.PK).

- SINOTRANS LTD. A majority-controlled subsidiary of the government-owned China National Foreign Trade Transportation Group, Sinotrans has an almost iron-clad guarantee to participate in the government's infrastructure investments. As one of China's leading logistics companies, it will do so by providing air, ocean, road, and rail freight forwarding, as well as through warehousing services. Its international partners include UPS and DHL. Listed on: Hong Kong Stock Exchange (0598.HK); four German exchanges—Berlin (SIY.BE), Frankfurt (SIY.F), Munich (SIY.MU), and Stuttgart (SIY.SG); and U.S. pink sheets (SNOTF.PK).

- GUANSHEN RAILWAY. A way to participate in increased leisure travel within mainland China as well as the government's investment in infrastructure, Guangshan Railway Company operates the only railroad between Guangzhou and Shenzhen, and as such is the principal provider of passenger and freight transportation services in this lucrative and booming area near Hong Kong. Listed on: Hong Kong Stock Exchange (525.HK); Frankfurt Stock Exchange (GRC.F); and New York Stock Exchange (GSH).

Energy-related companies

At the same time that China is gobbling up energy in its efforts to give its people a comfortable living, it is also a world leader in promoting energy efficiency. In the government's latest Five-Year Program, announced in 2006, the country is committed to cutting energy consumption by 20 percent by unit of GDP. In addition, energy conservation is now officially an important performance assessment factor for local governments.

- CHINA PETROLEUM AND CHEMICAL CORP. (ALSO KNOWN AS SINOPEC). Described in detail in chapter 8, this petrochemical refining and production firm is an SOE under the close supervision of the government. Nevertheless, it should benefit under the current programs to encourage both production and conservation of energy. Listed on: Hong Kong Stock Exchange (0386.HK); New York Stock Exchange (SNP); and Shanghai Stock Exchange (800028.SS).

- SUNTECH POWER HOLDINGS. Established in 2001 by Dr. Zhengrong Shi, who was then thirty-eight, Suntech Power is one of the world's largest solar cell manufacturers and is continuing to expand. In 2006, it set up a wholly owned subsidiary in the United States and tapped into the rapidly growing U.S. solar market. Given the Chinese government's commitment to energy conservation, Suntech has enormous potential in its home country as well. Listed on: New York Stock Exchange (STP).

- CHINA NATIONAL OFFSHORE OIL CORPORATION (ALSO KNOWN AS CNOOC). The third largest national oil company in China and approximately 70 percent state-owned, CNOOC focuses on the exploitation, exploration, and development of offshore crude oil and natural gas. Under the leadership of its urbane chairman, Fu Chengyu, CNOOC has aggressively acquired numerous stakes in international oil fields. Listed on: Hong Kong Stock Exchange (0883.HK) and the New York Stock Exchange (CEO).

Leisure activities

According to United Nations projections, by 2015 there will be over 400 million mainland Chinese between the ages of twenty and thirty-nine. This group, almost the size of the entire population of the European Union, likes to spend and have fun. They enjoy—some might say are addicted to—the perks and pleasures of instant communications, and they are also starting to engage in vacation travel, particularly throughout their own vast country. This is the age group that will fuel the growth of nonbusiness activities.

- NETEASE.COM. Named *The Motley Fool*'s best international stock for 2007, NetEase serves millions of Chinese gamers with its extremely popular MMORPGs (massively multiplayer online role-playing game), free e-mail, news stories, blogs, and more. With over 500 million daily page views, NetEase is one of China's most visited Web sites. Its advertising revenue is growing, its PEG ratio, as this book goes to press, is low, and its operating and net margins are enviable, surpassing those of Yahoo. NetEase.com is also a classic example of why U.S. investors may want to stick to companies listed on their own exchanges. In 2001, NASDAQ was prepared to delist the stock because of financial reporting irregularities. William Ding, founder of the company, publicly apologized, promptly submitted a new statement, and declared, "We will try to prove that we are honest in handling the false reporting affair." Listed on: four German exchanges—Berlin (NEH.BE), Frankfurt (NEH.F), Munich (NEH.MU), and Stuttgart (NEH.SG); and U.S. NASDAQ (NTES).

- FOCUS MEDIA. This company (described in detail in chapter 2) captures leisure time rather than leisure activity by beaming advertising to captive audiences in elevators, hotel lobbies, train stations, etc. As this book goes to press, Focus Media has a very high P/E multiple but a moderate PEG ratio. Listed on: three German exchanges—Berlin (F10.BE), Frankfurt (F10.F), and Munich (F10.MU); and U.S. NASDAQ (FMCN).

THE COMPANY THAT STRUCK OUT

We have presented some exciting examples of Chinese companies that have enjoyed superior growth in the past and that, in the eyes of many professionals, offer excellent prospects for future growth. But in the extraordinarily volatile Chinese market, there have been many flameouts as well. Investors who try to buy undervalued stocks should do so only if they have a cast-iron stomach for risk.

Perhaps one of the most incredible rags-to-riches-to-rags stories is that of a Chinese company that started out in 1997 as a construction company with the name OLS Group Ltd. Two years later, it acquired a sexier moniker when it changed its name to China Prosperity Holdings and as such managed to get a NASDAQ listing with a ticker symbol of CPIH. Along the way, the construction business did not prosper. No problem. The company decided it would do better to get into the Internet business, and it did so by announcing it had acquired the exclusive rights to develop broadband Internet and cable television networks in Sichuan Province.

Talk about a ten bagger! The stock went from $1 to $36 just

EXHIBIT 11.2 *China Brilliance Automotive, 1992–2007*

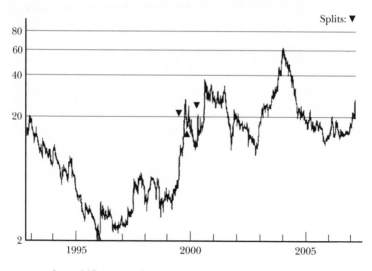

SOURCE: http://finance.yahoo.com.

like that, and in June 2000 the company became known as Prosper eVision Ltd. This time, there was a slight problem. The company did not, it turned out, have exclusive Internet rights in Sichuan. The SEC stepped in; the stock was delisted; and the name changed to a rather anonymous China Nan Feng Group Ltd. Recently it has changed its name once again to a catchy Green Energy Group Ltd. It is, however, back where it started from and trades as a "penny stock."

AND THEN THERE'S THE COMPANY THAT NEVER GOT TO SECOND BASE

In 1992, amid much fanfare, Brilliance China Automotive became the first Chinese company to list (ticket symbol CBA) on the New York Stock Exchange. As shown in Exhibit 11.2, the stock has essentially gone nowhere. Indeed, when inflation is factored in, original investors have lost buckets.

In the time period of the listing, the stock was suspended briefly for financial irregularities; the founder and chief executive officer Yang Rong was forced out; and the local Liaoning government bought a controlling interest at a purported 93 percent discount to the market price. Yes, indeed, buying Chinese stocks can be a manic-depressive activity.

A SUMMING UP

Buying individual Chinese stocks presents a host of problems. Few are listed on exchanges outside of mainland China and Hong Kong. Those that are often feature a convoluted structure and ownership. We do not in any way suggest buying individual Chinese stocks with your retirement money. Still, there are opportunities, and those who have money they can afford to lose might wish to take the slight chance of reaping huge rewards by investing in individual Chinese companies. The odds may be better than playing the lottery. For all other readers of this book, we recommend what we regard as the Optimal Investment Strategy, which is described in the following chapter.

CHAPTER 12

The Optimal Investment Strategy

> *He who would walk sanely amid the opposing perils in the path of life always needs a little optimism; he also needs a little pessimism.*
> —HAVELOCK ELLIS, *THE ART OF LIFE*

WE HOPE WE HAVE CONVINCED YOU THAT China is and will continue to be *the* growth story of the twenty-first century. And we hope that you agree that every portfolio, and yours in particular, should have some exposure to this economic powerhouse. We now get down to what we believe is the optimal strategy for you to profit from China's economic boom. We warn you in advance that it is not an exciting strategy that will make you a millionaire shortly after reading it—but it is a strategy that sharply curtails your risk.

Make no mistake about it. China is risky: corruption is rampant, corporate financial statements can be murky and misleading, and the heavy presence of the government's hand is not always in the shareholder's interest. With such risk comes hyperinflated volatility, or, paraphrasing the nursery rhyme about the little girl with a curl in the middle of her forehead, when the Chinese market is good, it is very, very good, and when it is bad, it is horrid. The mainland China stock market fell by 50 percent from 2001 through 2005 and then rose by over 100 percent during 2006. How's that for a roller-coaster ride? If you lose 50 percent in one period and gain 100 percent in the next, you have not made a dime, you have only broken even. Small wonder that cautious advisers have counseled, "The best China investment strategy: Forget about it."

We certainly don't think you should forget about China, but we firmly believe that you should use an investment strategy that substantially reduces risk. We tell you how to do that in this chapter by first presenting some general rules, then outlining an optimal mixed strategy that involves direct and indirect investments in China. We then present several model portfolio recommendations for investors with different amounts of resources available to invest in China.

THE PREPARATION REVISITED

Before we begin, recall the advice in chapter 8, "The Preparation." We assume that you have assessed your capacity and tolerance for bearing risk and have determined the proportion of your total equity portfolio that is to be devoted to a China investment strategy. For very risk-averse investors, that proportion may be only 5 percent. Investors with a high capacity and tolerance for risk might devote as much as 20 percent of their equity portfolio to China. Once you know how much money you wish to commit, this chapter tells you the least risky ways to expose your portfolio to China. Even risk-tolerant investors will not wish to take on any more risk than absolutely necessary. We also assume that you have invested the other 80 to 95 percent of your equities in a broadly diversified portfolio of common stocks. An investor living in the United States is likely to achieve above-average equity returns with index funds. A core equity portfolio might consist of two thirds of a U.S. total stock market index fund or ETF and one third of a total international market index fund or ETF. There is strong evidence that developed markets in the United States, Europe, and Japan are highly efficient, and that low-cost, low-turnover index funds provide returns that are likely to exceed those available from active managers. Such index funds would also contain the companies in the United States, Europe, and Japan, and in emerging markets that benefit indirectly from China. While we would not call this a China Strategy, it will at least give you a head start.

Four General Rules to Minimize the Risk of Investing in China

Four general rules follow that should allow investors to pursue an investment in China's growth strategy with minimized risk.

1. Diversify broadly

Buy funds rather than individual stocks. Accurate information is extremely hard to come by. In the past, some individual issues have lost almost their entire value. Moreover, there are many complications and additional fees involved for U.S. investors who purchase individual shares that are not listed on the New York Stock Exchange or the NASDAQ market. To avoid these problems, investors need broad diversification to contain risk and expense. That can be accomplished through mutual funds, closed-end funds, or exchange-traded funds.

2. Invest in Chinese securities gradually over time

Commit money to Chinese funds gradually over time, not all at once. We recommend that an initial investment be no more than one quarter of the total funds you plan to commit to Chinese securities. If you plan to commit $100,000 to a

Chinese strategy, your first investment should be no more than $25,000. Invest the remainder at periodic intervals as much as six months apart. Why such a cautious approach? By not investing everything at once, you lessen the risk of putting all your money in the market at a speculative peak. Market professionals call the technique of investing gradually over time "dollar-cost averaging."

Suppose, for example, that you invested $100,000 in a China fund over four six-month periods. We'll further suppose that the fund's prices were extremely volatile, as Exhibit 12.1 shows.

EXHIBIT 12.1 *The Benefit of Dollar-Cost Averaging*

PERIOD	U.S. DOLLAR PRICE OF CHINA FUND	INVESTMENT ($)	NUMBER OF SHARES PURCHASED
1	100	25,000	250
2	50	25,000	500
3	75	25,000	333⅓
4	125	25,000	200
Totals		100,000	1,283⅓
Average price	87.50		
Average cost of shares	77.92		

Final Portfolio Value

If invested all in period 1		125,000	(1,000@125)
If invested in four installments		160,417	(1283⅓@125)

By the process of dollar-cost averaging, you have purchased 1283⅓ shares at an average cost of $77.92 per share ($100,000/1283⅓). Your average cost is lower than the $87.50 average price of the shares during the period over which they are accumulated. It works because you purchased more shares when the price was low. Of course, if the price of the fund goes straight up after the first purchase, you would have been better off putting everything at risk at the start. And you need the courage to continue investing in periods 2 and 3 when the market is low. Dollar-cost averaging is a particularly useful strategy in a volatile market like China. You won't reap the benefit of investing all of your money at a market low, but you will avoid the regret of plunging in at a peak.

3. Be aware of costs — Lower investment costs mean higher returns for you

Investment costs play a crucial role in determining your net investment return. There's no evidence that buying a fund that charges high management and sales costs will lead to higher net returns. In the investment world you get what you don't pay for, not what you do pay for. So, buy funds with low management fees. Stay away from funds with a load fee (sales charge) attached. You can buy funds from companies such as Fidelity and Vanguard by mail or through the Internet. Exchange-traded funds have particularly low management fees. But when you buy them, do so through a discount broker. You can find the names of discount brokers from their newspaper, magazine, and Internet ads. You can also Google "Discount Brokers" for more information. Every fee or charge that you can keep to a minimum means a higher net return to you.

4. Employ a mixed strategy of both direct and indirect investments

Risk can further be reduced by employing a mixed strategy. Only half the monies devoted to China should be invested directly in Chinese securities. The other half should be placed in indirect investments. There are many indirect ways of investing to benefit from China's growth. We discussed in chapter 10 a large number of investments in China's trading partners or in commodity producers who benefit from China's development (as they will from the development of India, which is enjoying the world's second highest growth rate). Because these investments are domiciled in countries where transparency is greater and fraud is less likely to exist, the investment risk is substantially reduced.

THE OPTIMAL MIXED STRATEGY: SOME GENERAL GUIDELINES

The optimal strategy for most investors combines quite risky direct investments in Chinese companies with less risky investments in companies domiciled in other countries that benefit from China either through trade or direct investment or because they manufacture their goods there. These companies are likely to have fewer governance and corruption issues than some Chinese firms. We believe that risk can be reduced further if the following five guidelines are employed:

1. For the monies invested in Chinese securities, broad diversification is essential. Investors with limited means should not buy individual Chinese stocks but rather should focus on managed open- or closed-end funds or ETFs. Buyers of just one or two Chinese stocks should consider such purchases pure speculation.

2. If ETFs are used, we believe there are four feasible candidates as this book goes to press (as described in chapter 9). These are: FXI (a fund containing twenty-five Hong Kong listed stocks); EWH (another fund of Hong Kong stocks with a heavy proportion of property companies, providing the investor with real estate exposure); PGJ (a fund containing stocks of Chinese companies traded in New York); and GXC (the S&P China ETF). If only one ETF is to be purchased, we favor GXC, since it is broadly diversified and has the lowest

expense ratio. As we have stressed repeatedly, lower investment expenses mean more money in your pocket.

3. For actively managed funds, we suggest the following
   priorities:
   (a) If closed-end funds are available at substantial discounts,
       they are preferable to open-end funds. We believe closed-
       end funds are particularly attractive if they sell at dis-
       counts of 10 percent or more.
   (b) If open-end funds are used, choose funds with relatively
       low expense ratios and low turnover. You should avoid
       funds with a sales charge.

4. Commodities and their producers can easily be accessed
   through mutual funds and/or ETFs, an approach we recommend rather than buying individual companies. We prefer
   commodity producers rather than the commodities
   themselves.

5. Investors with substantial assets should buy stocks of companies domiciled in countries that are China's main trading
   partners; these will obtain a meaningful share of their future
   growth from China-related activities (see chapter 10). Alter-
   natively, country ETFs representing China's major trading
   partners may be purchased. Investors without enough
   resources to buy several different instruments would gain
   some benefits from the growth of China (and India) by purchasing an emerging market index fund or an index fund
   containing only Pacific region countries.

Optimal strategies for direct investment in Chinese stocks

Strategies for direct investment in Chinese equities will
depend upon whether the investors are Chinese citizens or
foreigners, and whether the foreign investors have a QFII
quota. The A-share markets are not yet efficient, and we recommend active management rather than passive indexing
strategies for those who can gain access to this market. In

chapter 8, we listed some managed open-end funds that we favored for investment, but we prefer managed closed-end funds when available at substantial discounts. As this book went to press, equities were available through closed-end funds at discounts of 25 percent or more. Since the funds have maturity dates in the future when they will liquidate, investors in closed-end funds should earn returns that exceed those available from the market as a whole. See chapter 9 for a sample of mainland closed-end funds that we favor.

For foreign investors who do not have QFII quotas, as well as investors who can buy A shares but who wish to diversify into the H- and N-share markets, we believe that either managed or index funds are viable solutions. We showed that the H- and N-share markets tended to have somewhat more profitable stocks, and that these markets were more efficient than the A-share markets. (You can find the names of the U.S.-domiciled China mutual funds and the closed-end funds we favor in chapter 9.)

If the closed-end shares are available at substantial (10 percent or greater) discounts, we favor those shares. Closed-end funds are easier to manage than open-end funds. The fickle whims of the investing public often force the open-end fund manager to buy at market peaks and sell at market troughs. (Public investors invariably tend to put money into mutual funds at market peaks when enthusiasm is widespread and to liquidate their holdings during market troughs.) Closed-end fund managers have more control over the timing of their purchases and sales. When investors liquidate their closed-end shares, the closed-end manager is not required to liquidate portfolio holdings. This characteristic offers an advantage when dealing with Chinese shares because of the large transaction costs of buying and selling. When these funds are available at discounts, it is time to open your wallets to closed-end funds.

Indexing can also be a useful strategy in the H and N markets. These markets are open to international institutional investors and tend to be more efficient than the A-share markets. Index funds and (indexed) ETFs tend to have relatively low expense ratios and low portfolio turnover. The ETF we particularly favor is the SPDR S&P China ETF (ticker GXC) because it is broadly diversified and has a low expense ratio. If one more China ETF is added, we would select the MSCI Hong Kong ETF (ticker EWH), because of its real estate exposure. Investments in Chinese property development companies can be risky, but that risk is considerably lessened with the diversification benefits provided by EWH.

Indirect strategies for investing in China

Investing in China does not have to be restricted to investing in companies domiciled on the Chinese mainland. Investments in commodities and their producers and in companies domiciled in Japan, Taiwan, Hong Kong, and China's other trading partners represent an indirect method to benefit from the growth of China. Many U.S. companies have also derived an important share of their growth from China-related activities.

We believe that diversifying the Chinese portion of a portfolio with as much as half dedicated to indirect investments provides an excellent risk/reward balance. Portfolios arranged in this way will be far less volatile than a portfolio restricted to direct Chinese investments. A mixed portfolio including indirect investments is more likely to produce generous returns even if China's growth falls short of our optimistic forecasts.

The indirect investments in non-Chinese companies will ensure that a substantial share of the investments is subject to better corporate governance. Indirect investments will also benefit from India's growth, as well as the growth in other developing countries of the world.

SOME PRACTICAL PORTFOLIO STRATEGIES
FOR U.S. INVESTORS

Institutional investors can use the general guidelines outlined above and the detailed recommendations from earlier chapters to implement the mixed China strategy we recommend. That strategy envisions the use of many different instruments. It stresses obtaining exposure not only to the stocks of companies operating in China but also to commodity companies and to the stocks of companies in other countries that benefit from China's growth. Using active strategies, such as buying portfolios of stocks in Japan, Taiwan, and the United States that derive substantial benefits from China, requires including large numbers of individual investments.

The optimal mixed strategy, however, would be prohibitively expensive for small investors. Are there easier ways to implement this strategy we recommend in order to benefit from the continued growth of the Chinese economy?

We believe so, and in what follows we describe specific investment strategies and concrete recommendations for investors with very different resource levels: (1) investors with no more than $5,000 to $10,000 to invest in a China strategy; (2) investors with $25,000 to $50,000 to invest; and (3) investors with substantial resources of $100,000 or more to devote to direct and indirect investments geared to China's growth.

1. Strategies for investors with limited means

Even if you have only $5,000 to invest, you can position your portfolio to benefit from China's development. The strategy can be implemented through open-end or closed-end funds, active or passive funds, or with exchange-traded funds. The simplest strategy for obtaining direct exposure is to make one investment in a diversified fund that invests in the stocks of Chinese companies available to international investors. Indirect exposure can be obtained by purchasing a fund broadly diversified in countries representing China's major trading partners. If closed-end funds are available at a discount of 10 percent or more, we favor those vehicles. The following portfolio mix, if available at attractive discounts, provides a good example:

50% Templeton Dragon Fund (direct investments in Chinese companies)
50% Morgan Stanley Asia Pacific Fund (investment in China's Pacific region trading partners)

Though the Asia Pacific Fund does not give you exposure to companies in the United States and Europe that benefit from China, it does offer a diversified portfolio of Asian companies, many of which have significant exposure to China's growth.

If the closed-end funds are not selling at attractive discounts, open-end funds can be used. Any of the funds listed in chapters 9 and 10 may be candidates. Here is one such mixed portfolio:

50% Matthews China Fund
50% Vanguard Pacific Stock Index Fund

A third strategy for investors with limited means is to purchase low-expense exchange-traded funds. Any of the ETFs listed in previous chapters would be suitable. One specific portfolio, for example, consists of:

50% SPDR S&P China ETF (GXC)
50% Vanguard Pacific Stock Index ETF (VPL)

The Vanguard Pacific Stock Index ETF provides substantial exposure to Pacific region countries that do trade with China (and India) and it has a very low expense ratio. The Vanguard ETF does not encompass U.S. and European companies with significant China exposure. But we assume that investors in the United States and Europe will have a diversified core portfolio of stocks domiciled in their home country that does include significant numbers of those multinational companies.

2. Strategies for investors with $25,000 to $50,000 to invest in China

For investors with somewhat larger resources, more options are available. Of course, an investor could use the same instruments recommended above. Exhibit 12.2 presents a slightly more complicated strategy that would be low-expense, well-diversified, and contains elements of the mixed strategies we favor.

Again, while the portfolio listed above does not include multinationals domiciled in developed markets in the United States and Europe, we assume that the investor's core portfolio will contain some of these companies. Note that recom-

EXHIBIT 12.2 *A Simple All-Indexed Equity Strategy for U.S. Investors*

Direct	
CHINA FUNDS[*]	50%
SPDR S&P China ETF (GXC)	
iShares MSCI Hong Kong (EWH)—an ETF with heavy real estate exposure	
Indirect	
EMERGING MARKETS TRADING PARTNERS	40%
Vanguard Pacific Stock Index ETF (VPL)	
COMMODITY PRODUCER FUNDS	10%
Vanguard Energy ETF (VDE) and Vanguard Materials ETF (VAW)	

[*]Closed-end managed funds may be substituted for ETFs, if the funds are available at attractive discounts.

mendations do include exposure to commodity producers that we believe will enjoy favorable long-run returns.

3. Strategies for investors with $100,000 or more to invest in China

Investors with substantial resources can more fully implement a mixed strategy involving investments in Chinese companies as well as portfolios of companies that benefit from China's growth through trade and investment. But even investors with substantial reserves may not wish to make the effort to put such a portfolio together. Fortunately, there are simpler ways to achieve similar results.

Open- or closed-end investment funds are readily available. Once again, we would favor closed-end funds if they are available at discounts. The investor could diversify over several funds such as the Templeton Dragon Fund and the Greater China Fund. Indirect exposure as well can be obtained from the broadly diversified Asia Pacific Fund or some of the Pacific region country funds.

The China strategies can also be implemented with low-cost index funds. Recall that the Chinese companies traded in Hong Kong and in other international markets did appear to be reasonably efficient and index funds tended to outperform actively managed China company funds. Index funds can be used, too, to access China's major trading partners. Exhibit 12.3 presents an all-ETF indexed strategy that gains exposure to China both directly and indirectly. Particularly if actively managed closed-end funds are not available at substantial discounts, an ETF strategy is likely to be optimal.

Half of the portfolio is invested in China company shares traded in Hong Kong or New York. The other 50 percent is invested in China's major trading partners, not including the United States. Ten percent of the portfolio is invested in com-

EXHIBIT 12.3 *An All-ETF Portfolio to Exploit the Growth of China*

	TICKER	EXPENSE RATIO (%)	PROPOSED WEIGHTING (%)	
SPDR S&P China ETF	GXC	0.60	30	China and
iShares MSCI Hong Kong	EWH	0.54	20	Hong Kong 50%
Vangard Pacific (70% Japan)	VPL	0.18	15	
Wisdom Tree Pacific Ex Japan (over 75% Australia, Singapore, and New Zealand)	DND	0.48	10	China- linked
iShares MSCI South Korea	EWY	0.74	5.0	50%
iShares MSCI Taiwan	EWT	0.74	5.0	
iShares MSCI Malaysia	EWM	0.59	5.0	
Vanguard Energy ETFs	VDE	0.26	4.0	
StreetTracks Gold Shares	GLD	0.40	3.0	
Vanguard Materials ETFs	VAW	0.25	3.0	

Blended expense ratio: 0.51% based on a 100% ETF portfolio.

SOURCE: Authors' calculations.

modities and their producers, including gold, which is a favorite savings vehicle in China. This ETF portfolio has tended to produce generous returns with only moderate volatility.

The recommendations in Exhibit 12.3 do not make use of two very promising strategies covered in chapter 10. We refer first to the strategy of buying a portfolio of Japanese companies that greatly benefit either from trade with China or from offshoring their manufacturing to China. The second strategy was to invest in a subset of U.S.-domiciled companies that benefit substantially from their association with China. We showed that portfolios of such companies have handily outdistanced the market averages in Japan and in the United States. Portfolios of European companies with considerable China exposure would also be useful.

Investors with substantial resources can—and should—adopt such strategies. But as yet no funds are available to permit a small investor access to these portfolios. We hope that such funds are developed soon. They would be a welcome addition to the portfolio choices available for international investors.

A Summing Up

The transformation of China is the economic miracle of the twenty-first century. The pace of growth is so rapid that it takes less than a year for China to build a new city equivalent to the size of Houston. China is now central to world commerce; and even if its growth rate slows, it will be the largest economy in the world by the 2020s, as measured in terms of purchasing power.

The Beijing Olympics in 2008 and the Shanghai World Expo in 2010 will focus the eyes of the world on China. No well-diversified investment portfolio can afford to ignore the investment opportunities that China offers.

BIBLIOGRAPHY

Anderson, Kym, and Anna Street. "China's Economic Growth, Policy Reforms and WTO Accession: Implications for agriculture in China and elsewhere by 2005," International Agricultural Trade and Research Consortium, 1999.

Baumol, William J. *The Stock Market and Economic Efficiency.* New York: Fordham University Press, 1965.

Bergsten, C. Fred, Gill Bates, Nicholas R. Lardy, and Derek Mitchell, under the auspices of the Center for Strategic and International Studies and the Institute for International Economics. *China: The Balance Sheet* New York: Public Affairs, 2006.

Brook, Timothy. *The Confusions of Pleasure: Commerce and Culture in Ming China.* Berkeley: University of California Press, 1998.

Chen, Zhiwu. "Stock Market in China's Modernization Process—Its Past, Present and Future Prospects," Unpublished paper, Yale School of Management, June 2006.

"China's Private Sector: Where The Future Lies?" Asia Pacific/China Strategy, Crédit Suisse Equity Research, October 2006.

Chow, Gregory C., *China's Economic Transformation.* Oxford: Blackwell Publishers, 2007.

———. *Corruption and China's Economic Reform in the Early 21st Century.* CEPS Working Paper No. 116, Princeton University, October 2005.

————, and Yan Shen, "Demand for Education in China," *International Economic Journal*, vol. 20, no. 2 (June 2006), 129–47.

Clissold, Tim. *Mr. China*. New York: HarperCollins, 2004.

Congressional-Executive Commission on China 2006 Annual Report. Washington, DC: U.S. Government Printing Office, 2006.

Datz, Christian, and Christof Kullman. *And Guide Shanghai: Architecture and Design*. New York: Te Neues Publishing, 2005.

Deng, Thomas, and Kinger Lau. "The Case for Chinese Equities," Global Strategy Research, Goldman Sachs, November 2004.

Dimson, Elroy, Paul Marsh, and Mike Staunton. "Economic Growth and Global Investment Returns," London Business School, November 2005.

Du, Julan, and Chenggang Xu. "Administrative Governance and Financial Development in China: Evidence from Regional Analysis," Incomplete paper, June 2005.

Gao, Sheldon. "China Stock Market in a Global Perspective," Dow Jones Indexes Research, September 2002.

Groenewold, Nicolaas, Yanrui Wu, Sam Hak Kan Tang, and Xiang Mei Fan. *The Chinese Stock Market Efficiency, Predictability and Profitability*. London: Edward Elgar Publishing, 2004.

Hinton, William. *Hundred Day War: The Cultural Revolution at Tsinghua University*. New York: Monthly Review Press, 1972.

Laing. Jonathan R. "What Could Go Wrong with China?" *Barron's* (July 2006).

Landes. David S. "Why Europe and the West? Why Not China?" *Journal of Economic Perspectives* (Spring 2006).

Leckie, Stuart, and Tony Zhang. *Investment Funds in China*. New York: FinanceAsia Publications, 2001.

Ma, Shiguang. *The Efficiency of China's Stock Market*. London: Ashgate Publishing, 2004.

Ma, Winston. *Investing in China: New Opportunities in a Transforming Stock Market*. New York: Haymarket House, 2006.

Malkiel, Burton G., Jianping Mei, and Rui Yang. "Investment Strategies to Exploit Economic Growth in China," *Journal of Investment Consulting*, vol. 8, no. 1 (Winter 2005–06).

Massey, Michael. "Analysis of the Efficiency of the Hong Kong Equity Markets," Unpublished manuscript, Princeton University, April 2007.

O'Neill, Jim, Sandra Lawson, Dominic Wilson, Roopa Purushothaman, Mike Buchanan, and Lord Griffiths of Fforestfach. *Growth and Development: The Path to 2050*. Goldman Sachs Group, 2004.

"Overview of Portfolio Investment Opportunities in China," Individual Investor Group Research, Morgan Stanley, April 2005.

Raskin, Amy, and Brad Lindenbaum. "China: Is the World Really Prepared?" AllianceBernstein Investment Research and Management, December 2004.

"REITs Around Asia," CB Richard Ellis Research, May 2006.

Schell, Orville. *Mandate of Heaven*. Simon & Schuster, 1994.

"Stratfor Decade Forecast 2005–2015," Strategic Forecasting Report, January 2005.

Thomas, William Arthur. *Western Capitalism in China: History of the Shanghai Stock Exchange*. London: Ashgate Publishing, 2001.

2006 Report to Congress of the U.S.-China Economic and Security Review Commission. Washington, DC: U.S. Government Printing Office, 2006.

Tyler, Patrick. *A Great Wall: Six Presidents and China*. New York: Public Affairs, 1999.

Vaknin, Michael, Zhong Sheng, and TengTeng Xu. "Bonding the BRICs: The Ascent of China's Debt Capital Market," Global Economics Paper No. 49, Goldman Sachs, November 2006.

Walter, Carl E. and Fraser J. T. Howie. *Privatizing China: The Stock Markets and Their Role in Corporate Reform*. New York: John Wiley & Sons, 2003.

Wang, Jiangyu. "Dancing with Wolves: Regulation and Deregulation of Foreign Investment in China's Stock Market," *Asia-Pacific Law & Policy Journal*, 5 (2004).

Wu, Guojun. "Manipulative Trades in Equity Markets." Working Paper University of Michigan, January 2004.

Zeng, George Xiangwen. "The Efficiency of Chinese Financial Markets: A Cross-Market and Time-Varying Analysis," Unpublished Manuscript, Princeton University, 2006.

Zhang, Tao, Jian Li, and Phil Malone. "Closed-End Fund Discounts in Chinese Stock Markets," *The Chinese Economy* (May–June 2004).

Zheng, Joan, Yifan Hu, and Andy Zhao. "China in 2007–2010: Key Trends and Risks," Investment Strategy Research, Merrill Lynch, November 2006.

Zielinski, Richard. "Chinese Telecommunications Policy Examined: The Case for Reform," A Periodic Commentary from The Progress & Freedom Foundation, April 2005.

ACKNOWLEDGMENTS

THIS BOOK WOULD BE but a pale compilation of facts without the assistance and contributions of individuals in both China and the United States. In addition to those who we interviewed and who are named in the text, we would like to thank the following.

First, we acknowledge our debt of gratitude to Xiao Feng, president of Bosera Asset Management Company, for graciously arranging and supporting our research trips to China. These visits gave us the opportunity to personally view the dramatic and exciting changes taking place within the country as well as to meet with government officials and talk to private entrepreneurs.

In conference rooms and in luncheon and dinner meetings, with each meal featuring delicacies from a different geographical area of China, we benefited not only from the extraordinary food but also from the knowledge of numerous veteran regulators of China's equity market, including

Gao Xiqing, Jiang Yan, Liu Xinhua, Zhang Yujun, and Zhu Congjiu. While in Beijing, we were fortunate to meet with Gui Minjie, vice chairman of the China Securities Regulatory Commission, who shared his insights about local fund market development. And we are deeply indebted to Qi Bin, CSRC's Deputy Director General, Fund Department, for explaining the nature of the complex evolution of China's financial markets.

We learned firsthand about the investment climate in China from Conrad Yan, Zhang Xi, and Harold Kim. We are especially indebted to Andrew Yan for explaining the operations of private investors on the Chinese mainland. We also gratefully acknowledge the hospitality of Fan Yonghong, Wu Yan, Zhao Wei, Yin Rong Yan, Peng Yue, Zhao Yong, Li Ming, and Wu Zhizhe. Senior officers and the research staff of Bosera Asset Management took time during our Beijing stay to explain the rules and regulations of China's mutual funds as well as to reminisce on the extraordinary changes that have taken place within their lifetimes. Several also worked on compiling data for many of the tables and charts that appear throughout the book. In addition to Executive Vice President Li Quan, we would like to thank Xia Chun, Wang Yan, Zeng Sheng, Liu Jianwei, Gui Quan, Yin Qinjun, and Zheng Bo. Two Bosera support staff, Xia Yingjie, administrative assistant, and Dong Songhe, chauffeur, cheerfully ensured that we were able to attend our various meetings on time and meet all our schedules—no small feat given Beijing's notorious traffic jams.

We would also like to acknowledge the generous support of the Cheung Kong Graduate School of Business and its faculty and students for providing a fruitful atmosphere for understanding the broad nature of both the China economy and its financial markets. In our forays into the countryside, we acknowledge the assistance of Wang Kang of the Beijing Botanical Garden for explaining the country's reforestation efforts and for taking us to rural areas where few Chinese have trod. And we thank Ruidon Jin, consultant to the Natural Resources Defense Council, for arranging our visit to the National Research for Science and Technology, as well as serving as an interpreter.

In Shanghai, we are indebted to Chian Q. Li, head of international affairs at the Shanghai Stock Exchange, for making our visit to that institution such an informative one, and for her translation services. In Hong Kong, we thank Dr. Winnie Yu for arranging our visit to the Ace Style Institute of Intimate Apparel at the Hong Kong Polytechnic University, and Paul Chow for his invaluable insights into the workings of the Hong Kong Stock Exchange.

China scholars at Princeton University were generous in donating their time and expertise to read and comment on our manuscript. We particularly appreciate the contributions of Professor of History Susan Naquin and Emeritus Professor of Economics Gregory Chow. And we acknowledge the insights provided by Princeton graduate student Tang Xian, art historian Virginia Bower, Jonathan J. Masse, CFA, and Princeton history professor Michael Mahoney.

Abby Cohen and Kathy Matsui of Goldman Sachs and Joan Zheng and Wendy Stimpson of Merrill Lynch were instrumental in allowing us to use research data from their respective institutions. Brett Masters and Uhang Wang spent many hours calculating U.S. financial data and preparing tables and charts. We also appreciate the research assistance provided by Amie Ko, Michael Massey, Daniel Tso, Laurissa Yee, George Zeng, and Damien Zhang. And we thank three Taylors—Anne, Katherine, and Toby—and Princeton's Joseph Henry Professor of Physics Philip W. Anderson for providing numerous research materials and reports and ensuring that we were aware of them all.

Several people in the United States were instrumental in arranging our interviews in China. We acknowledge here the help of Rob Watson, chairman and chief executive officer of EcoTech International; Dr. Yash Kamath, editor of the *Textile Research Journal*; Bendetta Roux, vice president, Christie's New York; and Tomasz Anisko, Janet de Grouchy, and Carol Weg.

And, of course, behind every manuscript there are hours of typing, proofing, and correcting. Kudos then to Phyllis Fafalios, Karen Neukirchen, and Melissa Orlowski for the time, energy, and patience they devoted to this task and to deciphering our handwritten notes and edits. By far the most important contribution to the production of this manuscript was made by Wendy Allard. She not only kept track of numerous drafts, inserts, tables, and charts, but put them all together flawlessly into a final manuscript. Wendy also updated almost all the tables and charts so that the book contained the most recent data available when the book went to press.

We acknowledge with deepest thanks the support and encouragement of W. W. Norton, particularly that provided by Drake McFeely and Brendan Curry. We are also much in debt to Ann Adelman, our copy editor. We have never experienced a more careful and professional job of editing in our many years of publishing. Finally, we acknowledge with enormous gratitude the numerous hours spent by Nancy Malkiel in reading many versions of this manuscript and ensuring that all had a consistency of style and clarity of exposition. Nancy has carefully reviewed every draft of each chapter of this book and has made countless suggestions that have clarified the organization and vastly improved the writing. She has played a critical role in bringing this manuscript to completion.

Though we come from many countries and from different

backgrounds, we all share an interest in understanding and explaining to others the modern phenomenon that is today's China. It was the enthusiasm, the diligence, the work ethic, and the entrepreneurial spirit of the Chinese people that proved so infectious and made us all the more eager to tell the amazing story of the new China and its prospects for continuation of its unprecedented record of growth. It is therefore to the Chinese people that we have dedicated this book. We only hope that we have been able to give our readers at least a partial picture of why we share the enthusiasm and optimism of these remarkable people.

INDEX

Page numbers in *italics* refer to illustrations and tables.